SOCIAL MEMORY AND HISTORY

SOCIAL MEMORY AND HISTORY

Anthropological Perspectives

EDITED BY
JACOB J. CLIMO AND MARIA G. CATTELL

ALTAMIRA PRESS
A Division of Rowman & Littlefield Publishers, Inc.
Walnut Creek • Lanham • New York • Oxford

ALTAMIRA PRESS
A Division of Rowman & Littlefield Publishers, Inc.
1630 North Main Street, #367
Walnut Creek, CA 94596
www.altamirapress.com

Rowman & Littlefield Publishers, Inc.
A Member of the Rowman & Littlefield Publishing Group
4720 Boston Way
Lanham, MD 20706

PO Box 317
Oxford
OX2 9RU, UK

British Library Cataloguing in Publication Information Available

Library of Congress Cataloging-in-Publication Data

Social memory and history : anthropological perspectives / edited by
Jacob J. Climo and Maria G. Cattell
p. cm.
Includes biographical references and index.
ISBN 0-7591-0177-9 (cloth : alk. paper) — ISBN 0-7591-0178-7 (pbk. :
alk. paper)
1. Ethnopsychology. 2. Learning, Psychology of. 3. Social learning.
4. Memory—Social aspects. 5. Cognition and culture. 6. Social
values. I. Climo, Jacob, 1945– II. Catttell, Maria G.
GN502 .S64 2002
153.1—dc21

2002007336

Printed in the United States of America

∞™ The paper used in this publication meets the minimum requirements of American National Standard for Information Sciences—Permanence of Paper for Printed Library Materials, ANSI/NISO Z39.48-1992.

For Marea Teski

Contents

Preface

THIS BOOK AROSE from a conversation between Jacob Climo and Maria Cattell about organizing a symposium to honor the memory of their colleague, Marea C. Teski. The symposium was held in 1999 at the annual meeting of the American Anthropological Association in Washington, D.C.

Marea Teski was one of the first sociocultural anthropologists to recognize the potential power of social memory studies. Her early involvement led to a coedited volume with Jacob Climo *The Labyrinth of Memory: Ethnographic Journeys,* published in 1995. Shortly before her untimely death in 1996, Marea was developing her concept of "memory repertoires" as a binding force in some societies and a way of passing on social memories endowed with meaning. Marea believed that ethnographers of memory would find a fertile arena if they asked their informants directly to explain their memories, which memories they chose to share, how they learned them, and how they passed them from one generation to the next. In her last papers, she was developing her interest in cross-cultural comparisons of social memory.

This book is dedicated to Marea Teski. We miss her enthusiasm, her intellect, and her company. We believe she would be pleased that we have continued the project she began so well.

Many others contributed to the formation of this book. We thank our chapter authors and others who contributed to the 1999 symposium: Marjorie Schweitzer and Robert Rubinstein, who were discussants, and John Conway, Hannah Kliger, Rakhmiel Peltz, and Dena Shenk, who presented papers not in this volume. All helped in the development of our ideas concerning social memory. Maria Cattell thanks especially Jack Mongar, Marjorie Schweitzer, and Nancy (Penny) Schwartz for their loving support, responses to queries, and comments on drafts of this introduction, and her daughter, Kharran Cattell, for assistance in the library. Jacob Climo acknowledges the support of his wife, Martha, and sons Avi and Simi. In countless ways, Nicole A. Clemen and Gail Barricklow, of Michigan State University's Department of Anthropology office staff, have provided assistance on this project. We are grateful to James Bielo for creating the index.

The editors, as authors of this volume's introduction, "Meaning in Social Memory and History: Anthropological Perspectives," wish to thank each other for the great effort each put into the writing of it. We regard each other's contributions as equal.

How the Book Is Organized

We begin with an interdisciplinary overview of social memory theory. This introduction includes discussion of the nature and processes of social memory, the current "crisis in memory," the relationship between social memory and individual or autobiographical memory, and the personal and political implications of memory. Special attention is given to anthropological approaches to memory and history.

Each of the ten chapters is a case study of social memory, culture, and history. Though arranged by themes, the chapters, individually and collectively, embrace continuums ranging from continuity to contestation to reconciliation and redress of memory, from individual to social memories, and from the relationship of memory to concrete places such as neighborhoods, hometowns, gardens, and cemeteries, to more intangible sensory experiences such as song, language, and creative expression.

Part I stresses continuity in specific places that are resonant with memories and cultural and historical meanings. The first two chapters, by Carole Crumley and Marilyn Cohen, focus on continuities of memory and history in Burgundian gardens and Irish households. Chapters 3 and 4, by Robert Archibald and Maria Cattell, turn our attention to individual memory and continuities and disjunctions in personal meanings and self-identity in relation to the author's home place (Archibald) and older white ethnics' urban neighborhood (Cattell). Chapter 5, by Doris Francis, Leonie Kellaher, and Georgina Neophytou, on ethnicity and cemeteries and chapter 6, by Jacob Climo, on migration to Israel focus attention on multiple linkages between individual and collective meanings and include reconstructed as well as continuous memories.

In Part II, chapters 7 and 8, by Eric Lassiter and Adina Cimet, deal with memories reconstructed in song, language, and symbols that are instruments of resistance and contestation. Lassiter focuses on the symbolic meanings of Kiowa song, dance, and story as protests against white domination. For Cimet, language symbolically represents both current and historical Mexican memory in contemporary political confrontations between subordinate native language-speakers and the dominant Spanish-speaking government elite.

Part III considers issues of reconciliation and redress arising from situations of contested memory and history. Cheryl Natzmer, in chapter 9, focuses on the processes of reconciliation in post-Pinochet Chile, as opposing national groups find different meanings in creative cultural expressions. In chapter 10, Larry Nesper delineates the empowering and validating impact of the repatriation of their schoolhouse on individual and tribal memories of Miami Indians.

Introduction
Meaning in Social Memory and History: Anthropological Perspectives

MARIA G. CATTELL AND JACOB J. CLIMO

"When I use a word," Humpty Dumpty said in rather a scornful tone, "it means just what I choose it to mean—neither more nor less." "The question is," said Alice, "whether you can make words mean so many different things." "The question is," said Humpty Dumpty, "which is to be master—that's all."

—LEWIS CARROLL (1982:136)

Memory and Meaning

MEMORY IS THE FOUNDATION of self and society. We are always "steeped in memory" (Casey 1987:ix), and without it there can be no self, no identity. Without memory, the world would cease to exist in any meaningful way, as it does for persons with amnesias or dementias that make them forget the self through inability to remember some or all of their past and or to create new memories in their ongoing life. Without memory, groups could not distinguish themselves one from another, whether family, friends, governments, institutions, ethnic groups, or any other collectivity, nor would they know whether or how to negotiate, fight, or cooperate with each other. From the simplest everyday tasks to the most complicated, we all rely on memories to give meaning to our lives: to tell us who we are, what we need to do, how to do it, where we belong, and how to live with other people. But memory, whether individual or collective, is constructed and reconstructed by the dialectics of remembering and forgetting, shaped by semantic and interpretive frames, and subject to a panoply of distortions. Such complexities are what make memory of such compelling interest to so many—that and the question Humpty Dumpty raises: who is to be the master of memory and, with it, the master of meaning? For the masters of memory and meaning also control much else.

Interest in memory, both individual memory and social or collective memory, is found in many scholarly disciplines. In the literary world, memories are the basis of memoirs, autobiography, life histories, travel and nature writing, and often are the inspiration for fiction and sometimes its explicit subject. Philosophers and social scientists focus on the personal, social, and political significance of memory. Memory studies also offer opportunities for multidisciplinary collaboration. For example, cognitive neuroscience integrates research on the physiological basis and functioning of memory with research on the psychological aspects of memory (Schacter 1995b, 1996). Indeed, the many and varied approaches to memory render the challenge of understanding it almost overwhelming. Yet memory studies provide a rare opportunity to move beyond narrow disciplinary boundaries, an opportunity for scholars to share insights that would otherwise be relatively inaccessible to those outside each discipline.

Within anthropology, scholars have called for a return to the remembered (and perhaps idealized) past, to a time when anthropologists from the various subdisciplines shared common intellectual problems and theories and engaged in broad discourses that unified the entire field. In recent years, these mutual exchanges have been absent, mainly because of the increasing specialization of anthropology's subfields. Studies of social memory and history can respond to the call for greater unity within anthropology by bringing sociocultural and physical anthropologists, archeologists and linguistic anthropologists together to consider topics of mutual interest.

This book is an exploration of social memory and history from the perspectives of cultural anthropology, perspectives shaped (like those of any discipline) by conceptual and theoretical concerns, by methodology, and by the accumulated knowledge of the field. For sociocultural anthropologists or ethnographers, this means culture as the key concept, research—known as participant observation—carried out through immersion in local cultures, and a holistic and comparative approach to the human social universe. We look for contexts and connections and for the meanings people find in their lives. Anthropologists often find themselves working on the edges, where the boundaries between anthropology and sociology, ethnography and history, memory and culture, are fuzzy. But in common with scholars from other disciplines, we realize that people everywhere seek meanings in the past, that memories mold, create, and sustain meanings, and that those meanings inform the present and guide the future. It is the human search for meaning that serves as the basis for our discussion in this overview of social memory and history from an anthropological perspective.

We begin our overview with a discussion of the theoretical emergence of social or collective memory, followed by examinations of postmodernity and the current crisis in memory and the relationship of cultural anthropology to history and memory. The introduction is then organized around four key themes useful for examining the ways that memories mold, create, and sustain meaning: (1) the construction of meaning in individuals' memories and the implications of these findings for social memory; (2) the sites of memory, which include places and objects, human bodies and autobiographies, rituals, bodily practices, language and symbols; (3) the search for meaning through the dynamic processes of memory, processes that include remembering and forgetting, contestation of memories, and the search for truth and justice through reconciliation and redress; and (4) memory and identity as expressed, claimed, and contested through representations of the past, in voice and text, for and by various persons and groups. In explicating these themes, which are threaded through the case studies of this book, we explore the nature of both individual and collective memory and related theoretical developments, particularly in the disciplines of anthropology, history, psychology, and sociology.

Social or Collective Memory

> *[H]ow easy it is to forget when there are no collective occasions for remembering.*
>
> —LAURENCE KIRMAYER (1996:188)

Social memory is a widespread and profoundly important phenomenon, of great interest to many persons from politicians to academics. Not surprisingly, it has many names, and in recent years much has been researched and written about social memory, its characteristics, processes, and functions, under its assorted nominal guises from various disciplinary and theoretical perspectives. Scholars have analyzed social memory from a number of thematic perspectives: for example, as moral knowledge and practice (Lambek 1996; Werbner 1998b); as a strategy to cope with traumatic experiences (Antze and Lambek 1996) or to deal with ancestors and death (Battaglia 1992; Davies 1994; Taylor 1993); and as local forms of historical interpretation constituting present communities and identities and as strategies in economic and political struggles (e.g., Abercrombie 1998; Amoss 1981; Boyarin 1991, 1994; Brundage 2000; Buruma 1994; Daniel 1996; Herzfeld 1991; Kammen 1991; Rappaport 1990; Steedly 1993; Stoller 1995; Sutton 1998; Tonkin 1992; Werbner 1998c).

In 1925, French sociologist Maurice Halbwachs published the first of his two books on collective memory; the second appeared in 1950 (Halbwachs 1992). Revived in the current memory boom, both have become classics. Collective memory, said Halbwachs, is "not a metaphor but a social reality, transmitted and sustained through the conscious efforts and institutions of groups" (Yerushalmi 1982:xv). Social groups, he said, construct their own images of the world through agreed upon versions of the past, versions constructed through communication, not private remembrance. He rejected the individual psychology approach of the philosophers and psychologists, not in favor of a supraordinate group mind, but in favor of shared or collective thought arising from interactions among individuals as members of groups.

A proliferation of terms has attached to the phenomenon of collective memory: cultural memory, historical memory, local memory, official memory, popular memory, public memory, shared memory, social memory, custom, heritage, myth, roots, tradition. Some writers stick with one of these terms or draw distinctions among two or more of them, while others regard them as more or less interchangeable. Halbwachs distinguished autobiographical memory (personal experience), historical memory (the "dead" past known only through historical records), and collective memory (the active past that informs our identities) (Olick and Robbins 1998:111). French historian Pierre Nora (cited in Olick and Robbins 1998:120–21) makes the same clear distinction between memory (living) and history (dead). On the other hand, Burke (cited in Olick and Robbins 1998:110) refers to history as social memory, "a convenient piece of shorthand that sums up the rather complex process of selection and interpretation." American historian Fitzhugh Brundage (2000:24) accepts collective, historical, public, and social memory as equivalent when they are applied to any "organized, explicitly public representation of the past." Thus vocabulary seems to be related to one's "lumper or splitter" taxonomic leaning, except for those (such as Halbwachs and Nora) whose theoretical interests led them to greater precision.

If it is impossible to fix this concept with a single name, it is also impossible to define it, though it has general contours that are recognizable across disciplines, substantive issues, and geographic areas (Olick and Robbins 1998). Even if we cannot say exactly what it is, we seem to recognize it when we see it. Collective or social memories are shaped by social, economic, and political circumstances; by beliefs and values; by opposition and resistance. They involve cultural norms and issues of authenticity, identity, and power. They are implicated in ideologies. Social memories are associated with or belong to particular categories or groups so they can be, and often are, the focus of conflict and contestation. They can be discussed and negotiated, accepted or rejected. Collective memories are expressed in a variety of ways. They create interpretive frameworks that help make experience comprehensible. They are marked by a dialectic between stability or historical continuity and innovations or changes (see Brundage 2000:5–13).

Social, collective, historical memory is provisional (Schudson 1995), malleable (Olick and Robbins 1998), contingent. It can be negotiated and contested; forgotten, suppressed, or recovered; revised, invented, or reinvented. Examples include suppression of memory in the Chinese Cultural Revolution; ongoing controversies over German guilt and Japan's role in World War II; human rights investigations in many nations such as Nigeria or the former Yugoslavia; South Africa's postapartheid reexamination of the Afrikaner version of history that silenced African art, history, and culture; and denial in the face of all evidence that the Holocaust happened (see, for example, Brundage 2000; Buruma 1994; Cimet, this volume; Hobsbawm and Ranger 1983; Kammen 1991; Klein 1997; Natzmer, this volume; Nuttall and Coetzee 1998; Paris 2001; Schudson 1992; Vidal-Naquet 1992).

But social or historical memory can also be cumulative (Halbwachs 1992) and persistent (Olick and Robbins 1998). Some aspects of the past are highly resistant to efforts at revision (Schudson 1992), while some persistence results from inertia and the force of habit (Olick and Robbins 1998). The past of individuals tends to build around a persistent central core (Kaufman 1986; Middleton and Edwards 1990; Pillemer 1998). Generational or cohort experiences that differentiate cohorts from each other tend to endure (Schuman and Scott 1989; Uhlenberg and Miner 1995). Subordinate groups often retain many elements of their history and their culture and traditions, in spite of the efforts of dominant groups to impose change. While not evidence in a scientific sense, the dystopias of George Orwell's *1984* (1949) and Ray Bradbury's *Fahrenheit 451* (1967) show the necessity for totalitarian regimes to control memory and the powerful resistance to such control. For example, in *Fahrenheit 451*, individuals make themselves into books through memorization, holding their knowledge for a future freedom.

All this suggests imprecision of concept, lack of disciplinary hegemony, lack of theoretical development—a fair enough assessment. As Jeffrey Olick and Joyce Robbins (1998:106) have expressed it: "Social memory studies is . . . a nonparadigmatic, transdisciplinary, centerless enterprise." Nevertheless, social memory is deeply implicated in important contemporary issues: the truth of memory, history, and culture, who owns them, and their roles in identity, nation building, hegemonic relationships, and other situations. Memories can create "communities of memory" (Bellah et al. 1985) or bring together a broken community, but they can also tear a community apart.

Postmodernity and the Crisis in Memory

We speak so much of memory because there is so little of it left.

—PIERRE NORA (QUOTED IN OLICK AND ROBBINS 1998:121)

Built on the foundations laid by late-nineteenth- and early-twentieth-century thinkers, especially French sociologist Maurice Halbwachs, a widespread scholarly interest in social or collective memory developed in Europe and North America in the late twentieth century (Olick and Robbins 1998). Memory is currently of great general interest in the United States, as evidenced by such things as the popularity of history, biography, and historically based films and television programs; by the pursuit of family history; and by memorials such as the Holocaust Memorial Museum and the Vietnam Memorial with its list of names of the dead. These are all examples of not forgetting, of avoiding oblivion, achieved through profound and often highly public remembering.

Impetus for the current boom in memory studies comes, in part, from what has been called the crisis of memory, a crisis involving on the one hand enormous attention to memory, and on the other, disjunctures between contemporary life and the remembered past. The memory crisis is usually viewed as a condition of modernity, or postmodernity, or both. Richard Terdiman, in *Present Past: Modernity and the Memory Crisis,* originated the term "memory crisis." He located the origins of the crisis in modernity, in Europe's nineteenth century upheavals that involved the loss of innocence and tradition and created a sense of emotional detachment (Lambek and Antze 1996). Historian Michael Kammen (1991) views post-1945 nostalgia and the "roots" and heritage phenomena in the latter twentieth century as responses to heightened anxieties in times of transition when a society feels disconnected from its own past. In *Twilight Memories: Marking Time in a Culture of Amnesia,* Andreas Huyssen sees the current obsession with memory as indications of an effort to slow down in a world of high-speed communication, information overload, and epistemological unease (Olick and Robbins 1998).

Others see the crisis as an aspect of the postmodern condition, especially the postmodern attack on linear historicity, truth, and identity (Schwartz, cited in Olick and Robbins 1998), with the consequences of epistemological uncertainty and the loss of stable communities and the sense of the collective (Lambek and Antze 1996). In his monumental seven-volume *Les lieux de mémoire,* French historian Pierre Nora refers to the paradoxes of memory in postmodernity and sees the crisis of memory as a separation from the continuous or living past. This separation has brought postmoderns to a condition where "[w]e speak so much of memory because there is so little of it left" (Nora, quoted in Olick and Robbins 1998:121).

For Halbwachs, like Nora, the disconnected past is dead memory, which he equates with history (Olick and Robbins 1998). In another view, anthropologist Richard Werbner (1998a) locates contemporary Africa's memory crisis in postcolonial situations where colonial nostalgia, state memorialism, and popular countermemory (differing from the official memory of political regimes) are important forces in postcolonies, ranging from collapsed states to repressive and authoritarian governments.

With the current memory crisis being, in many respects, "the flip side of rapid social change" (Lambek and Antze 1996:xiv), whether it is theorized in post-modern, sociological, or historical terms, it is no wonder that memory engages the attention of so many people: individuals seeking roots, groups constructing or re-constructing identities and claims to political autonomy and material prosperity, writers, researchers. What more appropriate response to feelings of social dislocation and intellectual uprootedness than the anchor of memory?

Anthropological Perspectives on Social Memory and History

Culture . . . may be seen as memory in action.

— MAREA TESKI AND JACOB CLIMO (1995:2)

Anthropologists share much with other social sciences. Like scholars in other disciplines, ethnographers have been affected by new theories and research methods and shifts in the political and economic climates for research (Jenkins and Csordas 1997). They have, for example, joined the recent boom in scholarly explorations of social memory. As we will see, social or collective memory, history, and culture appear to be similar phenomena with fuzzy boundaries and overlapping issues and themes that are relevant in various fields of research. Research methods may be borrowed, concepts may be shared. So one may well ask: what is distinctive or unique about anthropological perspectives? To explore this question we will discuss methodological and conceptual issues and anthropology's relationship to history.

Participant Observation as Liminal Practice

Susannah Radstone (2000:13) notes that memory work is often done in "liminal spaces," that is, in spaces between disciplines, and is carried out by "liminal practices" or "hybridized" methods. The notion of liminality embraces the idea that being in interstitial spaces, betwixt and between, promotes creativity (Turner 1967). Anthropologists, having left their usual sociocultural context to do fieldwork in other cultures, are quintessentially in liminal spaces, and over the past century, anthropological methods have developed as liminal practices in Radstone's sense. The basic method of "participant observation"—participating in activities while trying, at the same time, to maintain the more objective stance of an observer (Keith 1986)—has come to embrace a wide range of methods, many borrowed from other fields, especially history and sociology. We may combine archival research and or surveys with fieldwork, intensive interviews, and the collection of oral traditions that are used to reconstruct the past of a group—as seen, for example, in the work of anthropologist Jan Vansina (1965). Memory also plays a major role in anthropological research.

Anthropologists "go to the field," to another culture, with the aim of understanding that culture, what the inhabitants of a given place do, what is important to them. We also collect data directly through observation, conversation, in-depth interviews, focus groups, surveys, censuses, and in other ways (e.g., Bernard 1988; Naroll and Cohen 1970; Pelto and Pelto 1978). In all of this, memory is intimately implicated. We rely heavily on others' memories to provide us with information about the present and the past, including customs that have changed or disappeared. We consult other memory sources such as archives, written histories, photographs, and demographic records. Not least, we depend on our own memories for note taking, analysis, and writing up. The unwritten form of fieldwork memories is what Ottenberg (1990) calls "headnotes." Headnotes are information stored only in our heads, subject to the usual vagaries and distortions of memory, yet they play a crucial role in shaping ethnographic understandings as we analyze our written materials and write them up.

Contributors to this volume illustrate various kinds of methodological overlap. For example, Marilyn Cohen explored the construction of memory among working-class women in northern Ireland in the early twentieth century; she combined archival records with fieldwork and the collection of oral histories from thirty-five contemporary villagers who are elderly survivors living "with the ghosts and remains of a century-old factory culture surrounding them." Doris Francis, Leonie Kellaher, and Georgina Neophytou, in exploring London cemeteries as sites for the construction of memory, identity, and ethnicity, collected data through observation, interviews, and surveys. In her examination of the struggle over memory practices in post-Pinochet Chile, Cheryl Natzmer used participant observation along with materials from the media, popular culture, and literary works; she also considers the silences in the record. Such methodological heterodoxy enriches our data and enhances our knowledge, while at the same time retaining the anthropological approach of fieldwork and participant observation.

Culture and Ethnography

> *[M]an is an animal suspended in webs of significance he himself has spun.*
>
> —CLIFFORD GEERTZ (1973:5)

A discipline's conceptual framework is another powerful influence on research. For example, American anthropologists—in common with sociologists—trace their intellectual roots back to the European sociologists, to Emile Durkheim, social facts, and the possibility of discovering social laws; and to Max Weber and social class. However, from its late nineteenth century beginnings, American anthropology's dominant concept, and its subject matter, has been culture. The concept of culture has varied through time as changing theoretical frameworks and research concerns have led to differing views of culture (e.g., Kroeber and Kluckhohn 1952), research methods, and ethnography. In spite of such shifts, however, the anthropological concept of culture has steadfastly embraced the importance of contextualizing information about people and their lives in specific times and places, understanding interconnections holistically, and working within a framework of comparison. At the very least, researchers compare their own worldview with the worldviews they encounter in the field (Weisner 1997). However, anthropologists often make more explicit and formal cross-cultural comparisons, including comparative field studies (Munroe and Munroe 1991) and comparisons based on the ethnographic literature, made in either a discursive style (e.g., Albert and Cattell 1994; Foner 1984) or through statistical analysis (Ember and Levinson 1991). In any case, the aim is to make generalizations about human cultures and societies.

Current understandings of culture are informed by the work of anthropologists Clifford Geertz and Victor Turner. "Believing, with Max Weber," said Geertz (1973:5), "that man is an animal suspended in webs of significance he himself has spun, I take culture to be those webs, and the analysis of it to be therefore not an experimental science in search of law but an interpretive one in search of meaning." In addition, Geertz argued that ethnography should be "thick description," a dense accumulation of facts that can be interpreted to reveal the meanings in those self-spun webs. A second approach to cultural interpretation through symbolic analysis comes from the work of Victor Turner, a British social anthropologist who investigated the role of rituals and symbols in conflicts and in maintaining social order (e.g., Turner 1967).

These interpretive and symbolic approaches foreshadowed postmodern anthropology, which abandoned earlier views of culture as homogeneous, well-bounded units, and proposed a view of culture as ambiguous, filled with inconsistencies, only partially shared, and often contested (Bruner 1999; cf. Greenfield 2000). Postmodernists questioned ethnographic authority and urged self-reflexivity so readers can evaluate data and conclusions. They viewed ethnographies as texts subject to layers of interpretation, deconstructed long-held ideas, and focused attention on issues of voice and representation, power and hegemony (see Clifford and Marcus 1986). As a consequence, recent ethnographies have become more humble. They are multivocal, more precise in revealing the positions of both researchers and researched, often highly introspective, and interpretive rather than omniscient.

Postmodernist questioning of basic assumptions has led us to examine more closely our ethnocentric biases and consider voice and representation, including self-representation or reflexivity. But ethnography has endured these—and many other—transformations because ethnographers are open to "the surprise of fieldwork," to the discovery of other cultural worlds and other perspectives that we can use in our comparative framework (Shweder 1997). It has endured because the findings of ethnography matter: they matter in the cross-cultural comparative enterprise, and they matter to our research participants, the people among whom we do our research (Weisner 1997). For example, an older ethnography can be a useful guide to their own past by those about whom the ethnography was written, as anthropologist Igor Kopytoff (1995) learned when he met, in Belgium, several Suku intellectuals who were children forty years earlier when Kopytoff did fieldwork among their people in the Republic of Congo. For these modern Suku, the value of Kopytoff's work lay in his preservation of "a picture of their society as it had been several decades ago . . . in a way that rang true to them in terms of what they themselves knew" (12). For them, surely, Kopytoff's picture of their past revealed important meanings for their current lives.

The view of culture that emerges from this book is that of a social or collective manifestation of complex shared memories, memories that belong to particular groups and may be remembered, forgotten, or silenced, contested or revised. We agree with anthropologists Michael Lambek and Paul Antze (1996:xvii) that memory "always depends on cultural vehicles for expression" and, like culture, is always found in context.

Anthropology and History

. . . the disciplinary borderlands where ethnography and history meet.

—THOMAS ABERCROMBIE (1998:14)

Anthropology has had a long and often ambivalent relationship with history, beginning with the early interest in social evolution and the historical reconstructions of American Indian cultures in Boasian anthropology; life histories; acculturation studies (from mostly documentary sources, though not acknowledged as history); and a flood of research since the 1950s variously labeled ethnohistory, folk history, historical ethnography, and even "anthrohistorical" (Friedrich 1986). Hudson (1973) argues that admitting to historical research has been perceived as a threat to anthropologists' identity, that anthropology may well be a kind of history, and that "one can separate the work of social anthropologists from that of historians . . . only in the most arbitrary fashion" (131). Perhaps Hudson should have spoken of "some" social anthropologists, since many still subscribe to what Vansina (1970:165) called the "zero-time fiction," the synchronic study that ignores time, dates, change. However, Abercrombie (1998:14) can rightly refer to "the disciplinary borderlands where ethnography and history meet." With the growth of oral, social, and cultural history in the late twentieth century, these borderlands would seem to have expanded right into the heart of both disciplines, so that ethnography is often close to, and sometimes entirely congruent with, historiography, especially history "from below" (Daniel 1996:196).

Despite such affinities between anthropology and history, many early American and British anthropologists ignored history and change. Franz Boas, regarded as the founding father of American anthropology, and his students did intensive fieldwork among American Indians whose original communities had been shattered by colonialism and postcolonial expansionism. The Boasians were driven by the idea of salvaging or rescuing information of the vanished past before it was too late. Their ethnographies were historical reconstructions or culture histories, but they were static since they ignored the colonial part of the story and portrayed Indian cultures as frozen in time, in an unchanging ethnographic present. In fact, the ultimate goal was historical: to understand the origins and development of each culture. What was produced, however, were descriptions of remembered cultures, what Roger Sanjek (1993) calls "memory cultures."

During this same period, roughly 1920 to 1960, some Africanist anthropologists were working in what Sally Falk Moore (1993) calls the "contemporary-historical mode." These ethnographers focused on historical and ongoing transformations in African societies through case studies, life histories, statistical information, and other data. Their ethnographies were history, though based in part on different methods and evidentiary standards from the histories written by historians. Yet another historical approach is invoked by long-term fieldwork in a particular site, making the ethnographer a witness to history over many years or even decades (Foster et al. 1979). Such ethnographers record social history as it unfolds.

Ethnography and academic history are more remote from each other. For example, Robert Archibald's training as an academic historian taught him the process of scholarly inquiry that relies on written records to produce "scientific history" (Collingwood 1956). In time, this kind of history seemed to Archibald to lack the authenticity of memory and the reality of personal experience: "In the absence of empathy, emotion, concern, and caring, history becomes an exercise in nostalgia or an academic sidebar of limited use in the real world" (Archibald 1999:22). For him, history became an activist discipline, a process of constructing useful narratives that "explain the past, evaluate the present, and project the future" (109, 166).

Anthropology and Memory Studies

An increasing number of ethnographers are focusing their research on the meanings of social memory and history, rather than teasing them out as interesting but unintended byproducts of their conceptual orientations, field methods, or research directed at other goals (e.g., Abercrombie 1998; Bailey and Bailey 1986; Friedrich 1986; Herzfeld 1991; Rappaport 1990; Spyer 2000; Steedly 1993; Stoller 1995; Sutton 1998, 2001). Such ethnographers use anthropological fieldwork to discover memories, document how memories are created and transmitted, and interpret the role and significance of memories in people's constructions of the past and coping with the present. They also consult archival and historical records; for example, Abercrombie (1998) gave colonial documents an "anthropological re-reading." In such inquiries, which emphasize the meaning of the past to contemporary people, memory is conceived as both cultural process and historical artifact.

The Meaning of the Past: Individual Memory, History, and Culture

Our first theme deals with the workings of individual memory, the meanings of the past for individuals, and the implications of these findings for social memory, history, and culture. Because individual and collective memories are inextricably intertwined, we begin with a brief consideration of memory as organic process. Given the current conventional wisdom that all memory is social, individual memory can be viewed as an aspect of social memory. Some of the vocabulary of collective memory is taken from the vocabulary of individual psychology, and individual memory processes are both analogous to and different from collective memory processes. Epistemological and hegemonic issues of truth, ownership, and power come up in regard to both individual and social memory. Thus, understanding individual memory, "vivid with existential immediacy" (De Boeck 1998:39), enhances our understanding of social memory.

For anthropologists, the stories of individual lives are important dimensions of both personal and social identity. Memories define our being and our humanity as individuals and in collectivities. Moreover, the individual consciousness by which we recognize ourselves as persons, and the collective consciousness by which groups identify and organize themselves and act with agency, arise from and are sustained by memory.

For these and other reasons, individuals' relationships to time and memory are highly subjective and individual. They are, at the same time, profoundly social, for the exercise of memory very often involves others. For example, memories shared with others enables those who did not experience the events to include them among their memories vicariously (Climo 1995; Ishino 1995). In literate as in preliterate societies, vicarious memories such as myths, legends, songs, proverbs, genealogies, rituals, and other forms of knowledge extend memory across generations and beyond individual lifespans (d'Azevedo 1962). Or in another example, the memory performance of older adults in laboratory research has been consistently poorer than that of younger adults. However, in research that took into account the social context of storytelling, the memory of older adults was as engaged, adaptable, and active as that of younger adults (Adams et al. 2002).

Memory as Organic and Social Process in Individuals

> *The output of human memory often differs—sometimes substantially—from the input.*
>
> —DANIEL SCHACTER (1995A:1)

The human brain is an incredibly complex organ that creates, stores, and retrieves a person's memories in ways just beginning to be understood. Nevertheless, some things about individual memory seem reasonably certain. Memories are not replicas or documentaries of events; they are interpretations. Human memory is highly constructed, and individuals' sense of self and identity results from narrative constructions integrating past, present, and future. Memory is tightly connected with emotions, which lead us to create memories of things not actually experienced, reshape existing memories, and introduce other inaccuracies or distortions through blocking, bias, and other "sins" of memory (Schacter 1999). Distortions result from numerous other causes including selective forgetting and remembering; the effects of prior knowledge; aspects of the retrieval environment; and amnesia, trauma, and the workings of imagination (Schacter 1995b, 1996). Distortions also result from the shaping of individuals' memories by social norms and interactions, cultural practices, socially structured patterns of recall, and by the fact that memories largely operate through the consummately social medium of language. Many memory distortions are neither apparent nor verifiable. Some are harmless, others serve various personal and political purposes, still others can wreak havoc in people's lives, most notably the recovered (but false) memories of childhood sexual abuse (Pendergrast 1996) and the amnesias, dementias, and traumas that take away memory (e.g., Casey 1987; Sacks 1985, 1995).

Philosophers since Aristotle and psychologists for the past century have focused their attention on individual processes of remembering: how and what we remember, how accurately we remember, how and what we forget. Empiricist philosophers since the seventeenth century, from Hobbes to Hume and Russell, linked their conception of objective knowledge to a conception of objective remembering in which memories are retained sense data. Hume proposed that although these sense data are subject to inaccuracies, true memory can be distinguished from imagination by the "superior vividness and lifelike character of true memory" (Fentress and Wickham 1992:22), an idea refuted by recent research of cognitive psychologists (Schacter 1996; Pendergrast 1996; Pillemer 1998). Experiences are subject to misperceptions and interpretation as they are encoded and stored. Further loss and distortion occur with retrieval and reinterpretation, no matter how vivid the experience and later recall of it.

In the latter nineteenth and early twentieth centuries, important groundwork for memory research was laid. Ebbinghaus carried out the first experimental research on memory; Semon developed the concept of the engram as a memory trace in the brain. In 1928, Pierre Janet argued that narrative memories of everyday experience are always reconstructed and frequently distorted, whereas traumatic memories are likely to preserve exact details—the latter a focus of further research today (Schacter 1995a). Frederic Bartlett in *Remembering*, published in 1932, came to the similar conclusion that memories are imaginative reconstructions that are strongly influenced by preexisting knowledge structures that he called schemas (1995a). The notion of schemas called attention to the notion of reconstructive memory and the importance of present needs in memory process. Sigmund Freud developed hypotheses about memory repression as ego defense (1995a). In Freud's early model the objective truth of a memory was never lost although it might be masked or changed in its form and significance. Later he came to believe that patients' recovered memories were false, though he had no independent checks on the veridicality of the memories.

Freud observed that most adults have few, if any, memories from the first few years of life, a condition known as infantile or childhood amnesia. He explained this amnesia as the result of the repression of early memories. Late twentieth century cognitive and developmental psychologists explained childhood amnesia through the child's development of brain mechanisms, language, cognition, and perception, along with socially induced changes in categories of thought and an emergent sense of self. In particular, the rapid growth of linguistic ability from about age three shifts the child's memory system from cognitive and behavioral components to a narrative memory system enabled by language skills (Pillemer 1998:108). This shift occurs along with discovery of the cognitive self, initially represented nonverbally but increasingly, as language skills grow, represented through language (Howe and Courage 1997). The idea that memory is not based solely on language is compatible with the move away from linguistic determinism originally framed in the Sapir-Whorf hypothesis (Durbin 1973).

The last two decades of the twentieth century witnessed a paradigm shift in memory research. The idea that memory is a single mental faculty gave way to recognition of memory as composed of various distinct and dissociable processes or systems (e.g., short-term, long-term, episodic, procedural, semantic, implicit) within a complex and dynamic interactive network (Pillemer 1998; Schacter 1996).

Continuity and Change in Personal Memory and Identity

My life is created as I narrate, and my memory grows stronger with writing.

—ISABEL ALLENDE (1995:8)

Just as social memory is marked by a dialectic between stability or historical continuity and innovations and changes (Brundage 2000), individual memory is characterized by continuity and change.

Connerton (1989) discusses the ways communal memory in a French village (based on Marcel Proust's remembrances of Combray) encouraged continuity of behavior among villagers, whose individual identities were embedded in village social networks. Through lifelong familiarity, each villager's memories and experiences were closely connected to the collective memories and experiences of other villagers. Through daily recounting of events, the village constructed "a continuous communal history of itself: a history in which everybody portrays, in which everybody is portrayed, and in which the act of portrayal never stops" (17). Since individuals remembered in common to such a great degree, the situation left little room for uniqueness or flexibility in behavior or for transformation in the meaning of an individual's memory and life story.

By contrast, in the world of mobile strangers that many moderns inhabit, people must continually inform others of their history and origins (Berger 1963; see also Gross 2000). Berger identified modernity as an impetus for ongoing reinterpretations of lives through what he calls "alternation," the possibility of choosing between varying and sometimes contradictory systems of meaning—a possibility not present in Connerton's French village. People on the move physically are frequently people who are also on the move in their self-understanding. Transformations of identity and self-image can result from a single change of residence or through moving into a social world utterly different from that of one's parents. Berger saw as an inevitable consequence of massive physical and social mobility in America the fact that many Americans tell themselves and others, over and over again, the story of what they have been and what they have become. The past is changed or corrected where necessary or left untouched if it can be incorporated into a person's present self-image, although in a haphazard process of which the rememberers often are only partly aware. In the postmodern world, even people who are not highly mobile, who remain in the same place for many years, may discover that they need to change and adapt their identities as places are transformed around them.

In many cases, however, reinterpretation of the past is part of deliberate, fully conscious, intellectually integrated activities, such as happens with conversion to a new religion or ideology and relocation of an individual's biography in the new meaning system. Born-again Christians, for example, may view the past as evil and want to break from it, motivated by personal and or political considerations (e.g., Cattell 1992; Meyer 1998; van Dijk 1998). Among their discourse strategies are autobiographical narrations aimed at confronting their own past life and reforming it to suit their new, born-again selves.

Truth and Meaning in Autobiography

Biography is fiction. (Auto)biography is hopelessly inventive.

—MICHAEL GAZZANIGA (1998:2)

Autobiography or life history, written or oral, is blossoming in the United States. It is a common denominator in a number of disciplines, including the humanities and the medical, psychological, and social sciences. It is widely used in reminiscence therapy and intergenerational programs. Inevitably the question comes up: "But is it true? Is that the way it really was?" Often enough the answer is no, in regard to factual accuracy (if it can be determined), but yes, in regard to personal truth.

Through reminiscence and narration, individuals are continually reshaping their past lives to fit present needs and concerns. "[A] life is not 'how it was' but how it is interpreted and reinterpreted, told and retold" (Bruner 1987:31). Or, as Ruth Ray (1998:118) expresses it, autobiography "represents a complex interplay of language, memory, culture, and the conventions of storytelling. Autobiography is, above all, not experience written down, but a *discourse* on original experience" (emphasis in original). Coherence and meaning are what matter.

We are fictional selves, in the sense that we create and recreate ourselves, and yet, so long as we have our memories, we are true selves. While details may be lost or distorted in autobiographical revisions, the central meaning or "core truth" tends to be consistent over time (Pillemer 1998). "On balance . . . our memory systems do a remarkably good job of preserving the general contours of our pasts and of recording correctly many of the important things that have happened to us. We could not have evolved as a species otherwise" (Schacter 1996:308). Thus the past, present, and future dwell within us, and we use memory to maintain a consistent individuality through imaginative reconstructions (Archibald, this volume; Kaufman 1986).

Given the above, combined with numerous possibilities for memory distortion, one would not expect a great deal of factual accuracy in autobiographical memories (Neisser and Fivush 1993). However, autobiographies usually provide an abundance of truth in regard to personality, self-expression, personal identity, future planning, and other self-oriented aspects of memory. As David Pillemer (1998) puts it, the details may be wrong but the story is true. "There is a fundamental integrity to one's autobiographical recollections" (Barclay, cited in Schacter 1996:95). For example, anthropologist Sharon Kaufman (1986), using in-depth interviews with sixty older women and men, found a continuity of self across the life course that the interviewees themselves emphasized. They said the continuities gave meaning to their lives. In fact, meaning is given priority over truth in various contexts where autobiography is the connection between memory and history. In therapeutic settings, autobiographical memories are elicited, not to develop a true life story, but to use reminiscence as a healing process. Such therapeutic techniques are notable, for example, in cases of recovered false memories of childhood sexual abuse (Pendergrast 1996) or repeated stories of recovery from alcoholism told in Alcoholics Anonymous (AA) programs. This AA method keeps the past "detemporalized"—that is, the past is viewed as being in the present; it is current reality, not history—in order to discourage forgetting and lapses back into drinking (Swora 2001). In both therapeutic processes, the truth that matters is not the details of individual accounts but the shared narratives about problem drinking or intergenerational conflict.

Again, when guided autobiographical memories and narrative therapy are used in clinical practice with frail older persons and individuals with dementia, meaning rather than objective truth prevails (Haight and Webster 1995; Hendricks 1995; Kenyon, Clark, and de Vries 2001). Other invocations of individuals' autobiographical memories occur in programs aimed at fostering intergenerational relations and, at the same time, benefiting elder storytellers (e.g., Teicher 2001) whose lives are enriched through reminiscence with an appreciative audience (Bluck 2001). And in a natural setting, younger Coast Salish of the Pacific Northwest sought out elders' stories during a process of cultural renewal (Amoss 1981). In such settings, truth is unlikely to be an issue, since the truth expected is the core truth of individual lives and the cultural truths that emerge from elders' narratives.

The Sites of Memory

The second theme concerns the sites of memory. Where are memories kept? In one sense, human memory resides only in the human brain and its imagistic-behavioral and linguistic-narrative systems. But humans are cultural beings, not limited to biological understandings, and memories are everywhere. Memories reside in many mnemonic sites and practices—in language, songs, and ceremonies, bodies and bodily practices, places and things. Memories are associated with many different inanimate objects, from ordinary household items with personal meanings to art objects, monuments, and museums and other public buildings with collective meanings (Attfield 2000; Csikszentmihalyi and Rochberg-Halton 1981; Miller

2001; Myers 2001). The memories and meanings stored in buildings became acutely obvious to Americans following the terrorist attacks on the World Trade Center and the Pentagon that occurred as this introduction was being written.

Literate people put many memories into documents of various sorts, though oral culture continues to shape memories even among highly literate people (Brundage 2000). People without writing have developed a variety of mnemonic systems and practices in addition to the oral traditions found everywhere. For example, the tattoos of Melanesian groups record genealogies and clan affiliations on the body (Fentress and Wickham 1992). In Kilimanjaro, Tanzania, *mregho* sticks, carved with inclined and vertical lines, circles, and triangles, were "read" during the formal initiation of Chagga adolescents into adulthood (Kerner 1995). Food has a significant place in the interactions of culture and memory (Sutton 2001), and even the seeds of plants may be sites of memory because of the "nutritional, aesthetic, cultural, and ecological values embedded in them" (Nabhan 1992:159; cf. Crumley, this volume; Nazarea 1998).

The sites of memory are important to truth claims, identities, and many other aspects of human life. They are important for social and cultural continuity within ethnic, religious, national, and other groups, and across generations, occupational categories, and other identities. At the same time, the sites of memory can, and often do, become the focus of contestation, as in current debates over different histories of the American South—black, white, Hispanic—and symbols such as the Confederate flag and the Alamo (Brundage 2000), and reconsiderations of nationhood and power through memory work in African postcolonies (Werbner 1998c) and elsewhere (e.g., Abercrombie 1998; Rappaport 1990; Steedly 1993).

Language as Memory

All languages are fictions.

—SINFREE MAKONI (1998:245)

Languages are fictions because they are symbolic systems that are created and recreated. They are fictions because, like the English language as described by Pennycook (quoted in Makoni 1998:245)—and like other forms of memory—they are "fragmented, struggled over, resisted, rejected, diverse, broken." As fictions, languages encode historical formations and meanings, thus constituting psychocultural memory. For example, in Mexico, the Spanish conquest and indigenous resistance to it are symbolized by the languages—Spanish and indigenous—that perpetuate structures of domination and subordination through symbolic reenactments of 500-year-old hegemonic patterns. In contemporary Mexico, speaking Spanish is a tool of domination, not speaking Spanish is a tool of resistance—a reenactment of the old confrontation between Spanish and Indians (Cimet, this volume). At the same time, in an ironic polysemy, the national narrative of *mestizaje* (the blending of Spanish with indigenous cultures) makes the Spanish language the principal symbol of a unified, homogeneous nation.

Language loss is another issue, where native or vernacular languages actually cease to be used because of repression by a politically dominant group or from attrition when the dominant language takes precedence in education and daily life. Cultural revivals often include efforts to restore the use of indigenous languages. For example, tribal historian Lora Siders envisions the repatriated schoolhouse as a site for teaching the Miami language (Nesper, this volume).

Linguist Sinfree Makoni (1998) describes the colonization of African languages by missionaries who included in their dictionaries, teaching materials, and standardizations of vernacular languages the terms that suited their own ideological programs, thus transforming Africans' views of themselves as they spoke their transformed languages. In another linguistic shift, some contemporary Africans hide their ethnic origins by speaking various pan-ethnic forms of language, rather than the local forms of their place of origin, thus reinventing their pasts and creating new identities for themselves.

Thus language is an important arena for confrontations of subordinate and dominant peoples and social classes. It is a key symbol of personal and political identities and the means to define or redefine identity through the languages spoken. It encodes everyday memories and is the usual medium of rehearsing and expressing those memories, ranking perhaps with food (Sutton 2001) and bodily practices (Connerton 1989) as an emotionally evocative, person-centered (or endogenous) triumvirate of memory sites.

Embodied Memories and Meanings

[K]nowledge and remembering [are] in the hands and in the body.

—PAUL CONNERTON (1989:95)

Recent anthropological research on memory has focused attention on experiences and emotions that are inexpressible through language (Climo, Teski, and Stafford N.d.; Rosaldo 1984) and the idea that memories are not stored solely in the brain, but in the body and bodily practices (e.g., Connerton 1989; Csordas 1994; Stoller 1995; Sullivan 1995). "We do not gaze outside ourselves to discover preexisting stories," says Archibald (this volume); "instead we construct the stories around the sensory impressions we receive." For him, remembering involves all the senses. His memories of his grandmother, for example, include hearing the echoes of her voice and smelling her fragrance. Crumley (this volume) notes that culture is often transmitted in intimate, nonverbal, and informal ways, as when a child helps grandfather transplant lettuce: "It is everything in the moment: the person, the place, the time of year, the smells and sounds, the feel of the earth, the sensed ritual as well, as the practical importance of the act." The physical rhythm, the bodily practices of gardening, become part of Burgundian social memory.

Connerton (1989) stresses the importance of incorporated or embodied memories and the transmission of social memory through bodily practices such as posture, gesture, and habit, and commemorative ceremonies, which he views as ritual reenactments of meaningful cultural experiences or "performative memory" (:71). Memories are embodied in a great variety of performances such as libation sequences (Abercrombie 1998), spirit possession (Stoller 1995), and religious liturgies (Sullivan 1995); in mnemonic systems such as the Ifa divination of Yoruba people (Bascom 1980) and age-set rituals among Borana Galla of Ethiopia (Legesse 1973); and in everyday bodily practices such as posture, gestures, eating behavior, and clothing (Connerton 1989). Further, as anthropologist Paul Stoller (1995) shows, ritual (in this case, Hauka spirit possession among Songhay of Niger) not only conveys meaning and memory, but also becomes "a sensory arena of counter-memory" for ongoing and unresolved existential issues in the postcolonial context of political repression and economic struggles.

Lassiter (this volume) takes a sensory approach to Kiowa songs. For Kiowas, to know a song's power is "to *feel* song's power . . . to sense the past in the present, to *participate through sound* in a Kiowa continuity story of struggle and survival that is generations old" (emphasis in original). Social memory as song achieves meaning through a process of enactment and becoming real in the bodies of individuals. Lassiter tries to convey to readers some sense of this embodied power of song by using poetic transcriptions, storytelling, breathing pauses, and changes in topic and emphasis.

Philip Stafford (in Climo, Teski, and Stafford, N.d.) suggests that gerontologists doing reminiscence therapy and life reviews rely too heavily on a cognitive model of memory; an ethnographic perspective on memory should involve the whole body. "[E]very fiber of our bodies, every cell of our brain, holds memories—as does everything physical outside bodies and brains, even those inanimate objects that bear the marks of their past upon them in mute profusion . . . memory takes us into the environing world as well as into our individual lives" (Casey 1987:ix).

Meaning in Places

> *[Places] are fertilized into being through a confluence of voices. Places are complex constructions of social histories, personal and interpersonal experiences, and selective memory.*
>
> —MIRIAM KAHN (1996:167)

People become emotionally attached to places, and places have the power to evoke forgotten memories and even forgotten selves (Bourguignon 1996; Schneider 1998). Many different kinds of places hold memories, for example, the natural world (e.g., Boyd 2001; Lyon 1989; Trimble 1995), created landscapes (e.g., Korp 2000), and urban spaces and other sites of human habitation (e.g., Feld and Basso 1996; Rotenberg and McDonogh 1993; Rowles 1978; Zeleza and Kalipeni 1999). Specific places support continuity of memory and history as they become invested with meaning for specific individuals and groups, though such meanings may be contested within groups or between competing groups. And places can be "un-remembered," as when buildings or other landmarks are demolished and can no longer support the memories and meanings stored in them (Archibald 1999; cf. Klein 1997).

Every chapter in this book is grounded in particular "memory places" (Archibald this volume) or "memoryscapes" (Nuttall and Coetzee 1998:xii). For example, family vegetable gardens and rural landscapes in Burgundy hold many meanings for residents (Crumley, this volume). Gardens are "places of recreation, creative personal expression, and escape; they represent a resistance to the industrialized production of food. Gardens . . . reduce anxiety about food, encourage practical experimentation, and are the source of personal pride. They encourage reflection on larger issues of family, history, and Providence; they inevitably represent . . . the rhythms of lives lived within the seasons and with death." The vegetable gardens are also sites for transferring from older to younger generations the emotional and practical knowledge, behaviors, and attitudes that will enable them to continue to live on family land. Features of the landscape thus retain ecological understandings and are classrooms for younger generations.

For older white ethnics in a Philadelphia neighborhood, personal memories bound up personhood and identity with place, in spite of the fact that many elders felt alienated from newcomers of different ethnicities and ill at ease in their rapidly changing community (Cattell, this volume). The older residents achieved a sense of stability through their own homes and objects in them that helped evoke the past (cf. Miller 2001), their own past selves, and important persons, especially spouses who had died and adult children who had left home—a form of intense and emotionally vivid remembering that helped them reconstitute their families and communities. Barbara Myerhoff (1992) called this process "re-membering." Through re-membering, their urban neighborhood continued to give the older people a sense of continuity, ongoing identity, and meaning.

Connecting Biography and Social Memory

Individual and collective memory come together in the stories of individual lives. The process of constructing a life story is heavily mediated by social construction; for example, it usually occurs in a social setting that shapes the stories told. A life history writing group becomes a minisociety with its own norms for encouraging and discouraging elements in the stories told (Ray 2000). Or a story told as true but easily proven to be erroneous can nevertheless express important truths or serious concerns to the audience (Rosenberg 1997). Even solitary writers of autobiography are likely to have an audience in mind, and that imagined audience affects what the writer chooses to remember and write.

Personal narratives can aid the reconstruction of nearly forgotten social institutions, demonstrate continuities and changes in memory and identity over time, and reveal individual and collective reactions to historical events. In this era of rising resistance to global cultural flows and growing assertions of local distinctiveness (Harrison 1999), life stories raise issues about intellectual property rights and how (auto)biographical texts are authored, read, and interpreted (Denzin 1989) and also reflect the recent surge of experimental writing in anthropology (see Mattingly 1998 for a review).

Connerton (1989) distinguishes the memoirs or autobiographies of famous citizens or political elites and the oral histories of individuals from subordinate groups. Elites see their lives as worth remembering because they made decisions that had a wide influence or visibly changed the world (Connerton 1989). In contrast, the life histories of persons from subordinate groups have a different rhythm, a rhythm "not patterned by the individual's intervention in the working of the dominant institutions" (Connerton 1989:19). Even the terms autobiography (of elites) and life history (of lower classes) reflect status differences. Elites frequently produce their own narratives, but often subordinate groups such as the poor, ethnic minorities, and women are rescued from silence and invisibility through the efforts of social historians, sociologists, anthropologists, and others (e.g., Bailey and Bailey 1986; Bozzoli and Nkotsoe 1991; Personal Narratives Group 1989; van Onselen 1996). Even in academe, rescues from silence may be needed through biographical and autobiographical narratives, as in the case of women anthropologists (e.g., Behar and Gordon 1995; Parezo 1993; Schweitzer and Cattell N.d.) and women historians (e.g., Boris and Chaudhuri 1999; Kammen 1997:38–44) .

Today (auto)biographical techniques are a common denominator in many disciplines, including the humanities and the medical, psychological, and social sciences. They take many forms: medical histories, psychological case studies, novels, biographies of great men, life histories and portraits, psychohistory and psychobiography, oral history (Langness and Frank 1981), therapeutic life review (Kenyon, Clark, and de Vries 2001), family memoirs (e.g., Horowitz 1996), and life stories used to understand the life course and the aging of self and others (e.g., Black and Rubinstein 2000; Gubrium 1993; Kaufman 1986; Laird 1979; Myerhoff 1980; Savishinsky 2000).

Halbwachs was the first to theorize that individual memory is socially mediated and structured. For him, the idea of an individual memory totally separate from social memory was "an abstraction almost devoid of meaning" (Connerton 1989:37). He saw individual memories existing idiosyncratically only to the extent that a given person is the unique product of a particular intersection of groups (Fentress and Wickham 1992). Individuals, said Halbwachs, acquire, localize, and recall memories in the associational contexts of various groups, from kin affiliations to nations and transnational groupings. There is no neutral ground; every person has affiliation bias that "colors the form and content of remembering at all ages and across generations" (Ross 1991:197). "[N]early all personal memories are learned, inherited or, at the very least, informed by a common stock of social memories" (Brundage 2000:4; see also Casey 1987; Connerton 1989; and Schudson 1995, inter alia). Halbwachs believed that human dignity, statuses, and distinctiveness can emerge only in social settings (Coser 1992).

Growing numbers of social scientists are following Halbwachs in looking at memory as a social phenomenon. They have learned that collective memory is a process, just as individual memory is a process, that it is constructed and reconstructed by the dialectics of remembering and forgetting, shaped by semantic and interpretive frames, and subject to a panoply of distortions that make accuracy and truth major issues. But a persistent challenge in using life stories as social and cultural exemplars is sorting out individuals' typicality and uniqueness. American anthropologists and sociologists have recognized this problem at least since publication of *The Polish Peasant in Europe and America*, a monumental work by sociologists William Thomas and Florian Znaniecki (1918–20) that was based on life histories of Polish immigrants to Chicago. Sociologists and anthropologists are still struggling to understand the relationship between the individual and the collective, an enterprise in which they have been joined in recent times by many scholars from other social sciences and the humanities (Denzin 1989; Frank 2000). The chief difficulty arises from tensions between life history as the portrait of a unique individual with special abilities, problems, or achievements and that person as representative of sociocultural, economic, and political configurations. Oral historians skirt the problem to a degree when they focus on the unique contributions of individuals to a central theme such as labor or military history. Anthropologists and sociologists, trying to portray culture and society, find that exemplary lives are hard to find, if indeed they exist.

Nevertheless, individual lives can be explicated ethnographically so that variations show, by comparison and contrast, cultural patterns of thought and behavior along with the individuals' unique experiences. Early American anthropologists turned to life history in the 1920s to illuminate cultural patterns and typical behaviors among American Indians, as in *Crashing Thunder* (1926), the autobiography of a Winnebago man chosen as a "representative middle-aged individual" (Radin 1926). Of numerous ethnographic life histories (Langness and Frank 1981), probably the best known are those of Oscar Lewis and Marjorie Shostak. Their works are extraordinarily vivid portrayals of individual lives and, at the same time, the social groups in which the individuals live. Lewis's *Five Families* (1959) and *The Children of Sanchez* (1961) pioneered the use of multiple autobiographies and hence multiple perspectives on a shared past. Shostak's *Nisa* weaves together the autobiographical memories of Nisa, a !Kung (or Bushman, now called Ju/'hoansi) woman with ethnographic descriptions of Ju/'hoansi social organization and cultural dynamics (Shostak 1981, 1989). Through this device, Nisa's narrative becomes "part of an interconnecting set of narratives; it is embedded in the story of [her] group"—the group from which she derives her identity (Connerton 1989:21). These life stories thus express both personal and cultural truths and reveal connections between individual memory and social memory, culture, and history.

Jacob Climo (this volume) addresses the continuity of individual and collective memories over two generations in an ongoing ethnographic study of American Jewish migrants in Israel and their parents in the United States. In narrative interviews, both parents and children expressed the meaning of *aliyah* (migration to Israel) in a discourse of individualism, with individuals explaining their desire to "make aliyah" as rising from highly personal and subjective experiences and motives. At the same time, generational continuities in memory construction are common when parents and children in a family share strong attachments to American Jewish ethnic identity and collective Zionist ideology, memory, and history.

In another chapter, Larry Nesper explores the relationship between the memories of Lora, a Miami Indian tribal historian, and the history of the tribe's schoolhouse. Lora Siders, the sole living person who remembered the schoolhouse in its original location, mediated the transition. The transfer ceremony, involving photographs from Lora's life and old pictures of the schoolhouse, linked Lora's memories with deep social memories of her people. For other chapters that consider both individual and group levels at the same time, see Crumley; Francis, Kelleher, and Neophytou; Lassiter; Natzmer.

The Processes of Social Memory

Our third theme concerns the processes of memory involved in maintaining or seeking and constructing meaning from the past. These processes include remembering and forgetting and a multitude of distortions, as discussed earlier. Makoni (1998) prefers the term "unremember" to "forget" because it emphasizes that forgetting is an active process. Archibald (1999; this volume) identifies several memory processes that he experienced during his return to his home place after a thirty-year absence: "co-remembering," or remembering together with other persons; "re-remembering," or reexperiencing places and people, sights and smells, evoking emotions as well as fresh memories (rather than just recalling memories of memories); and "un-remembering," or finding nothing to stimulate and confirm his memories because the landscape or built environment had been altered beyond recognition. Schudson (1995) describes four memory processes: distanciation, the fading of details and emotional intensity over time; instrumentalization, putting the past to work in service of the present; narrativization, the encapsulation of the past in cultural forms (most often, narrative); and cognitivization and conventionalization, making the past knowable through cultural conventions such as autobiography, monuments, and memorialization. Other concepts include flashbulb memories (Brown and Kulik 1977, cited in Pillemer 1998), personal event memory (Pillemer 1998), re-membering (Myerhoff 1992), sociobiographic memory (Zerubavel 1996, cited in Olick and Robbins 1998), and vicarious memories (Teski and Climo 1995). So many attempts to identify and label memory processes are indications of the complexity of social memory, the difficulties of trying to describe and analyze it, and the need for conceptual and theoretical clarification in memory studies.

We do know that social memory is, on the one hand, cumulative and continuous, and on the other hand, changing, provisional, malleable, and contingent. In this section we briefly discuss some issues of truth and meaning in social memory and several general types of memory processes, with the proviso that these processes overlap, interact, and in various ways do not confine themselves to rigid categories.

Issues of Truth and Meaning

> *[T]he same words that constitute truth for some are, and always will be, myth for others, who inherit or embrace different assumptions and organizing concepts about the world.*
>
> —WILLIAM MCNEILL (CITED IN ROSS 1991:166)

A significant impact of postmodernity and the crisis of memory is tensions concerning accuracy and truth in representations of the past. Historian Michael

Kammen (1995:342), for example, has found empirical verifiability of both individual and collective memory "equally elusive." Nor is academic or scientific history—dependent mainly on written records—free from distortions and inaccuracies, since both the makers of records and the historians who consult records have interpretive frameworks that bias their selection of information. As historian William McNeill (cited in Ross 1991:166) said, in a discussion of the nature of historical truths: all history should really be called "mythohistory."

Sometimes social memory is extremely accurate, for example, when American baseball fans discuss the history of a game and insist on accuracy down to the minutest detail. But different standards of truth are applied to different genres and narrative styles, in different social or political contexts, and among different groups. Some memory traditions are regarded as entertaining or instructive, useful but fictional accounts of the past; others are seen as authoritative, factual claims about past events (Fentress and Wickham 1992). Political agendas may drive views of the past, as in the Holocaust denial by rightwing extremists and anti-Semites (Stern 2001) and international protests over new, officially authorized Japanese history textbooks for middle school children (Baker 2001; Prusher 2001). In the latter case, South Korea protested the description of 10,000 South Korean women taken to Japan to serve soldiers as prostitutes during World War II. The text called them "comfort women." South Korea said they were "sex slaves." While the Japanese government stood by the text, in the end the Japanese people turned it down: only 6 of Japan's 532 public school districts adopted the text. In this instance, as in many others, the social meanings of memories, the beliefs about them, is what matters, not their factual truth. And different groups have different and often conflicting needs to be met by their constructions of the past.

Putting aside issues of fact, Archibald (this volume) asks: "Can we stop demanding that memory be a surrogate for truth and acknowledge it as a faculty for defining meaning?" Of course, concerns for truth in the sense of factual correctness will not go away, as there are numerous situations (in law and elsewhere) where truth matters, and decisions about what is true have economic, political, or other consequences for individuals and groups. However, often the search for truth may in fact be a search for meaning.

For example, Lassiter (this volume) discusses Kiowa efforts to remedy what they regard as false memories about their ancestor Satethieday's arrest and death. The United States government's memory is that Satethieday murdered seven men, for which he was arrested, and that he committed suicide while in jail. Kiowas dispute this official record, saying that Satethieday neither murdered the seven men nor committed suicide. Their dispute takes place through song and stories, stories "told by . . . my great-grandmother": "We feel that was *wrong*. And we're going to have to find the documents to substantiate *our* facts" (emphasis in original).

Underlying the dispute about the facts in the case, for contemporary Kiowas, is a concern for the meaning of their ancestor's life, especially as it relates to their own search for meaning and identity.

A Sense of History: Continuities of Memory

Memories perceived as continuous with the past provide a sense of history and connection, a sense of personal and group identities. Whether such memories are true, reconstructions, or inventions seems to matter less than whether people accept them as truth or, at least, as useful and meaningful. Nevertheless, while reconstructions, revisions, and inventions of the past are possible and common, research suggests that various forces inhibit revisions and reinterpretations of the past, that some pasts are remarkably persistent over time, even surviving the imposition of new versions of the past, and that some persistence is the result of inertial forces such as habit and custom (Olick and Robbins 1998). Thus memory is the outcome of both dynamic processes and stasis.

Where cultural memories have been forgotten or lost, or are no longer appropriate, memory reconstruction provides continuity. The process of reconstruction may vary from a barely conscious restructuring of the past to the fully self-conscious activity of tradition building, as in the construction of a national cultural identity (Swiderski 1995) and the inventions of traditions to support political legitimacy (Hobsbawm and Ranger 1983) and for many other reasons (Kammen 1995). Memory reconstruction frequently has a role in everyday situations, such as the cultural management of death and remembrance of the dead. For example, London cemeteries express historical continuity and traditional values for various ethnic groups and, at the same time, reveal transitions and transformations in cultural patterns and identities (Francis, Kellaher, and Neophytou, this volume). American Jewish migrants to Israel include memories of ritual and symbolic reunification and reincorporation into the Zionist world following their migration, thus reconstructing and completing Jewish collective memory through discourse on reunification—a completion those remaining in diaspora cannot achieve (Climo, this volume).

In another example, Cohen (this volume), through interviews with elderly Irish working-class women, reconstructs the pervasive "culture of control" found in early twentieth century Great Britain. This culture perpetuated an unequal gender system, rigid gender roles, and clear boundaries between "the respectable and the rough." In the framework of this larger historical context, Cohen examines the roles of Irish working-class women in orchestrating the culture of control at the household and community levels through their reproductive and household survival strategies. Today, as elderly survivors, the women's memories serve to validate their struggles to themselves, to each other, and to their children, and to give meaning to their lives both past and present.

On the scale of national politics, Cimet (this volume) suggests that a reconstructed view of memory and history is possible in spite of Mexico's embedded, ongoing structure of violence committed by Spanish-speaking elites against indigenous-language speakers. The rebels' ability to engage the powerful structure of the government represents a new dialogue that has opened up "a space uncharted in Mexican history," a space in which memory is the basis for contesting the dominant, authoritative "official voice of history."

Silences and Forgetting

> *If the Party could thrust its hand into the past and say of this or that event, it never happened—that, surely, was more terrifying than mere torture and death.*
>
> —GEORGE ORWELL (1949:35)

Connerton (1989) notes that the mental enslavement of the subjects of a totalitarian regime begins when their memories are taken away; Kundera (1980) speaks of "liquidating a people" by erasing memory. Forgetting can be a profoundly political act, a rewriting of history to make it support existing or new power relationships (Smith 1995). The powerful use "forced forgetting" (Connerton 1989:12) to silence or displace memories inimical to their projects, replacing them with history of their own choosing or invention (Hobsbawm and Ranger 1983). The struggle of citizens against state power, of memory against forgetting, is powerfully portrayed in George Orwell's novel, *1984*, and Ray Bradbury's *Fahrenheit 451*. In the latter, when books—repositories of countless memories—were burned by the state, dissident individuals committed the books to memory, thus making themselves into the books and keeping the memories alive against a future freedom when books again can be printed.

Memories that exist as silences or gaps in the records (Pincheon 2000), as countermemories or alternative histories, are clearly connected with the exercise of economic and political power. For example, in the late nineteenth and early twentieth centuries, white Southerners in the United States depicted a benign view of slavery with honorable masters and contented slaves—a view that, because it was the public memory, effectively silenced "alternative memories of violence, exploitation, and cruelty" (Brundage 2000:7). African Americans' countermemory—kept out of sight of whites—was largely ignored by whites until the 1960s, when blacks had enough political power to insist on a more inclusive history. Forgetting and silences may also result when memories, such as the Holocaust and the violence of South African apartheid, are at the same time too terrible to remember (Climo 1995) and too terrible to forget (Tutu 1999).

During the long centuries of colonialism, history was written mainly by the conquerors, and the histories of subordinate groups were hidden or silenced.

These groups became "people without history" (Wolf 1984; cf. Connerton 1989; Lambek and Antze 1996). Such hidden histories may be recovered by the groups whose voices have been silenced, as in the case of African Americans in the South, or through the writing of oppositional histories by others such as historians and anthropologists (e.g., Abercrombie 1998; Brundage 2000; Daniel 1996; Rappaport 1990; Steedly 1993; Werbner 1998c). In this volume, Natzmer examines the role of the "untold stories, the voices that remain silent" in Chile's memory struggles. Many individuals choose invisibility and silence over the possibility of further government repression if they speak out. Others may be ignored by the powerful; for example, the indigenous Mapuche, comprising 10 percent of Chile's population, have been engaged in a long struggle to reclaim their ancestral lands and with them, their cultural heritage. But their voice is absent from the reconciliation dialogue and from other national discourses.

While the same is true of Mexico's indigenous peoples, the Chiapas Indian rebels used silence as a resource in their confrontation with Spanish-speaking government representatives. The rebels, appearing as a symbolic army in folkloric attire and masks and carrying old guns and broomsticks as weapons, began by not speaking at all—not speaking Spanish, the language of conquest and not speaking their own language, the language of resistance. Cimet (this volume) interprets the Indian presence and initial silence as a challenge that put the Indians on equal footing with the government representatives in the ensuing dialogue. Following the American Civil War, there were two decades of silence, in both North and South, about the war and its causes—a case of amnesia being used to allow some reconciliation and bonding in preference to remembering (Kammen 1995).

National museums, which tend to validate the perspectives of the politically powerful, have many silences in terms of material objects either not shown or shown in such ways as to reinforce the political rulers. Chilean museums do not display *arpilleras,* patchwork wallhangings that include images of police brutality and abduction of loved ones. Arpilleras were smuggled out of Chile and displayed throughout the world, but they are not shown in Chile, which lacks a national narrative rejecting past violence and supporting the idea of reconciliation (Natzmer, this volume).

In South Africa, museums under the apartheid government reflected white history favorably and black Africans as specimens with little human dignity. By the late 1980s, as apartheid was unraveling, history and memory were no longer the prerogative of whites. Museums were rethinking their representations of South African history and expanding their collections to tell a more inclusive story of the past (Davison 1998). One of the most interesting of these "unsilencings" is the District Six Museum, where former residents of the District Six area in Cape Town put together an exhibit with the district's old street signs and other memorabilia rescued from the physical destruction of what had been, before apartheid, a vibrant multiracial, multiethnic community. The reconstruction, in the museum, of District Six is an instance of "a diaspora community intent on reassembling, and asserting, its public memory" (de Kok 1998:63).

Perhaps the most notorious historical silence was that surrounding the Holocaust in Nazi Germany during the war years. One of the most notorious of more recent historical silences involved the persecutions of South Africa's apartheid government, which went to extremes to silence the voices of those it oppressed (though it was certainly not alone among national governments in silencing and disappearing opponents and marginalized people). The legacy of those forced silences and forgettings will undoubtedly—for years to come—haunt South African efforts to become one nation, the rainbow nation, as some memories are rescued from silence and others fall into it in the process of evoking and reshaping the South African past (Nuttall and Coetzee 1998).

Contested Memories, Contested Meanings

> *[H]ow fiercely people will fight to chronicle their personal and collective experience in the face of an official history that has been falsified.*
>
> —ERNA PARIS (QUOTED IN ROSE 2001).

Any memory can be challenged—and many are. Just as sharing is an aspect of collective memory, so too are discussion, negotiation, and conflict (Brundage 2000). Struggles over identity, political power, and legitimacy often revolve around memory sites and practices. Political elites and others in positions of power try to be "the master[s] of memory and forgetfulness" (LeGoff 1992, quoted in Brundage 2000:11) because to control memory is to control history and its interpretations of the past. Resistance to such control is widespread and may express itself in silences, as discussed above, or in more confrontational ways, both subtle and overt (e.g., Watson 1994).

For example, American Indian history has usually been told from the framework of "white history," which privileges the written record (Lassiter, this volume). In contrast, Kiowas' understanding of their history and identity, as expressed through song and story, is grounded in social relationships, in memory, and experience. Kiowas resist white efforts to assimilate them by expressing their countermemories: "*We have a rich history. No one* can ever take that away." "*They've taken our land.* They've taken everything they could. [But] I will never let them have my language." This song "belongs to your ancestor. A *great* war leader of the Kiowas." (emphasis in original). Thus Kiowas are setting for themselves the boundaries of group memory and identity, rejecting the historical narratives of white history, and making their own interpretation of history.

Cimet (this volume) sees contemporary Mexico as haunted by history and memory, especially by the fundamental historical confrontation between indigenous peoples and dominant Spanish-speakers that originated in the conquest. This confrontation, Cimet argues, is reenacted daily in speech and symbolically in the relations between indigenous groups and the government. Each group has its own view of Mexican history. The national narrative of mestizaje leaves no room to recognize the centuries' long subordination, ill treatment, and repression of indigenous groups because, from its perspective, no one has been intentionally omitted from Mexico's development and self-definition. Indigenous groups have survived by virtue of historical and cultural memories that articulate their plight, shape their story, and are the basis for intense resistance and eventually, at least in some cases, recognition.

Healing Memories: Reconciliation and Redress

True forgiveness deals with the past, all of the past, to make the future possible.

—DESMOND TUTU (1999:279)

Ultimately, in the face of injustices, the question arises of possible reconciliation and the redress of history and memory. Can truth and reconciliation commissions, such as those established in Chile, South Africa, and Serbia, reconcile alternative, opposing, conflicting versions of the same historical events? Can they redress wrongs, atrocities, gross injustices? Can "the truth of wounded memories" be a healing truth (Judge Ismail Mahomed, quoted in Tutu 1999:25)? In a despairing postmodern voice, Milan Kundera (1969:245) suggests that "most people deceive themselves with a pair of faiths: they believe in eternal memory (of people, things, deeds, nations) and in redressibility (of deeds, mistakes, sins, and wrongs). Both are false faiths. In reality the opposite is true: everything will be forgotten and nothing will be redressed."

Natzmer (this volume) takes a more pragmatic and hopeful view, claiming that the ability to create a social history or national narrative that can accommodate the conflicting memories of opposing groups may well determine the success of reconciliation efforts in Chile. She describes conflicts over the ownership of memory in Chile, develops a model for analyzing the construction and reconstruction of the past through creative expression, and asks, in a voice of hope: Do creative expressions help resolve conflicts between those who committed atrocities and those who suffered them? Or does remembering intensify the differences and increase the conflicts?

Natzmer argues that creative expressions (pop culture, the media, literature, rituals in public spaces, personal narratives) are potent symbolic representations in struggles over memory that offer possibilities for reconciliation. After seventeen years of military dictatorship, Chile is now working to uncover the truth about disappearances, executions, tortures, and murders through the National Commission on Truth and Reconciliation. Yet no consensus exists. Supporters of former dictator Pinochet justify past violence as necessary to maintain state sovereignty against communism. Pinochet himself has called for both sides to forget. But those who wish to remember demand a public admission of guilt and contend that "only through truth and justice can the healing process begin."

From a different perspective, the answers to Natzmer's questions are context specific, dependent upon the possibilities of redress and the perceptions and forgiveness of the individuals and groups who have been harmed. Nesper (this volume) portrays the repatriation of a Miami schoolhouse under the National American Graves Protection and Repatriation Act. This act, passed by Congress in 1990, requires the return of Indian skeletal remains and material objects in federally funded museums to federally recognized Indian tribes. The return of the schoolhouse to the Miami Indians of Indiana, who are no longer a federally recognized American Indian tribe, represents a transformation of the relationship between political communities. Nesper shows how tribal memories of the schoolhouse, and its eventual repatriation, empowered the Miamis to "re-imagine themselves" as a people in the twentieth century "along deeply traditional and ancient lines." The schoolhouse is a physical and spatial representation of their past that legitimates the present. Today the schoolhouse is a pilgrimage site for Miamis and a place where healing ceremonies—and hopefully the healing of memories—take place.

Another model for reconciliation is found in the work of public historian Archibald (1999; this volume) at the Missouri Historical Society. Archibald works to develop for St. Louis communal narratives, narratives that will redefine the community of St. Louis to include, in particular, African Americans. For Archibald, history is not an immutable fact, but "an inclusive conversation of multiple perspectives on enduring concerns" (1999:166). In his view, diverse voices must be heard, multiple perspectives must be included. The result may be cacophony—or it may be community. Brundage (2000), looking at similar issues over the wider American South, wonders if the reconciliation of Southerners' sharply divergent memories is possible. A particular impediment is the "moonlight-and-magnolia" view of the Southern (white) past which is a major tourist commodity and a major impediment to the creation of a community of memory. The South, says Brundage (19), needs "a redemptive, inclusive reinterpretation" in order to heal the open wound of its past. Whether this can be achieved, he feels, depends to a considerable degree on the extent to which the South's "heterogeneous memories" can be acknowledged (20).

In South Africa, postapartheid efforts to recover and reconstruct memories have included museums, commemorative events, biographical accounts, and most particularly, the Truth and Reconciliation Commission, whose production of memory itself imposed new silences in the name of the reconciled new nation, the "rainbow nation," and its new national narrative of inclusion (Krog 1998; Nuttall and Coetzee 1998; Tutu 1999). The new openness in South Africa has inspired various countermemories such as the museum commemorating the razing of the multiracial District Six community (de Kok 1998); the rewriting of Afrikaner history to include nonwhite ancestors (Coetzee 1998); rethinking and reimagining exhibits in existing museums; and opening new museums such as District Six and Robben Island to explore South Africa's history and reshape memory and history, from the rainbow nation perspective (Davison 1998; Deacon 1998; Singer 2001).

Memory and Identity

The fourth theme concerns social memory, its voices and texts, as representations of the past of particular categories or groups of people in specific times and places. Such representations of the past have powerful relevancies for the present and the future in constructing or reconstructing and claiming or rejecting group identities, including family, ethnic and other groups, and nations; in making claims to land and other resources; and in various other issues. "National and other identities are established and maintained through a variety of mnemonic sites, practices and forms" (Olick and Robbins 1998:124). Nor is identity something achieved and completed; rather, it is an ongoing process of construction of self and other and of social groups.

Representations of the Past

> *Ours is a traditional goal of ethnography applied to the past: to journey with our informants through time as they conceptualize it.*
>
> —MAREA TESKI AND JACOB CLIMO (1995:1)

Postmodernism helped bring the issue of representation into prominence in the academic world, just as the struggles of subordinated people to be heard have brought the issue into prominence in the political world. In both worlds, the conversation is often discordant, even within groups, for individuals may act on their own behalf, rather than with the group in mind, and consensus is usually difficult to achieve. Questions arise: Who owns the story, the narrative, the history, the memories, even the names (as in current controversies over the use of American Indian names for football teams)? Whose voice or voices, whose texts are authentic or authoritative? Which voice, which text should be privileged or ignored? Can one person speak for another, or for a group, and if so, always or just sometimes?

These are difficult issues for anthropologists, who have been speaking for others in self-authorizing texts (ethnographies) for many decades. The *reductio ad absurdum* of postmodern and political interrogations of ethnography would be to say that no one can ever understand anyone else or speak for anyone else, a conclusion we do not accept. While a person can never be completely inside another culture, we do see value in attempting to understand The Other and sharing our understandings through the ethnographic enterprise.

In this volume, the contributors reach for understanding and sensitive representation through a variety of approaches to voice and text. They try to achieve a balance of insiders' and ethnographers' voices and also the voice of historical records; and a balance of texts—stories, songs, words spoken and written, interview material—that could loosely be called narratives. For example, in Nesper's account of the repatriation of a Miami Indian schoolhouse, the voice of Lora Siders as tribal historian is dominant as she shares her personal memories of the schoolhouse. Nesper speaks as ethnographer–witness, documentarian of contemporary events and critic of ethnographic and historical records. For example, responding to published ethnohistorical claims that the Miami Indians were "acculturated," Nesper issues a direct challenge: according to whom? and meaning what? Cattell uses several voices: historical sources, older longtime residents' stories, and her own ethnographic interpretation of the meaning of elders' personal memories of their neighborhood and their sense of continuity of the self.

Another aspect of representation comes up when ethnographers' interpretations do not coincide with insiders' perspectives on the meanings of their past and present lives. Climo (this volume), for example, fully expected his informants to narrate their experiences of migrating to Israel in terms of collective memory and ideology; instead, they expressed themselves in a discourse of individualism. From Cattell's (this volume) outsider analysis prior to doing interviews, the Philadelphia neighborhood of Olney looked capable of providing everything its older residents might need, but the elders themselves pointed to deficiencies and claimed they no longer felt at home. In such cases, it is wise to defer to the insiders, or at the very least, to look closely into the discrepancies.

Issues of Identity

> *[W]e can speak of a real community as a "community of memory," one that does not forget its past . . . [and] which is involved in retelling its story, its constitutive narrative . . . and it offers examples of the men and women who have embodied and exemplified the meaning of the community.*
>
> —ROBERT BELLAH ET AL. (1985:153)

Identity begins with individuals. "We increasingly invent ourselves," says Archibald (this volume), "and we modify the story of ourselves to maintain consistency." Thus, a person's memory and life story become "myths that will not stand the test of objectivity and accuracy when tested against recorded facts." Such stories, true or not, are "the sources of my consciousness and my identity, the stuff of me." Yet even the most individualistic persons—such as Archibald and the American Jewish migrants to Israel (Climo, this volume)—situate their personal identities within social and cultural frameworks, where memory plays a similarly significant role in constituting the identity of groups. Everyone is socialized into "mnemonic communities," where we learn to remember much that we did not experience as individuals; that is, we develop our "sociobiographic memories" (Zerubavel 1996, quoted in Olick and Robbins 1998:123).

Sociobiographic memories cross time and space, linking individuals within generations (cohorts) and across generations and tying individual identities to social identities. For example, Francis, Kellaher, and Neophytou (this volume) found that London cemeteries are sites that reveal the "intertwined processes of memorialization and identity construction of both self and other." Through the nexus of cemeteries, individual and family identities become ethnic and communal identities, and local group history is linked to larger historical processes. For those whose ethnic identities are centered in distant homelands, the cemetery is a memoryscape, a diasporic bridge, which is "a reflection of their homeland and an expression of collective experience."

In the contemporary world, national identities are of great importance. Like other identities, they are established, maintained, and renewed through various mnemonic practices and sites, such as centennial celebrations, clothing, heritage, heroes, language, national anthems, monuments, and museums (Olick and Robbins 1998:124–125). The past thus serves as the basis for social cohesion among groups, including nations, or creates the illusion of consensus, such as legitimizing a government (Kammen 1991). For example, Crumley (this volume) demonstrates continuities in memory and identity among Burgundians that are achieved through their garden practices. She draws parallels for all French people, urban and rural, whose devotion to their vegetable gardens symbolizes a "refutation of globalizing corporate control." Gardens link the French to their mythic past, "when smallholders controlled their own food resources. . . . In France, it is impossible to disentangle national and regional identity from the powerful mythic images that center on the garden, so enamored is the entire nation with expressing emotion and personality through the production and consumption of artisanal food and drink."

While nation-states use history to establish, maintain, or renew their identity and power, hegemonic struggles also go on within national borders, such as those described in this volume by Cimet, Lassiter, Natzmer, and Nesper. For example, in the United States, American Indians wrestle with issues of identity, economic opportunity, and political autonomy against losses such as land, languages, and customs. Among Kiowas, as fewer people speak the Native language, song has become the crucial link between the memories of contemporary Kiowas and their ancestors and the dominant symbol of the Kiowa past and Kiowa identity in the present. Though songs are individually owned, they are sung and experienced in communal settings and thus become bridges between the individual and the collective, the past and the present. Through song, Kiowas remember their past and are empowered to renegotiate their past and their Kiowa identity in community-centered dialogue (Lassiter, this volume).

Memory and the Search for Meaning

What is the future of memory studies? And what is the future of memory?

In many important ways the human future depends on our understandings of the meanings of culture, social memory, and history (whether they be separate categories or similar), especially in regard to identity and hegemonic relations and recovery of the past—including hidden and repressed pasts—in a world where many are disconnected from their pasts. Surely a crucial issue is to find ways to resolve contested representations of the past and the claims and counterclaims arising from such contestation. The cross-cultural and culturally sensitive approach of anthropology can be of value in constructing visions of the past that support visions of a future embracing distinctive group identities and a more cooperative interdependence among groups—a hopeful, perhaps wildly optimistic, recognition that it may be possible to create communities of memory even from pasts as complex, contestational, and divisive as those of Germany, South Africa, the Balkans, the American South, Indians in the United States and Mexico, and many others.

Given the processual nature of memory and identity, a processual or narrative approach is appropriate, but "some theoretical order and clarification" are needed (Vinitzky-Seroussi 2001:495). At present, memory studies are—as noted earlier—" a nonparadigmatic, transdisciplinary, centerless enterprise" (Olick and Robbins 1998:106). One could equally well characterize the field as being in a liminal state, a state of creativity and searching, on its way to a more comprehensive theoretical approach. As it is, there is much yet to learn about social memory, history, and culture, their details and their interconnections, and the human impulse to remember and to find meaning in our remembering.

I

CONTINUITY IN MEMORY, HISTORY, AND CULTURE

Exploring Venues of Social Memory

I

CAROLE L. CRUMLEY

All inquiry and all learning are but recollection.

—HERRMANN AND CHAFFIN (1988:28)

Social Memory and Environmental Change

ONE LEARNS CULTURE—but how? Which elements and events of everyday life transmit values, beliefs, techniques, strategies? While anthropology's answer in the nineteenth and much of the twentieth century was to study public institutions and ritual practice, today's answer highlights new sites and contexts of transmission. Much of the information passed between generations is practiced away from public view, in intimate rituals that few discuss, but everyone knows. To acknowledge such transmission sites, we must reframe our questions, exploring different voices and different conditions of existence through knowledge and memory.

Some of the new questions are: What circumstances fix individual memory? How does memory enable and shape communication among individuals, within groups and among groups? How does memory serve intergenerational communication? How does memory facilitate community redefinition and change? How does memory enable societies to adapt to environmental change? It is with this last question I propose to examine the others.

Social memory is the means by which information is transmitted among individuals and groups and from one generation to another. Not necessarily aware that they are doing so, individuals pass on their behaviors and attitudes to others in various contexts but especially through emotional and practical ties and in relationships among generations (McGaugh 1995; Schacter 1995). To use an analogy from physics, social memory acts like a carrier wave, transmitting information over generations regardless of the degree to which participants are aware of their roles in the process.

Rather than a definition of social memory focusing on the written and oral transmission of information (Goody 1987; Tonkin 1992; Vansina 1965, 1985), I employ a definition that includes other means of transmission that are, in whole or in part, nonverbal. Intentional, performative expression (e.g., dance) as well as intentional practices (correct use of a tool) and unintentional forms of expression (body language) would be included (Connerton 1989; Searleman and Herrmann 1994). Of special interest is the observation of practice and the identification of metapractice or guiding principles of practice, linking memory studies to practice theory (Bourdieu 1977). Like other modes of communication, these more visual and physical transmissions are a tangle of intentional and unintentional messages delivered through the cultural sieve of class, gender, ethnicity, and the like. Further tempered by individual experience, social memory provides fundamental measures (ideas, practices, beliefs, capabilities, histories) by which social change and spatial transformation are evaluated. Thus defined, social memory (the carrier wave) may be employed to examine transgenerational knowledge (the content).

Framed by a cognized nature that is place dependent, community perceptions, attitudes, behaviors, values, and institutions are communicated across generations. The category of environmental knowledge is especially important because it sets the parameters, in a specific geographic context, for evaluation of past, current, and prospective production and other transformative technologies. Cultural understandings undergird decisions about which environmental practices are maintained, which are modified, and which ideas are given substance. Environmental knowledge may be studied using the principles of historical ecology (Balée 1998; Crumley 1987, 1994a, 1994b; Egan and Howell 2001). Historical ecology traces human–environment relations in a particular place and over a specified period of time by integrating evidence from the physical, biological, and social sciences and from the pivotal interdisciplinary fields of anthropology, archaeology, history, geography, and ecology. The historical ecology of specific places renders explicit both the contexts in which the environment impacts communities and the effects of human activities on the environment.

In stable societies technological information about production (e.g., carpentry, stock raising) is passed quite transparently from one generation to another, often in specialized learning contexts such as apprenticeships and schools. In contrast, place-specific environmental information, such as local climate, soils, and moisture regimes, is less publicly visible and has specialized forms of transmission. The term *capturing* refers to such information, amassed over generations of observation and experimentation. The volume and sophistication of captured information—for example, the observed range of variation in a region's climate—is directly proportional to the length of time a group has inhabited the region (Gunn 1994:84; see also Crumley 1992). Climate, in that it modifies all other environmental phenomena, is a key ecological variable. For example, the frequency, duration, and intensity of temperature and moisture affect seasonality, soils, and the success of particular species. Considerable captured environmental information is transmitted orally, in casual discussions among neighbors, in instructional sessions between adult and child, in stories told and proverbs uttered. Another important route is nonverbal, encompassing the style in which something is done, the choices made among possibilities, the rhythm of work.

Like technical knowledge, the effective transmission of a community's captured environmental information requires a practical, although not necessarily formal, classroom. In this paper, I examine two aspects of the environment of rural Burgundy in France that serve as informal learning venues—vernacular gardens (family vegetable gardens) and the rural landscape. The fractal relation between these two scales of analysis and systems of knowledge will be explored. I demonstrate how social memory and historical ecology are mutually enriching, bringing advances in both social and ecological theory to bear on contemporary global issues.

Gardens and Landscapes as Transmitters of Social Memory

In the physical world, features of the landscape such as forests, mountaintops, pastures, and gardens concentrate and retain a community's ecological understandings, record both intentional and unintentional acts, and serve the younger generation as a classroom. Social memory, regarding the keeping of gardens and the maintenance of landscapes in Burgundy, teaches stewardship in a rich context that is simultaneously practical, empirical, spiritual, and emotional.

Like a coaxial cable on the ocean floor, bundles of cultural information are arranged around a central concept. Manifested as both a practice and as an ideal, such concepts elicit a variety of reasons for their existence. This multiplicity of rationales for engaging in certain practices ensures the transmission of fundamental information, but also leaves room for individual differences in experience, perception, and conviction. The idea of the garden, the many rationales for which range from practical utility to cosmic meaning, is such a concept. Vernacular (vegetable) gardens, ubiquitous in the landscape, are an excellent instructional site. At a more inclusive scale, landscape is similarly rich, both in meaning and in reality. Landscape is the spatial manifestation of the relations between humans and the environment, the visual signature of a territory—a vista—that both forms and is formed by the people who inhabit it (Marquardt and Crumley 1987). Inasmuch as the meanings attributed to the past and to nature give periods and societies their character and inform their actions, a critical narrative of human–environment relations can also be read in the landscape and its constituent elements, within the integrative framework of historical ecology.

The information contained in gardens and landscapes is conserved in the character and spatial arrangement of their respective elements, such as groupings of certain species and the siting of structures. Examples of garden elements are cold frames, medicinal plant groupings, potato patches; landscape elements are wood lots, springs, marketplaces. Inasmuch as initial conditions support and constrain human activity, these elements reflect both the distant and the recent history of the human–environment relation. Arranged in patches or mosaics at many scales (fractals) and documented through time and across space, such elements constitute practical units of analysis.

The focus on elements and their relations to one another enables pattern recognition at any spatial scale from microorganismic to regions and ecological zones (Hammett 1992; O'Neill et al. 1991; Pielou 1975, 1984), and even more broadly to phenomena at the continental (e.g., air mass patterns) and global (ozone layer) scales (Gunn 1994; Turner, Dale, and Gardner 1989). Similarly, pattern may be recognized at various temporal scales, as has been amply demonstrated by the Annales school of French history (Burke 1990).

In addition to geography (space) and history (time), cognition (mind) is a third important analytic dimension. For example, in cultures where class differences are marked, elite gardens—comprised of flowers, trees, and shrubbery—serve symbolically as miniature landscapes; they display and enhance status and are sources of pleasure, not subsistence (Leone 1984, 1988). Employed almost like stage sets, pleasure gardens manifest individual attempts to transmit identity, taste, and style (Le Dantec and Le Dantec 1990; Pugh 1988; Thacker 1979); like all dramatic creations, they are subject to marked shifts in fashion. If pleasure gardens are theaters, then vernacular gardens are schools. The vernacular garden (French *potager*, literally soup maker) is a conservative form, being home to vegetables, fruit trees, and other elements useful in the maintenance of the household (Erp-Houtepan 1986; Hunt and Wolschke-Bulmahn 1993; Miller and Gleason 1994). These gardens sustain traditions, store hard-won solutions to local conditions, and represent real household wealth. Both vernacular and pleasure gardens represent in miniature a vision of the owner's cosmic order but in the vernacular garden, the gardener who labors and the owner who enjoys are one and the same.

Vernacular gardens produce diverse benefits, and their role in traditional agrarian and agropastoral societies is primordial. They offer gardeners a rich, personalized mnemonic that is "good to think" (Levi-Strauss 1963:89; see also Francis and Hester 1990). The greater the range of thoughts and behaviors and the richer the meanings that concepts such as the garden evoke, the greater likelihood that diverse information bundled around that concept will be transmitted. An individual gardener's knowledge and experience, in an interplay with the environmental mosaic, ensures both substantive and stylistic variation. In the same way that a cable gains strength from myriad individual strands, the more reasons there are to value the garden, the more likely its messages will be transmitted.

In the vernacular garden, complex information about ecosystems and practices that ensure their maintenance are adapted to the region and the locale. This knowledge passes from one generation to another out of sentiment as well as good sense: vernacular gardening is an intimate activity, and kin share both the work and the harvest. Vernacular gardens act as reservoirs of social practice (e.g., age and gender roles) and ecological knowledge. So, too, do landscapes.

Unlike vernacular gardens, entire landscapes are rarely molded by a single person; instead, landscapes preserve the record of many individual actions, ideas, and societal practices. Even when elites have the means to alter many aspects of the countryside, others are still free to attach their own meaning to various landscape elements and spaces and manage to turn them to other uses (Crumley and Marquardt 1987, 1990; Schama 1995). Thus vigilance and stiff punishment have never been enough to ensure that even a royal preserve could be kept safe from poachers and gleaners.

Rural elites can adorn their estates with exotic plants and animals, and create or modify bodies of water, forests, and fields, but such activities are usually limited to the elites' places of residence. An exception is when disparate properties are owned and rented out, or the land is put up as collateral, under the same management scheme; then, the renter or debtor may be obliged to follow the wishes of a distant and ill-informed landlord or deed holder.

Institutions can shape landscapes by replicating activities in several locations. For example, religious institutions are frequently large landowners. It is estimated that during certain periods of the Middle Ages, the Church owned over 50 percent of French land. Monastic orders and royal estates, while engaged in essentially the same kind of activities as surrounding farms, nonetheless undertook these activities on a scale far beyond that of farm families (Harvey 1981). Former royal and monastic holdings can still be discerned on the French landscape from the air, although ecclesiastical policy and royal privilege are no longer major influences in shaping the landscape.

More essential to the shaping of landscapes and more enduring are activities associated with widespread patterns of subsistence, such as grain agriculture or stock raising. This is because many individuals and families, not just elites, find economic utility in the same elements of the landscape and foster their continuity from generation to generation. In contrast to industrial agriculture, in which particular crops or animals are raised exclusively for market, traditional farming, termed smallholding, meets the majority of domestic subsistence needs (Netting 1993). Vegetables, cereals, meat, and condiments are produced on the farm, most of them (excepting grains and herd animals) within steps of the farmhouse door. In the absence of electricity and community water supplies, a farm's woodlot, springs, and ponds provide heat, light, and water.

Spatial concerns are central to the efficient management of all farms, but they are especially important on traditional farms, where numerous daily activities are the responsibility of relatively few individuals (Van Deventer 2001). Frequent tasks must be undertaken as close to one another and to home as possible. The less frequent the activity, the further it can be away from home (von Thunen 1966; Chisholm 1962). Over generations, the spatial organization of farms in a region becomes consistent with a particular suite of activities, and the landscape takes on a visible regularity.

Learning Burgundy

Burgundy, in east-central France, has been in the political and economic mainstream for millennia, its natural resources supporting the enduring presence of both industry and agriculture. Always a prize because of its physical diversity, wealth, and strategic location, the region was often taken, but rarely destroyed.

Great polities, beginning 2,500 years ago with the Celtic Aedui (whose ancient territory corresponds with contemporary Burgundy), forged long-distance trade and military alliances. Artisans among the Aedui sold steel weapons to the Roman army and supplied Rome with grain, hams, and other comestibles. The viticulture for which Burgundy is famed throughout the world dates to at least Roman times. Burgundian forests supplied ships' masts for the Roman fleet, scaffolding for medieval cathedrals, and roof beams for early modern Paris. Burgundy boasted the first Christian bishopric (Autun) after Rome itself, and the region's wealth supported powerful Burgundian, Frankish, and Carolingian polities.

Beginning in the tenth century, the Dukes of Burgundy were eponymous with cultural refinement and political power. Great monastic houses (Cluniac, Cistercian), whose influence and holdings later spread through all of Europe, were founded in Burgundy. Burgundian iron and coal resources were of strategic importance in World Wars I and II, and radioactive materials for Marie Curie's experiments and for Cold War arsenals came from the region. Throughout its history and continuing to the present day, much of the wealth of this politically and economically important region of Europe has been in the hands of smallholders.

Neither France's consolidation as a monarchy in the fourteenth century nor the subsequent French nation-state has entirely subsumed Burgundy's independence. Today the region sends two representatives, apart from the French national delegation, to the European Union; its smallholder farmers may be seen on CNN in the streets of Paris and Seattle, protesting global agricultural policies. During the last two centuries, the industrial revolution and the need for labor in the world wars have diminished rural Burgundian population and modified farm production strategies. One of the most profound influences on agricultural production in the region occurred after World War II, as France sought to rebuild its economy by modernizing agriculture in order to compete globally.

Modernization entailed reducing the number of smallholders, replacing ancient peasant methods of production with more intensive technologies, and promoting formal agricultural education to replace local knowledge. Our project has documented local resistance to these efforts now and in the past (Van Deventer 2001; see also Bové and Dufour 2000). This region, long open to the outside world, provides insights on how durable land use in the hands of a self-reliant farming population has been—and can still be—compatible with global economic goals of sustainability (Netting 1993).

Burgundy is particularly sensitive to global environmental changes that affect human and other living populations and can serve as a laboratory in which contemporary issues—diversity and sustainability—may be studied, and where local, regional, and global spatial scales may be linked. Burgundy is situated at a global climatic triple point where three major regimes—the Atlantic, the Continental, and the Mediterranean—meet; the first two are temperate-latitude regimes, the last subtropical. The region's climate history reveals that the boundary between the temperate systems and the subtropical system, termed an ecotone, has shifted several hundred kilometers in response to extended periods of globally cool (southward movement) or globally warm (northward movement) conditions. For example, environmental, archaeological, and documentary evidence indicates that the ecotone has traversed Burgundy several times in the past two millennia (Crumley 1993; Gunn et al. n.d.). At the broad temporal (2,500 years) and spatial (region, continent) scales, the population's ability to adjust to profound and often rapid change appears linked to the biotic and economic diversification of smallholders (Crumley 1993, 1994a, 1994b, 1995, 2000; Holling 1986; Magny 1995).

Since my research group began working in Burgundy in 1975, we have examined changes in settlement, economy, environment, and demography that historic, long-term shifts in the Western European ecotones entailed. From these data, we have projected changes that would accompany contemporary global warming. We have monitored contemporary practices that count as ecological successes (gardening) and as failures (Cold War radioactive waste dumps, extensive gravel mining in river valleys).

Our research methods include archaeology, a variety of paleo-environmental studies, ethnohistory, demography, and ethnography. We have three millennia of archaeological evidence for biota, land use, and settlement, and over three centuries of detailed population data. For the work on contemporary gardens and landscapes, we have interviewed thirty gardeners and farmers and amassed documentary evidence (e.g., from almanacs) for older plants and practices. Our spatial data are aggregated into a geographic information system with over 100 layers. Since the 1970s, we have been accumulating LANDSAT and SPOT imagery of the region, as well as data from AIRES and other scanners. We have digitized a variety of contemporary and historic maps, the earliest from 1759. This extensive information offers a unique opportunity to look closely at how the region's economies, both domestic and industrial, have been sustained for the past two thousand years. The ethnographic research reported here allows exploration of an important tension between smallholders' traditional practices and contemporary pressures on their way of life.

Gardening Lessons

Like most French households—and many regions throughout Europe—rural and urban Burgundians have a garden, despite the ready availability of quality produce at open-air markets and in stores. In urban areas, garden space is rented along railroad right-of-ways; in towns, backyards are much more often gardens than lawns. In the countryside, the garden is a few steps from the kitchen door. This tradition of domestic production appears to be unbroken at least as far back as the first millennium B.C. It offers a remarkable opportunity to study the role gardens have played in allowing households a means of autonomous adaptation to social upheaval and Burgundy's unpredictable weather.

Research indicates that among the effects of the global increase of greenhouse gases will be meteorological instability, seasonal slippage, and an increase in extreme events such as powerful storms and hail (Camuffo and Enzi 1992:153). Because of its position at the West European climatic triple point, inhabitants of Burgundy have for centuries been forced to both anticipate just such conditions and to rally in their wake. An important means of reducing risk associated with inclement weather is the garden. Unlike field crops, gardens shelter numerous species in special soils and under controlled microclimatic conditions. Plants receive individual attention and enable the gardener to develop an intimate understanding of soils, winds, and seasons as they relate to the garden plot.

In addition to volatile climate, Burgundy's varied geology and broken terrain yield a landscape in which microclimates play a crucial part in the success of all plant and animal communities. While a locale may benefit from high quality soils or abundant rainfall, advantages are easily offset by other circumstances, such as less favorable exposures or increased danger of frost and freeze. Disastrous late spring and early fall freezes, torrential rains, softball-sized hail, and extended droughts beset Burgundy.

Rural people know their community's microclimates well enough to draw them on a map, and gardeners can map subtle differences in their garden plots. Features, such as a hill that both breaks the wind and produces a rain shadow, or the elevation-related distribution of chestnut and cherry trees, give every farm its distinct microclimate. Farmers accurately recount the years in which cold or drought or floods took their toll, and they retell relatives' weather tales from as far back as the late-nineteenth century. One man, an amateur historian, knows the harshest winters and famine summers beginning in the seventeenth century. Most people can recount tales of storms and snowfalls, not only in their own lives but in the lives of their parents and grandparents.

Not surprisingly, Burgundian gardeners are keen observers of the weather, with a long tradition of weather-related sayings (Labrunie 1984; Taverdet and Dumas 1984). Many sayings (*dictons*) are tied to the seasons through the calendar of saints' days or the phases of the moon. For example, on St. Vincent's Day (January 21) and Candlemas (February 2), "l'hiver s'en va ou il se reprend" (winter goes or stays: a time of transition), and "il faut couper le bois á partir de la pleine lune" (cut wood when the moon is waning [to avoid wood worms]).

It makes sense that encoded environmental information takes the paradigmatic form of sayings, because they ensure that seasonal and annual differences are noted and that the right way to do a task is retained. Most people know the sayings and say that there is "something to them" but that they do not slavishly follow the advice or expect the prediction to prove accurate. Instead, the sayings serve as reminders, not laws, and produce contemplation on the situation at hand rather than a particular action. "Ça nous donne une raison á reflechir" (this gives us reason to reflect), said Jean Degueurce of Wooden Tower Farm (*la Tour du Bois*), as we stood one evening among his garden's neat rows.

Gardening and farming philosophy aids in the transmission of information by encouraging the recognition of and response to conditions. For example, to know in advance about changes in the weather, one Charolais cattleman asserts that one must simply "read the animals, which are no more beastly than humans." His neighbor remarks that plentiful hawthorn berries warn of a harsh winter. It is such observations, gained from the close scrutiny of all living things and of the land, that serve rural people as indicators of future conditions. It is this familiarity with all aspects of the mutable Burgundian environment that has made possible the long tenure of gardening and farming in this landscape.

Principles of intensive gardening practiced in the region (Crumley 2000) identify four critical categories of metaknowledge that ensure the harvest and undergird the practice of nearly any Burgundian gardener; retired factory workers, suburban managers, and Charolais beef cattle farmers all report very similar tactics. The selection of a particular suite of plants and animals has, over time, resulted in the traditional husbandry of species that have tolerance for a relatively broad range of conditions. The wide repertoire of species in local gardens ensures variation in the severity of weather and the impact of pests. Because a cool summer is better for cabbage than for garlic and a cold winter impacts rabbits less than pigeons, it would be a rare year that all husbanded plants and animals failed to thrive. Historically, gardeners saved seed from year to year and swapped seed with neighbors; today, while seed saving and trading are still practiced, gardeners also order from seed catalogues and buy bedding plants at the local agricultural cooperative or the weekly open-air market. The planting and harvest cycle allows for regular adjustments of the enterprise as conditions (e.g., severe or unseasonable weather) change. The individual gardener's diversity of practice—regarding expertise, taste, creative experimentation, region or country of origin, and the like—ensures regional and local diversity of produce despite the strongly shared gardening traditions observable throughout Europe.

The complex ways gardens are used and what they represent explains some of their enduring fascination. In addition to the historic ability of garden produce to get families through hard times, Burgundian gardeners cite the convenience of year-round produce, the assurance of quality and economy, the known circumstances of production (which they consider especially important regarding pesticides), the advantages of daily gardening exercise, and the opportunity to supply friends and family with edible proof of affection.

As my research advanced, I became concerned that this rich gardening tradition was disappearing because so many experienced gardeners are in their sixties and seventies. I was relieved to discover that intensive gardening is associated with a particular stage in life; while people are taught how to plant, hoe, and weed at a young age, it is only later—once many chores are turned over to younger members of the household—that virtuoso gardening is practiced. In two-generation households, this is when a collectively tended garden moves to the sole purview of a single individual. Since farm households often have three generations living under the same roof, there is usually someone who can devote the time and thought to careful gardening.

The instruction of young persons begins at five or six years of age, and often the teacher is a grandparent or someone else from that generation. Teaching a child to garden is the perfect means by which grandparent and grandchild can build memories together. One younger gardener told me that he saves worms for his son's fishing expeditions, thereby fostering an early interest in the garden. An older gardener confided that his father had taught him to garden, and now his own garden serves as a place of meditation not only on the evoked memory of his father but as a place in which personal tranquility may be found. Not only does the child learn a practical skill, but all the lore—weather sayings, tricks of practice—become a part of the childhood memory of that adult. Adults report that as children they enjoyed learning to garden in that context, then disliked garden work in their teens and early adulthood when the labor increased and the enchantment diminished, and eventually took it up again after starting their own families. At retirement, most men in small towns and rural areas increase their gardening activities, growing more than their household needs, so as to be able to supply visiting grown children and their families, and elderly neighbors.

Even the work itself must be undertaken in a certain way. M. Dauvergne, a retired mason of our acquaintance, confided to me that the hardest gardening lesson he had to teach a 20-year-old friend of our project was that "La cadence, c'est tout!" (The rhythm, it's everything!) This means that the effort that goes into a project should be spread out over an appropriate period of alternating work and rest that ensures that not too much energy is expended all at once. The result of such pacing is that individuals in their seventies and older can work a 12-hour day—hauling earth, pulling weeds, preparing beds, planting seedlings, pruning—with periodic stops to chat, drink a glass of wine with a friend, eat a leisurely lunch, take a 20-minute nap in the shade. A gardener in his early sixties said that for his parents' generation, gardening was the main subject of both conversation and lively competition: "*Chaq'un a sa combine*" (Each [gardener] has his tricks) replied one gardener, when asked which local gardens were the prettiest. Yet no leading questions could cause gardeners to comment on others' *oeuvre*. Once, in late March, when I mentioned that a neighbor had already planted his garden, but that another friend had declared it too early to plant, my host replied with a smile that he had nothing at all to say.

While the great majority of the gardeners I interviewed were men, nearly everyone insisted that to like gardening is a matter of taste, not gender. Some people gave me examples of woman gardeners in their family, but in nearly every instance there seemed to be another reason that the woman in question might have taken up gardening: a husband who was incapacitated or who put in long hours at a factory job, or a habit taken up in the absence of men during wartime. A few couples garden together: a farm wife who gardens together with her husband prefers gardening to the local retirement club because, unlike noisy card playing, she can see the results of invested time and energy.

These responses led me to the realization that while gardens are in every sense an extension of domestic space, garden space is not under the equal control of everyone in the domestic unit. While the Burgundian kitchen is almost invariably women's space, the garden—although not inevitably so—belongs to men. Male friends and neighbors are offered something to drink and a tour of the garden when they visit; one gardener's elderly uncle, born in 1908, is still vexed if someone declines when invited to view his garden. A clear majority of gardeners report learning to garden from their male relatives, and a few insist that they taught themselves, but no one claims to have learned gardening from his mother. Women harvest garden produce infrequently, with the exception of lettuce and a few other vegetables that will be eaten immediately and require particular freshness. Rather, women's role is to prepare and preserve the harvest. When garden produce moves from garden to kitchen, it falls under the control of women, and men rarely help with canning and other preparations. The final product—beautiful jars of green beans, tomatoes, fruit jellies and jams—is the pride of both the men who grow it and the women who preserve it.

Gardens, then, hold myriad meanings. They are places of recreation, creative personal expression, and escape; they represent a resistance to the industrialized production of food. Gardens (and the resulting stocked larders) reduce anxiety about food, encourage practical experimentation, and are the source of personal pride. They encourage reflection on larger issues of family, history, and Providence; they inevitably represent, in the most immediate fashion, the rhythms of lives lived with the seasons and with death.

Thus is the garden both carrier wave and classroom, transmitting ecological information across generations. This is accomplished in small but important acts: learning to garden begins with helping grandfather transplant lettuce from the cold frame to the neat, awaiting garden rows. It is everything in the moment: the person, the place, the time of year, the smells and sounds, the feel of the earth, the sensed ritual as well as the practical importance of the act. It is myriad meanings and emotions that fix the event in memory, and it is through memory that the garden is recreated.

Landscape as Garden

Burgundian farmers must think on a larger scale than their gardens. In some regards, the farmer's control over many hectares of pastures, fields, hedgerows, woods, and ponds resembles that of the estate owner. There are, however, several significant differences. No more than serious gardeners can farmers follow whimsy too far; rather, they must engage in careful calculations that sustain the profitability of the land. Farmers' large bank loans mean that land, farm equipment, crops, or animals may not be entirely theirs to deploy. Because subsidies account for as much as 40 percent of farm income, the French government is a de facto participant in every farm decision.

After World War II, the French government began a program to move farmers away from what Paris saw as the peasant mentality of smallholders. First, farmers were to be educated in modern farm management, which included a healthy dose of culture—literature, music, the arts. Children who would inherit the farm were required by law to complete two years at an agricultural *collège* (high school); soon two years became four. *Paysan* became *exploitant agricole* (farm manager). These reforms took a while to be manifest but between 1970 and 2000, the number of French farms was reduced by half; those remaining were first mechanized, then industrialized. In hilly southern Burgundy, the grain agroindustry of the Centre and elsewhere in France and Europe is not feasible, but nonetheless French government policies have pressed farmers to increase the regional specialty: Charolais beef cattle. The European Community's Common Agricultural Policy (CAP) and the 1992 General Agreement on Tariffs and Trade (GATT) have forced herd owners to adopt practices completely counter to ecologically sensible customs handed down for generations.

For example, the unique soil, vegetation, and moisture characteristics of Burgundian pasturage counsel a ratio of one animal per hectare; this calculus has been scrupulously respected for centuries as a part of a larger tradition of landscape maintenance, which Burgundian farmers term *l'entretien du paysage*. Along with much larger contemporary herds come the increased risk of infectious bovine diseases, overuse of pasturage, and the digging up of hedgerows. Fewer hedgerows means less shelter for cattle and ultimately more health problems, a weakening of a key relationship between wild animals and wild plants, less plant diversity in the pastures, and more erosion.

This is ironic, especially in light of the government's most recent attempt to re-invent French farmers (Van Deventer 2001). Like the United States and Canada, France meets national demand for agricultural products many times over; farmers are no longer needed to feed the country. Instead, they are now to be *jardiniers du paysage* (gardeners of the landscape), producing regional specialties and preserving the picturesque, less agro-industrialized regions for tourists. Since France is the number one tourist destination in the world, this renewed attempt to manage the countryside and mold its inhabitants remains firmly rooted in the French national economy and reflects France's jockeying for position as a country of high-end products in the European Union and globally.

But the greater irony is to know the sustainable practice and be paid to ignore it. Farmers seek price supports and protection from competition for their best known regional products and are often successful due to powerful agricultural unions' lobby of the French government and the European Union. The government, by granting or withholding subsidies, dictates herd size, health standards, and market conditions. French farmers' ire is deflected away from their own government, and GATT has further inflamed fury toward American products and practices. These include pesticide use, industrial monocropping, the loss of the family farm, seed stocks containing genetically modified organisms (GMOs), and a persistent reputation for bad food (*malbouffe*), hence local support of activist-farmer José Bové, best known for manuring a Paris McDonald's.

Caught up and sometimes compromised in national and global economic struggles, the French, both rural and urban, give enormous significance to their beloved vegetable gardens because they symbolize a refutation of globalizing corporate control. Inasmuch as most French people have agrarian origins, gardens also harken back to a (mostly mythical) past when smallholders controlled their own food resources. While the role of class and church in the history of Burgundy and of France belies peasant sovereignty, it can hardly be disputed that domestic vegetable gardens everywhere, even among enslaved peoples, retain an autonomy not necessarily mirrored in the landscape (Westmacott 1992). In France, it is impossible to disentangle national and regional identity from the powerful mythic images that center on the garden, so enamored is the entire nation with expressing emotion and personality through the production and consumption of artisanal food and drink (Terrio 2000).

And so the garden finds yet another purpose, this time as a powerful symbol that links individual personality, family and regional history, and national identity. The question is whether the French can use the symbol of the garden to demonstrate how place-specific environmental knowledge undergirds sustainable landscapes, to champion smallholders everywhere, and to save themselves and the rest of us from the global corporate control of comestible resources. It may be that finally the French government has gotten the farmer's image right: *jardiniers du paysage.*

"It Wasn't a Woman's World" Memory Construction and the Culture of Control in a North of Ireland Parish

2

MARILYN COHEN

PATRICK JOYCE (1991) ARGUES that the need to manage and bring dignity to poor working-class lives in the British Isles at the turn of the twentieth century generated a culture of control characterized by rigid gender roles, the need for order, and clear boundaries between the respectable and the rough. This culture of control was a working-class variation of the broader construction of feminine domesticity that shaped the social lives of all women during the Victorian and Edwardian periods. Working-class women, however, played significantly broader roles in their households' material survival than did middle- or upper-class women, resulting in a modification of the patriarchal sex-gender system. Women were pivotal in the orchestration of the culture of control since they were the managers of household budgets and fully shouldered the burden of reproductive work. Women were central figures in the creation of regionally specific working-class cultures at the family, workplace, and community levels. This paper will analyze how working-class women in the parish of Tullylish in northwest County Down, Ireland, constructed memories of their strategies to ensure the material survival of their households.[1] These memories functioned to acknowledge their contributions to themselves, to others in their cohort, and to their children.

There is an extensive literature relating to British working-class women's family roles at the turn of the century and the varied effects of gender inequality on their lives.[2] Men and women experienced class differently, performing different types of work and conforming to different work schedules and rhythms. Women's work formed the basis of family and community sociability partly because they shouldered the burden of coping with working-class material realities. Through women's networks, various forms of paid and unpaid work were exchanged that helped ensure material survival. Women-centered networks provided the "interface between the formal economy and the web of interpersonal community and familial relationships," helping to explain how working-class families made ends meet (Ayers 1990:271).

The concept of strategies used in this chapter retains the tension between agency and structural determination. Problems with the concept arise when the family is the unit of analysis since functional interdependence and the assumption that families are corporate groups can mask gender and age inequality and resulting conflicts. The decisions made by individual members of the working class were constrained by the structure of the local economy, class stratification, and unequal generational and gender relations. Household strategies relate to goals concerning size and security of income, wage earning activities, self-help networks, and gender-specific standards of respectability.

Research Methods and Site

The parish of Tullylish, located in northwest County Down, was part of a rural industrial region where the Irish linen industry flourished for over two centuries. During the long eighteenth century (1690–1825), the parish was densely populated by petty-commodity producers, bleachers, and linen drapers. In the pre-Famine period between 1825 and 1846, industrial capitalism was rapidly advancing along the intersecting Bann River where numerous mills and factories were built and operated until the mid-twentieth century when many ceased production. In the northern town lands, the handloom weaving of fine linen predominated, organized by manufacturers through the putting-out system until the mid-twentieth century.

Data for this paper were derived from a combination of archival records such as the 1901 Irish census enumerator's schedules, wage books, and school attendance registers, and oral interviews with thirty-five elderly residents from the parish carried out between 1982 and 1984. Respondents were male and female, Catholic and Protestant, and most lived in rows of small terraced houses formerly owned and built by their employers. While Protestants in general enjoyed certain privileges in this north of Ireland region, working-class women's lives were very similar on both sides of the religious divide since wages and the standard of living among the majority of employees in the linen industry were low. Residents of the factory villages and hamlets along the River Bann lived with the ghosts and remains of a century-old paternalistic factory culture surrounding them.

Although I am interested in the past, as an anthropologist I wanted to retain a concrete focus on real people who experienced and coped with the dominance of employment in the linen industry. The evidence derived from the oral histories served two purposes. One follows Paul Thompson's (1978:7) early empirical inspiration to "imagine what evidence is needed, seek it out and capture it." Thus additional qualitative evidence relating to family strategies, socialization practices, self-help, and women-centered networks was gathered to document and explore women's perceptions and reactions to their waged and unwaged working conditions, to the division of labor in the home, and to poverty. This evidence served to expand and flesh out a quantitative database obtained through record linkage among a number of nominal lists. A second purpose, less bound within empiricism, was to use popular memory to help reveal the hidden history and complexity of Irish working-class women's subjectivity. The concept of subjectivity, following the Popular Memory Group (1982:227), is a conceptual tool for exploring the contingencies of human agency at the level of consciousness.

Coping with Low Wages: Employment Strategies

The vast majority of Irish linen industry workers earned low wages, and most adult males did not earn high enough wages to support their families. Consequently, the struggle to make ends meet was a repeated theme along with the necessity for a family wage economy. The most common way this was expressed was: "It was just a matter of slavery at that time," or "They talk about the poverty line now. Nearly everybody was on the poverty line at that time." Two factors were seen to be of paramount importance in shaping family strategies to cope with poverty. One was the narrow employment base outside of the linen industry: there was nothing else for you. If one person left a job, there was always someone else to take the place. The second was that low wages demanded multiple contributions to make ends meet. All working class families expected and needed the wage contributions of their children, who began working at age twelve as half-timers, splitting their day between work and school, under the provisions of the 1844 Factory Acts. Some households needed the contributions of married women.

While contemporary upper- and middle-class reformers argued that working wives could not properly care for their children, homes, or husbands, economic necessity often required that married women work outside the home. In Tullylish, as in Ireland generally, the majority of married women, particularly those with children, did not work outside the home, conforming to Victorian middle-class norms. However, in 1900, 21 percent of married women continued to work.

The occupation of the male head of the household or the absence of a male head was the principal indicator of social stratification within the working class. At the turn of the century, it was a sign of financial well-being and status to have the women of the household, single or married, remain unemployed. In addition to the wives and daughters of the middle class remaining unemployed, skilled workers, the majority of whom were Protestant, were better able to keep their wives at home and daughters in school beyond the legal age of twelve. Only 6.8 percent of the wives of skilled workers were employed, compared with 23.1 percent of the wives of semiskilled workers and 20 percent of the wives of unskilled workers (Cohen 1994).

Given the asymmetrical wage scales for men and women and the double burden of employment and family responsibilities, paid employment did not lay the foundation for freedom or independence among working wives. To the contrary, keeping a woman at home increased her ability to maintain order in the household and reduced the risk of poverty. Since working outside the home meant double duty and no leisure, women who did so were viewed as objects of pity:

> I knew a woman who worked across from me. And she had a family of five boys, and she had hardly a shoe on her foot, and oh, I used to feel sorry for her. She had to go out to work, five boys to raise. (Sarah Campbell)

Supplementary Wage Earning

Scholars have analyzed the various means by which working-class women, in the role of "chancellor of the exchequer," supplemented their family's income and eased tight budgets (Ayers 1990; Black 1983; Lewis 1984; Rowntree 1913; Ross 1983, 1993). Since many of these supplemental activities were extensions of women's domestic labor, they articulate with the labor and commodity markets in numerous ways. For example, providing childcare for a woman who worked for wages outside the home in Tullylish would both enable that mother to work and earn the child minder about two shillings, six pence per week. Taking in boarders and lodgers, who were usually single and employed, was another way to earn supplemental income. Other wives took in laundry, cleaned the homes of wealthier families, dug potatoes, pulled flax, and gathered wild blackberries, at two shillings for fourteen pounds. Many kept animals such as pigs, hens, goats, or cows and grew vegetables in garden plots.

> A good many of the people whose husbands worked in the bleachgreens kept hens, and they laid eggs, and sometimes they could sell the eggs to supplement their husband's earnings which weren't very big. [Was it a common thing to keep hens?] Oh, it was. Nearly everybody and a good many people would have kept a pig. Now a pig didn't eat a whole lot of money. Where there's a family there's always refuse, and it didn't take too much of their own refuse to feed the pig. Over the months, it was sold. There was a man went round and killed the pig. The pig was killed and brought to market. They bought the pig for maybe five shillings or something and sold it for maybe a couple of pounds. There was always a few bob extra. (Arthur Patrick Burns)

Perhaps the most important way a married woman could contribute additional income in Tullylish was through homework. Homework has been a poorly remunerated alternative to factory work for many women.[3] Women who remained home could turn to homework sporadically, as available time arose in the course of their daily routine. This form of work is also undocumented in the census, but oral evidence suggests that it was very common in Tullylish in areas close to hemstitching factories where handkerchiefs were hemstitched or tea towels hemmed. In 1983, homework was still being done by married women who sewed handkerchiefs on sewing machines supplied by Blane's hemstitching factory in Ballydugan. The company earned additional profits in an extremely competitive market by reducing variable capital costs through low piece rates and by not providing sickness and unemployment benefits.

Because many supplemental wage-earning activities were undocumented, their full extent cannot be determined. The ideology surrounding the separate spheres of work and home impinged on the definitions of work counted in the census enumerators' schedules. Income earning strategies were linked to family position, and since married women's economic roles were often not publicly visible, their contributions were more likely than men's or single women's to be hidden. Finally, it was assumed that men would work for wages continually and women intermittently. The consequent undercounting of women's supplemental contributions hid the fact that most married women earned small amounts of money continually.

Managing Household Expenses

According to Laura Oren (1973), there were essentially two ways of dividing the household money in British working-class households during the nineteenth century. One way was to give the wife control. Her husband handed over all of his earnings and received back a fixed sum used as pocket money. The second way, more common in England, was for a husband to give his wife a fixed sum or wage each week based on his average minimum earnings. In this latter case, wives did not always know the amount of their husband's earnings. Oral evidence suggests that in Tullylish, the first system—where the husband and other family members handed over their pay to the wife and received back pocket money—was the most common arrangement.

> They would just bring it home and give it to her and they would've had whatever she wanted to give them out. The man, the husband, never opened his pay. Brought it home and give it to her, and she would've opened it. And she managed that, so she did. She'd give them their pocket money. (Adam Davison)

The biggest expenditures of a household's budget went to food and clothing. Rents were low since many lived in company-owned houses. Other landlord's rents were comparable, ranging from one shilling to two shillings, six pence per week for most terraced houses. Wives also had to factor into their budgets for pocket money. Pocket money, given to husbands and often spent on smoke and drink, enabled "moments of potential excess" that threatened a wife's careful control over financial order, since they could not refuse their husband's requests (Joyce 1991:151). Drinking by men in particular was a factor affecting working-class standards of living and marital relations since it was integral to male sociability in Tullylish and throughout the British Isles. "The poor man's drink was at the expense of his family's food and sometimes his own" (Ross 1982:42; 1993:42).

> She hadn't have enough money to pay for the food and clothes. And he would've wanted his tobacco, his smoking money, and he woulda had to get that. And then maybe there'da been words over that. He'd expect her just that she should have the food on the table, whether she had the money to pay for it or not. The men wanted their own way. In some cases there mighta been men who drank their money before they come home with their pay . . . all these mills and factories you see, they were near the pubs . . . they used to drink an awful lot in those days. . . . All the men were goin' home and had a drink. Some of them stayed on, and then they come home darting across the road. God help them. God help their wives. (Sarah Campbell)

When households had to make do with less it was usually the wife who ate less so that her husband and children did not feel the pinch. Working-class women often obtained a disproportionately smaller share of food, medical care, and leisure time (Oren 1973:197). The structure of the Victorian and Edwardian family economy gave men an illusion of independence, while women were buffers, absorbing the "blows of an insecure existence," ensuring the survival of breadwinners and children out of their own standard of living (Ross 1993:121).

> I wouldn't take an egg keepin' it for the children. Wouldn't take this or that keepin' it for the children. I remember one time. I don't remember if it was during the time he was in the hospital, musta been. And I wasn't eatin'. I was gettin' all for them. So long as I got food for them, until I let myself down too far. I didn't feel like I was ever hungry. I suppose I was nibblin' at bits and pieces, but I was never sittin' down to a big meal. It was all for them, six of them. (Sarah Campbell)

Although wives in Tullylish often made due with less, managing the household money did give them a measure of control and influence over decision making that middle-class wives did not share. Daily decisions regarding purchases for the household were made by wives independently. Both men and women acknowledged that money management was the special talent of women.

> Long ago, the men didn't realize like what was the value of the money. It took the women really for to know the value and how far the money was goin' to go. Men

> didn't like take any interest . . . the men never knew the value of money because they never really had any money. (Mrs. McCusker)

Women's Community Strategies: Credit and Shops

Most of the commodities consumed by members of working-class households were purchased in local shops by women. These shops were open until 7:00 or 8:00 p.m. to accommodate working wives. Since wages were paid either weekly or every two weeks, credit relations were established between women and shop owners. Women patronized the same shop to begin a credit relation called her "book." This would enable a woman to take what she needed for her household and pay the shop on a Friday when wage packets were received. For all households, but especially among those whose primary wage earner was paid every two weeks, this credit relationship was a critical strategy enabling wives to maintain financial order.

> The women would do the shoppin'. It was marked in the book, and they marked it in their own ledger, and at the end of the fortnight [two weeks], they paid the bill. The shop people would usually give a wee packet of sweets for the children. Each time they went to buy something, they brought the book. It got marked in the book, and then the shopkeeper went back to see if it corresponded to the house ledger, and the book was marked paid then till the end of the fortnight. . . . If a man was off sick, the way they worked was they put it to the back of the book, whatever was that couldn't be paid at the fortnight, and whenever he went to work again, they paid so much off what was at the back of the book, till that bill was reduced. Sometimes it took nearly a year. If a man was out for two weeks, it took nearly a year. They took a shilling or two each time until it cleared. As a rule there was never too many heavy debts unless a man was off for months. (Mrs. McCusker and Arthur Patrick Burns)

Everyone stressed the importance of credit and no one felt that shopkeepers were exploitative since they were enmeshed in the local web of social obligations.[4] People were tied to a particular shop through credit and debt. If a family did fall into debt, usually due to the illness of the primary wage earner, shopkeepers, who needed loyal customers, usually saw the family through this difficult period, expecting to be repaid in time. In theory, shopkeepers had the power to refuse credit, but they were under considerable pressure not to do so. Although some left the community to avoid paying their debt, on the whole, working-class households made an effort to repay their debts and sustain good relations with shopkeepers.

Women's Unwaged Work: Housework and Childcare

The principal reason why most wives did not work outside the home was that domestic work—childcare, cooking, washing, and cleaning—was very labor intensive and solely women's responsibility. Cooking was done by means of a griddle hung over an open fire. Washing was done by hand without the convenience of running water in the houses. Ironing clothes was a particularly arduous and disagreeable task, especially during the warm summer months when women would sweat profusely from the heat of the hot irons, done inside the house on tables covered with sheets.

According to Eileen Kane (1972), the rigid sexual division of labor in Ireland was linked to cultural conceptions of masculinity: "The wife controls the kitchen, the children, and the small animals and fowl. Men will have no part in women's work; masculinity is defined not by what he does as much as what he does not, and the tabooed area includes the whole range of women's work. Women, conversely, can do men's lighter tasks; if a woman takes on heavier work, she is an object of respect and pity, and her husband if he is living and able is despised."

In Tullylish, while some men helped their wives, the culture of control included a clear demarcation between women's and men's work. There was little daily change in the routine or quantity of women's work, resulting in the elimination of their leisure time. Even on the weekend there were particular tasks that had to be done, such as ensuring that the children and their clothes were clean for Sunday school and church. Although wives could expect help from their children, especially their daughters who learned early about the double duty of women, many tasks would be done after hours, on weekends and by lamplight in the winter months. A frequent reply to the question, "What did your mother do in her spare time?" was either another task like darning socks or knitting or that she hadn't any spare time. Another female—usually the eldest or second daughter—filled this role when their mothers worked outside the home. For example, I got this response to my question, "Did your father help with childcare?"

> Well you see with him bein' out workin'. He was workin'. He would be tired when he come home. Fathers in those days didn't take the same interest in the children as they do now. And they would hardly have held a child. They thought it was too much like a woman's work. And even after when I got married, the husbands wouldn't wheel a pram or anything. No, they thought that was too womanish to do that. We were just killed. Looking after children and doin' all that bakin' and washin' and ironin'. (Sarah Campbell)

The difficulties of domestic work were compounded by the lack of space in the rows of small "two up, two down" company-owned houses and by high standards of cleanliness. Standish Meacham (1977:87) states that among English working-class women, "no ritual assumed greater importance in the eyes of the respectable working class than the weekly house cleaning." Wives in Tullylish were no exception, and they expected to be assisted by their daughters. The heaviest burden fell on daughters in succession, with the younger ones taking over the lion's share from older daughters when they worked full-time. Sons were expected to do some heavy chores, like carrying water from the nearby pump or River Bann or firewood, but they were allowed more free time to play and engage in sports. Daughters "got very little time to play when you were growin' up" (Mrs. Fry). Since girls were not allowed to go out at night after dark, the evening hours were spent helping their mothers.

> When it got dark, the girls didn't go outside at night, and my mother used to make all the boys socks, black socks, and I would sit, and I would had took one from the top of the leg to the ankle. My mother woulda turned the heel in for me, and then the next night I woulda sat and done from the ankle to the toe, and she woulda knotted off the toe. Like when I was young, I didn't know how to knot the heel or the toe, and she did that. We all helped her out with the knittin' and everything. (Mrs. Fry)

Women-Centered Social Networks

The web of female-centered social ties between neighbors provided another support network vital to survival. When wives worked outside the home, they frequently turned to nearby kin and neighbors to care for their children. Although a small fee of half a crown a week was usually paid to the child minder, if the sum could not be afforded, help was given anyway. Such behavior was part of the larger norm of neighborliness, which in the north of Ireland often transcended religious boundaries, particularly in small communities.

> Every door was open. If I were short of sugar next door or flour or somethin' like that enough to do the bakin', I'd get the neighbor to give in. Didn't ask any questions who you were. You were a neighbor and you worked in the mill beside them every day in the week. Any trouble next door, you were in just the same as the other side, the Roman Catholic, was in to you. (William Quinn)

The critical evaluation of a neighbor depended on the general importance assigned to the role. In Tullylish, as elsewhere in Ireland, where the neighbor's contribution was indispensable, the role was strictly defined and highly significant, providing the model for the behavior of kin, referred to as "friends" (Buckley 1983; Glassie 1982).

Everyone stressed that the past was "far more neighborly than now," a statement that conveys the strength of social obligation rooted in the material realities of the time. Prior to 1920, services provided by the state for the poor were few and stigmatized, and people depended on one another in times of crisis such as illness, unemployment, childbirth, and death, and for daily needs like childcare, food exchanges, and companionship. These networks between neighbors were a form of working-class self-help. When a family faced financial difficulties they turned to their community.

> Generally your friends give you a handout. You see it was far more neighborly then than it is now. If there was a neighbor really far down, like you went around and you collected the whole locality. Just put your penny or tuppence or six pence or shilling. Then you went to the big boys, and maybe he give you a pound or something. Well, that do them maybe till someone got a job. (Adam Davison)

Married women were at the core of family and neighborhood self-help although men were also involved. Men visited with their friends and neighbors and would readily help when a crisis arose. Since married women's social activities were circumscribed by the volume of work they were responsible for and by a sharp cultural demarcation between male/public and female/domestic social spaces, visiting was the key form of social interaction open to them. Women were more likely to share scarce domestic resources and visit one another in their homes, seeking a break from children and the company of peers. Men usually met in groups outside along the road or in pubs.

Women neighbors always helped one another when they were giving birth since babies were born at home. The birthing room was strictly "handywomen" or midwives whose skills gained them a respected reputation among local women and health care practitioners.

> There was never anything such as doctors running, you know, if you were expecting childer or anything like that. I don't believe there was ever a nurse with any of them women in Banford. Johnny's mother went to deliver all them childer herself. She was very good at that. And very good at sickness. Anybody was ill and in bed she could make them comfortable and done for them. Just the same as a midwife, as we call them now. You see you had to pay your doctor. We always would have said you have to have the money, two and six, for the doctor when he comes. And if you needed medicine or anything, you had to pay him another two and six. It cost you what we would've said five shillings then. (Mrs. McCusker)

Women-centered networks formed during childbirth and postpartum recovery were a way in which women were able to regain a measure of self-control over their lives. Women spent much of their fertile lives pregnant and delivering babies, facing considerable risks to their health (Leavitt 1986). Women's networks provided care and comfort and helped defray the cost of health care during birth and confinement by contributing small sums of money into a fund.

> They started up a fund. You paid into this, you see, so much and like it wouldn'ta been maybe a whole lot of money, maybe as we'da called it ten pence. And maybe

> it was only five pence you paid. Well then when your confinement came, then you would have the money. One of those ones that would start it up and all, they give you the money then to pay your doctor for your confinement. I seen women comin' out of their work on a Friday night and them expecting a baby and havin' their baby on Saturday morning. Then, they maybe woulda had to go into their work beginning maybe the next week. The next day, maybe they woulda had to get up out of bed. They would stayed in bed the one day and they woulda been outa bed the next day to have done their washin' and had to look after themselves. You see, there was nobody who could stay at home for to look after you. (Mrs. McCusker)

The importance of self-help networks in defraying the cost of health care cannot be overstated. Working-class people did not turn to doctors unless it was absolutely necessary. Folk remedies such as wild herbs, porter, castor oil, flaxseed, and licorice were used to treat a variety of ailments.

Finally, if anyone died, it was women neighbors, not kin, who came out to help since it was strictly taboo for kin to be involved with laying out the dead body.

> Oh, they would go to their neighbors if there was anything wrong. Oh, they were the first to be there. If anybody died, they would have people engaged to lay them out and all. It's not like now with the undertaker. No, my mother was always on call for that. The people who died, their own people wouldn't touch them. Oh no. There was always two women went out and did it. Fixed the bed. It was white . . . the women in those days always left white sheets. If anything happens see, if the paper was faded on the wall where the bed was, they'd put a big white sheet against the wall, and everything was pure white. The women done that. (Sarah Campbell)

Conclusion

In conclusion, for working-class women in Tullylish at the turn of the century, "there was little distinction between work and home life . . . their families' survival depended on their incessant efforts" (Blewett 1990:38). Since women shouldered the full burden of reproductive work, they were key actors in the creation and reproduction of the culture of control, orchestrating household relations and social ties in the community. Because women were household financial managers, supplemental wage earners, and at times, full-time wage earners, men and women were economically interdependent, a reality that modified the patriarchal system in significant ways. Men were clearly household heads, and the extent of a wife's influence was seen by women to depend on how agreeable their husbands' temperaments were. Nevertheless, major decisions affecting the family were largely joint, and control over daily household expenditures was wholly in women's hands.

There was unanimous recognition that the realities of working-class life in Tullylish were experienced differently and unequally. While men were expected to work hard and be the principal wage earner, their work was over at the end of the day. In contrast, the labor intensive nature of domestic work and the high standards of cleanliness resulted in long hours of hard work for married women and their daughters, whether they worked outside the home or not. This gender inequality was voiced in the following way: "Men didn't give women a very good deal in those days. The women got it very hard. It wasn't a woman's world."

Nevertheless, attempts by women to preserve respectability, defined in mid-Victorian gendered terms, were at the heart of working-class agency and subjectivity and provided deep satisfaction for many. Because working-class women led lives of purpose and dignity readily acknowledged in the community, perceptions of hard toil and oppression were often tempered by memories of good times and close social ties, creating an ambiguous subjectivity among many of the women interviewed. Neighborliness and interdependence—despite their links to poverty and gender inequality—were missed, considerably more so than the local linen industry, which has ceased to dominate the region.

Notes

1. For a more detailed examination of women linen industry workers in the parish of Tullylish, see Marilyn Cohen (1997).
2. Studies of British working-class women include Black (1983); Lewis (1984); McDougall (1977); Meacham (1977); Oren (1973); Reeves (1979); Rice (1981); Roberts (1977); Rose (1992); Ross (1982:576; 1983; 1993); Stearns (1972).
3. Historical examinations of women homeworkers include Miriam Cohen (1977); Franzoi (1984); Lewis (1984:55–62); Neill (1994); Roberts (1977:310).
4. Anthropologists who have analyzed Irish shopkeepers and their relationships with customers include Arensberg (1959); Arensberg and Kimball (1968); Silverman and Gulliver (1995).

A Personal History of Memory 3

ROBERT R. ARCHIBALD

THINK FOR SIXTY SECONDS without using words. It is not possible.

My earliest memory is of the middle bedroom in my family's home in Ishpeming, a gritty iron-mining town on Michigan's Upper Peninsula. I know this is my earliest memory because I had developed words with which to encode and save the experience, "sensory experience tagged with language," as Paul Ableman (1999:106) describes it. The bedroom had two windows overlooking the pine trees on the west side of the house. It had three paneled doors: one through a closet to an adjoining bedroom, another to a different closet, and the third to the second-floor hallway. In one early morning's shadowy light, I stood and peered out from my crib toward a table set against the north wall. I was terrified, for there on the table top was the dark decomposing corpse of a dead bird. The more I stared, the more distraught I became. I cried and screamed with terror. This was a nightmare that did not easily succumb to reality in the light of day. My father came from my parents' bedroom. He picked up the gruesome corpse and brought it to the crib where I finally could see that my fears were unfounded, that the corpse was a crumpled multicolored handkerchief. I think I was about two years old.

But the handkerchief story is more than my first memory; it is the point in time over fifty years ago where "the story of me" begins, where I can first apply the pronouns *I* and *me*. It is the beginning of my self-consciousness, and, when I look back, it becomes the vanishing point of my identity. Every person has a beginning point, a place where the story starts; and the story always starts when we have the words. Words are not merely a means of expression; words are the raw material of thought, of self-consciousness, and of story. Without words there are no memories, and without memories there are no "stories of me" for anyone.

Thus, words are not incidental to memory or to narrative. And narratives are how we construct ourselves and how we order the world around us.

For each of us, the story begins with that first memory, the opening scene of a lifelong narrative that concludes only with death. The idea that stories have beginnings, middles, and ends derives from personal narrative and those stark signposts of beginning and end: birth and death. A story without a beginning and without an end is not a story. Yet no scientific evidence has been found for a narrative that explains the universe. If from our perspective the universe is infinite, there cannot be an explanatory narrative because narrative requires a beginning and an end. While we know that cause-and-effect does exist in the universe, there is no evidence for sequential time, that is, time as we understand and use the concept. In the absence of sequential time, and in an infinite universe, narration is not possible. Memory and story are characteristics of our brains, not attributes of the universe that enfolds us. So we are left with the conclusion that my memory of the handkerchief and the story thus begun are proof of how my mind works, not proof that the universe can be explained by a story. Thus we do not gaze outside of ourselves to discover preexisting stories; instead, we construct the stories around the sensory impressions we receive. As I make my way through my life and the world, I make narratives as my only way of making sense of it all.

I am conscious of how little I remember about my childhood or youth or even details from last week, but memory is not a rote recording of the entire past of any of us. My mind sorts between the pieces that it will add to my story and those that it will discard. But my story also changes daily, and those pieces that I can recall take on new meanings as I rethink the experience of my life and even my own identity. We unceasingly reinvent ourselves, and we modify the story of ourselves to maintain consistency. In some instances, the distinctions between what I really remember and what I was told are blurred. I do not know for certain now whether some memories are remembered experience or remembered conversation. There are other instances where I discover inaccuracies in my memory. My memory can be undermined by tests of objective fact, but objectivity and fact are not what my memory and story are about. In one sense, my memory and my story of myself are myths that will not stand the test of objectivity and accuracy when tested against recorded facts. Yet, verifiable or not, they are the sources of my consciousness and my identity, the stuff of me. If I could alter memory, remake the myth, I would not be me. I would become a different person.

Years ago, an older friend told me about an experience with his elderly mother. His parents were of the doughty World War I generation of eastern Montana homesteaders who settled on hardscrabble land near Roundup. While his mother remembered well and eloquently and told him stories of the homestead beyond the time limits of his own memory, he wanted to know more. So on a spring weekend, he drove his mother from Billings on the Yellowstone River, northeast to the dry land his family had simultaneously embraced and battled. Once out of the car and on the very ground that had once been home, his mother was transported back in time, traversing the now barren land and describing the place in present tense as it had been years before. With a torrent of reminiscences precipitated by the outlines of what was once her house, chicken coop, and even the undulating landscape so intimately a part of her just a half century earlier, she could reveal that life to her son. My friend was overwhelmed by the mnemonic power of this place. His mother's ability to recall fact and feeling was intensified, magnified, focused by standing on the ground that was the crucible of her memory and the story of herself. She stood upon the memory place of her young womanhood, her childbearing, her marriage, and widowhood—but now from the perspective of her old age and impending death.

My own grandmother was a denizen of graveyards, especially the one that held what remained of her own family, where each individual was commemorated with a gray granite marker near a matching obelisk deeply engraved with family names. Sunday at her house in Negaunee, Michigan, invariably included good food, a relaxed discipline, and a drive down the old highway to the cemetery. Her mood did not become somber there. She yanked weeds from the ground, complained about the dry brown grass, planted a few flowers, and incessantly talked about the people who were buried there with spaces left for those still living. She did not need my cousins and me as an audience, but I do think that we were the stimulus for making her remembrances audible rather than remaining silent meanderings. The cemetery was her mnemonic device. I think that she drew comfort from the weekly summertime excursions. I believe that in those granite marked graves, she found confirmation of her own memories and of her very own story of herself. Although even then I treasured time spent with my grandmother, I do now wish I had listened more intently to her cemetery stories. I go to the cemetery alone now and try to recall what she said about uncles, aunts, greats of all generations, and especially the personal stories about my own great- and great-great-grandparents. When Grandmother died in 1966, a part of me was lost; although now when I go to her grave in the exact spot where she told me it would be, I have my own cascade of memories of her and of our cemetery visits too.

A few years ago I went to the place of my birth, childhood, and young adulthood to write a book finally titled *A Place to Remember*. I had not returned to this natal place in nearly thirty years. I knew that in this place, memory would come. I used the landscape and the people as stimuli in a risky experiment with my own story of myself, my memory, and my identity. It was the most exhilarating yet excruciating experience of my life, and it still reverberates in my present. I did not escape unscathed, and I will not repeat the experiment. Memory is too powerful.

Almost twenty-five years ago, Saul Friedländer wrote a wrenching book entitled *When Memory Comes* (1979:102). One passage especially strikes me.

> It took me a long, long time to find the way back to my own past. I could not banish the memory of events themselves, but if I tried to speak of them or pick up a pen to describe them, I immediately found myself in the grip of a strange paralysis. When I finished my military service, since I could not forget the facts, I made up my mind to view everything with indifference; every sort of resonance within me was stifled.

Place is the crucible of memory. As Friedländer discovered and then recorded in his book, you can "view everything with indifference" and stifle every sort of resonance—until you go back to where it happened. Then the most carefully erected barriers crash. The places where things happened are stimuli to memory, and there in those places, memories will pour out with irresistible force. An individual will feel this sometimes overwhelming power in a place, and so will a family, even a community or a nation.

Remembering is not completely rational and objective. I am sure that it has to do with how our brains are structured, but memories have an emotional component; that is, we do not just remember facts, but we reexperience emotions associated with past events. The power of remembering rests not just in recall of specific events of one's life. So at the cemetery I remember what it felt like to be with my grandmother. I have a visual image of her, how her hair was arranged, the printed dresses and sturdy shoes she wore. Her voice quietly echoes, and I can even smell the fragrance of her again. So remembering is also memory of smell, color, sound, touch, temperature, all of those sensory components of experience. And every time I remember Grandmother, I see her from a different perspective. I remember her differently, and she assumes different meanings for me. I am now nearing the age that Grandmother was when I first remember her. She seems different to me now because I now can know her for the first time as someone my own age. As a child I would have said, "My grandmother is an old woman." Now I think of her as nearly a contemporary. The facts of her life have not changed, but I have. There is a principle of historical relativity here. My meaning of the past constantly changes because the past is always moving through time in relation to me. My life doesn't feel like it projects into the future anymore, perhaps because more than half of it is past, not future. Thus I think that the line is headed in the other direction. My children follow behind me, just as I trail after my grandmother and grandfather and my great-grandfather into the past. Sometimes, I think that we have time and history backwards.

So Grandmother's graveyard stories were not just auditory; they were visceral, multisensory stories. And her stories were never neutral, never objective.

They reeked of regrets, love, sorrows, joys. In them she recounted the lives and imposed judgments upon the people under our feet. Her inflections varied as she stopped, stooped, smiled, or grimaced. Grandmother was not recounting the past; she was reliving it and passing it to me. She was telling me who my people were, how Quinns and Archibalds behaved and what they believed, how they had struggled, how they defined successes and failures. She was telling me about buried tragedy, suffering, pleasure, fear, pain, and about faith. And she was relating to me who I was, subconsciously telling me how to find my bearings and which way to head. She was cautioning me but also encouraging me to follow these people, our ancestors, learning from their experiences and valuing the good things they exemplified.

Grandmother's stories were always stories with a point; remembrance was instructive and engaging. I rest on the green bench in my garden in St. Louis. The pungent, fuzzy green tomato plants are chest high now with nectarine-sized fruit in this early June morning. Colors of splashy reds, browns, golds, pinks, yellows, purples, whites, and subdued greens tumble around and over the patio. Grandmother and I did not spend all our time in graveyards. Often I trailed her around her backyard garden in Negaunee. She planted more vegetables than I do now, but like me she also grew flowers everywhere. I know now that I grow these things because she did and because my father, her son, did. I know that her father, my great-grandfather, did, too—I vaguely remember his garden. So the story of her values, her aesthetics, her hobbies are repeated in mine. Such stories, such patterns, endure through generations with palpable consequences—garden smells and colors. Generations of gorgeous roses and fine tomatoes, tended in gardens where her descendants live, are proof.

Memory and History

Pierre Nora (1989:9) argues in his essay "Between Memory and History" that the true intent of history is to destroy memory. "At the heart of history," he writes, "is a critical discourse that is antithetical to spontaneous memory. History is perpetually suspicious of memory, and its true mission is to suppress and destroy it." While his view may be overstated, it does describe a real dichotomy. History, relying upon evidentiary rules, is factually more correct and thus more "true," while memory is suspect because it fails the test of evidence and accuracy and hence can be dismissed as unreliable. In a scientific age, anything that flunks the test is discarded. And memory often fails the test imposed by the mountains of historical evidence compiled and sorted in archives and libraries, stored on museum shelves, and interpreted by scholars concerned with the pursuit of a perfectly accurate memory: history. So individual and shared memory cave into history because they must. But memories and the traditions, habits, and values they communicate are within the sacred and thus have authority. As many people now observe, our challenge is to define new relationships between memory and history.

David Thelen's essay "Memory" (2001) is a fine summary of disparate approaches to the distinctions between memory and history and their reconciliation. Can we find a balance between emotional value-bearing memory and the white lab coats of history? Can we agree that facts matter as crucial reference points, but that memory, with its evocation of emotion and empathy, is the only sure path to the past? Can we stop demanding that memory be a surrogate for truth and acknowledge it as a faculty for defining meaning? Can we admit that despite memory's historical fallibility, it nevertheless is an important determinant of the course of human events?

My interest in history has always had more to do with a fascination with history's evocative power, rather than the rigid rules that require an objective examination of the causes of the Civil War or the results of the Civil Rights movement or an analysis of Jacksonian Democracy. Those things are undeniably important, but they seem so remote, so past, so impersonal to me. However, all of us have looked at artifacts or visited historic sites that evoke an emotional and visceral response. Tears well up uncontrollably, goose bumps tingle, and a lump rises in the throat. My body reacts in this way when, for instance, I visit Ellis Island. I knew the history of the place long before my first visit ten years ago. But traditional history belies the impact of the place. It is not the museum part of Ellis Island with its abundant artifacts and documents that makes the most vivid impression. It is the place itself. Just the view from Ellis Island toward Manhattan is overwhelming. I can imagine thousands of people on crowded immigrant ships looking at the New York shore after a long voyage in miserable quarters below deck. That view must have been a symbolic concoction of fear, hope, homesickness, longing, and anticipation.

Many Americans trace their roots to this place or places like it. Ellis Island makes this central part of the American experience vibrantly clear to me. This process of becoming American was so unlike becoming anything else. Imagine: walk through the Ellis Island portal successfully, board a ferry for New Jersey or New York, and instantly become an American in the making. Standing in the Great Hall, I get a palpable sense of the emotions exuded by the masses of people from every part of the earth who passed through this place. It is as if the people moved on but left behind as a residue everything that happened here and the range of emotions they felt. I can sense it; my own emotions resonate with it. Here I can stand in the spaces where they stood and imagine what they felt. And I shiver at the symphony of feelings that surrounds me imbedded in this place by those who passed through here long ago. The resonance between me and those long-gone immigrants is like the sympathetic vibrations between stringed instruments when tones produced by one are precisely echoed in muted tones by the others. It reminds me of listening to music from an orchestra in another room.

Of course, my experience at Ellis Island, repeated with the same intensity on several subsequent visits, is distinct from my memory of cemetery visits with my grandmother. Those experiences happened to me, whereas I have no personal experience of arriving at Ellis Island as an immigrant. My own experience is vicarious, but it does draw on the recorded experiences of others. I have read diaries and official reports and even talked with a few individuals who are connected to Ellis Island through personal experience. But my Ellis Island experience rests on the same symbolic mnemonic referent, Ellis Island itself, upon which first-hand memories of actual immigrants rely. I can stand in the same place, with much of its ethos intact, and I can repopulate the place, imagine the smells and the murmuring voices. I can dress the immigrants in the clothing from photographs I have seen. I can recollect the motions, even the emotions, of real immigrants who once passed through this place. I can conceive Ellis Island not as it is but as it was by drawing on what I have seen and read about the experience. I can recreate the sensory experience and the emotions of those humans long gone from the place because I am exactly like them in my own humanity. Thus, I have incorporated the real experiences into my own memory.

Traditional history makes little room for such experiences since they are subjective rather than objective, stimulated by emotion and not evidence, with conclusions not verifiable according to the rules of the trade. But several historians, notably R. G. Collingwood and Wilhelm Dilthey, have considered them. Collingwood, whose writings were published mostly posthumously from his drafts and lectures of the 1930s, notes that in attempting to make sense of the past we are never eyewitnesses of what we desire to know. So what is it that we must do in order to know the past? "My historical review of the idea of history," Collingwood (1994:282) concludes, "has resulted in an answer to this question: namely, that the historian must re-enact the past in his own mind." Dilthey, born in the Rhineland in 1833, lived and thought about history in the nineteenth-century ferment of philosophy and history. Dilthey (see Rickman 1961:39–40) argues for historical "understanding," which may be more easily understood in English as "historical imagination." He insists that since we are all human, we all have a view of what it is to be human from the inside out. We know what it is to be angry, happy, disconsolate, fearful, joyful, to crave intimacy, fulfillment, and meaning in our lives. We all know about motivation and struggle, success and failure. In other words, we know what it is to be human. Further, we also know about the function of memory because we all have and use memory. We can understand that memory binds us to people and places and that remembrance can induce comfort, grief, desire, confirmation, and the impulse for action in the present or the future. Thus, other humans, dead or alive, are not inscrutable. In fact, they are knowable precisely because they, just like us, possess human faculties. It is possible to see the world from another's vantage point and to see it with some precision. We do develop empathy for others, not just with those whom we know well, but with others we know only indirectly, even some who died before we were born.

Just because we are human, we can think our way inside humans who lived in the past, just as we can have empathy for those we know personally and intimately because we coexist in the same time. But thinking our way into the past is not simply a pattern for knowing the past; it is also how we confirm our own understanding of ourselves. My recollection of my experiences as a toddler or of time spent with my grandmother is a means of confirming my own identity and of distinguishing myself from others. It is an expression of consciousness of self. In discussing what we remember with others, we further establish our own self-consciousness and individuality. History then is a means of self-confirmation through connecting oneself to a particular past.

A friend regularly gives me postcards depicting my hometown of forty, fifty, or more years ago. Most recently she gave me one entitled "Ishpeming, Mich. Lake Angeline Basin." My childhood home was within, literally, a stone's throw of Lake Angeline. The lake I remember was rimmed with the ruins of iron-mining operations that had ceased years earlier. The postcard perplexed me; there is no lake in sight. Instead it is an industrial scene with mine shafts, stockpiles of iron ore, trams, railroads, smoke, and a deep pit in the foreground. Despite the fact the postcard title implies that this picture is of some place that I should know well, it is an unfamiliar scene. But as I study the image, looking for any familiarity, I recognize the outlines of the background bluffs, and they match exactly my indelible mental image of where I played as a boy. I can see the road that I know well, winding sideways up the hill where I walked in the spring picking dogtooth violets and jack-in-the-pulpits. I begin to sense that there is something intimately familiar about the scene. I look intently. There, on the edge of this desolate picture of a mining and smelting operation, is a house. Its cream color jumps out against the green trees. It is my house. I remember the profile, and then I remember my older brothers brushing barn red paint over the cream color when I was about ten years old. The arrangement of the chimneys confirms my recognition. But in this image, the house is not perched near the blue water of Lake Angeline but instead near a deep mine pit. And yet it fits. My father told me that at one time the lake was drained so that the iron ore underneath it could be mined. He cautioned me about huge drop-offs hidden by the water. In this picture, I could see that the water that I knew had disappeared.

The presence of the bluffs and of the house confirm my memory of my childhood home. Yet this image is not just a memory confirmation; it also reinforces the history of the place as my father described it and in doing so extends my knowledge of my own place backward in time, to years long before I was born. The postcard supports my own memory, but only because it contains enough familiar elements to confirm that it is my home place. The rest of the scene is disjointed, alien, but I am able to connect the dots and restructure the place through time. Thus, I can understand how radically my place changed, and I now have a story that begins in one place before my time and continues into the present. The Lake Angeline postcard serves to extend memory into a past before my birth, but I can connect the scene to a place and events within my own memory. At the same time, the postcard image changes forever the way I think of the place, and hence my memories of it. For example, the ruins that I knew around the edges of the lake as a boy and that I imagined to be antiquarian and even antediluvian relics of all kinds of fanciful edifices, are now forever associated with the mundane mining and smelting facilities they once supported.

Ellis Island is an analogous place for me. Although I had no personal bond to Ellis Island as an immigration portal like the one I have with Lake Angeline, I did have connections through immigrant diaries and other historical recountings, and I did know people whose first footsteps on American soil were taken in this place. So this island, this tangible link to bygone events and experiences, becomes for me and for millions of others a memory place, verifying and confirming what we have gleaned in other places. The diaries, official records, and histories of Ellis Island, like the picture postcard of my home, extend my memory into a past I never knew.

I was a carriage driver on Mackinac Island one summer between college years. It was a marvelous summer, enchanting really. The place is beautiful, and most of those who worked there were college students too, given to long work days and long dreamy nights, enjoying freedom from the pressure of studies and exams. I recall standing on a high bluff overlooking this juncture of Great Lakes and suddenly understanding why this small island was of such value to native people, and then to French, English, and Americans. From the island you can see the lower Great Lakes and the narrow passage up to Lake Superior. It is a strategic point.

I gave tours of the island seven days a week from my perch on the carriage driver's seat, repeating day after day to tourist after tourist what I now know to be a partly apocryphal history of the island. The place itself, in general not part of the guide's patter, was the most important clue to its historical meaning. But the built environment, including the fort and other historic structures that I rattled on about, meant less, and it was hard to discern what was real and what was not. It was clear that much of what visitors see is reconstructed, that is, it was not authentic, and some of it was even fictional. The fictionalized parts of it made me suspicious of the whole thing. The literature about this island connected a visitor to the place but not to the reconstructed remains of human activity. So Mackinac

Island never became an extension of memory for me, not in the sense that Ellis Island, where I never stayed or worked, has become. Mackinac lacked the authenticity of my memories of Grandmother, the reality of Ellis Island's ghostly halls, and the credibility of the Ishpeming postcard. People value artifacts because of perceived authenticity. Once the assumption of authenticity is undermined, the aura of suspicion settles in, and the credibility of the artifact or—as in my experience with Mackinac Island—of an entire historic site is destroyed.

Memories and history always have referents, especially the places where the remembered or recounted events occurred. The place may be altered beyond recognition or otherwise unidentifiable. In those instances, the memory or history lacks crucial confirmation, but indirect confirmation may compensate. For example, a memory may retain validity because others confirm it, or the memory may be so vivid that it remains unquestioned, or the history may be substantiated by multiple sources. But when the referent is lost, despite whatever kind of corroboration we can find, an important emotional element of the past is dissipated, and the process of imagining the past is crippled. In addition to actual disappearance, many referents are mangled; places, objects, images, and other potential mnemonics that purport to be representations of the past are in fact reconstructions, manipulated images, reproductions, and interpretations. They are profoundly mediated and lose any legitimate claim to an authenticity based on integrity. Such places may even possess integrity of a scholarly variety, that is, they are based on the best research possible, and yet they still fall far short of my family cemetery plot or Ellis Island.

Places of memory possess authenticity and integrity. Perhaps this is what accounts for my own disdain for our ubiquitous homogenized suburbs and my unabashed proclivity for life in an older city neighborhood. Living in places that are authenticated by memory, places that have a history, induces and embellishes the feeling of connection to the past, and I like the notion of adding my own memories to a place that already embodies so many. I do not disdain newness, but I do not care to live in places that do not encompass sufficient memory to give me a sense of connectedness and of expansion beyond now. We all need memory places. In the absence of them, we are cursed by a sense of confinement, an isolation in the present.

It is difficult to describe the effect of the remembered past upon emotions. Perhaps Dilthey's concept of historical imagination is close, but it does not adequately describe the intense stream of emotions evoked by memory and its places. In a recent interview with a friend, a Comanche woman, we discussed the importance of certain objects and locales, now and in the past, for her people and thus explored an alternative way of envisioning the past. Certain principles guide my friend Evelyne and her people in talking about the past. First, those who are dead are never referred to by name. Second, they are called as a token of profound respect "old ones." Third, the chronology of events is not of particular import. Fourth, the past is in the present; the old ones can be called upon for advice or strength at any time. Fifth, the past is not a place of death; it is real and very much alive. Evelyne refers to the old ones as having gone on ahead. They are not in the past but rather in the future towards which the living are headed. Finally, for Evelyne, remembrance is sacred and spiritual because the process of remembering calls the living past into the living present. Evelyne's understanding of the past is subjective, personal, emotional, intimately linked to her people; and yet this perspective exudes integrity in the sense that it substantiates and validates an entire culture and world view. Most importantly, it explains existence in meaningful ways. And so Evelyne's memory is precisely what Nora has in mind when he claims that history and memory are in fundamental opposition and that history seeks to annihilate memory. Evelyne's remembrances and the rituals that sustain them are immediately destroyed by historical inquiry, proved to be either inaccurate or unverifiable. The fundamental truths that these rituals convey are undermined by historical methodology, and hence they are heaped into the intellectual sophisticates' trash bin as vestiges of a primitive age. Yet they continue to sustain the Comanche people as they have for countless generations.

The Vietnam Veterans Memorial in Washington, D.C., is not a historic site as usually defined, but it is surely a memory place. A display at the Smithsonian Institution shows mementos and notes left at the memorial in what is likely the most powerful exhibition I have ever visited. Tokens of love, friendship, longing, and regret—notes written as if to the living—have made this wall, encapsulating memory, a place for communicating with those who are gone from the earth. Here, memories conjoin those who are commemorated on the wall and all those relatives and friends and comrades for whom the wall is a place for remembrance. There is a sense of closeness to both the living and the dead as memories come in torrents and the past becomes contemporary, so much so that the dead are addressed as the living. It is as if this place, sanctified by the memories of all who visit, is somehow a nexus between the living and dead. Evelyne would understand this. Yet a historian could only evaluate the wall as a symbol, describe how the wall was built, count the hordes of visitors, and speculate about the power of the place. The metaphysical qualities of the place, which are really the source of its power, are not the topics of history and in fact are antithetical to the whole notion of history as a rational inquiry subject to specialized rules of evidence. History can describe what happens here but cannot travel inside of it. So, the experiences of visitors at the Vietnam memorial become social phenomena to be described, analyzed, and interpreted by historians and other experts, rather than acknowledged as a profound emotional outpouring that transforms the place into sacred ground, just as sacred as the battlefield at Gettysburg, the Great Hall at Ellis Island, or the cemetery where Grandmother brought me so often and where the bones of my ancestors molder. None of these is at all sacred when viewed from the outside. However, viewed from the inside, the way Abraham Lincoln looked at the battlefield at Gettysburg, as ground hallowed through events of a time before us, we can feel the "mystic chords of memory" that bind us to the past (Kammen 1991).

Although the Vietnam Veterans Memorial now has its own peculiar history as a monument, it is not a place that had any particular association with the Vietnam War nor with the veterans it memorializes. It is not the site of a battlefield, nor is it a cemetery. It is disembodied from the events of the war in Vietnam. Yet, it has become the preeminent memory place for those who seek to understand the war and remember those who were lost. While the shape and design of the memorial may cause the deepest emotions surrounding the war and its dead to surface, the place is hallowed not by the physicality but by the tears shed, the mementos left, the emotions experienced, the words exchanged.

Objects, letters, and photographs left at the memorial wall by friends, lovers, comrades, and even strangers provoke deep poignancy in all of us, often prompting tears of empathy, even now so long after the war. I am especially struck by those objects that are intimate and even erotic, left, I suppose, by wives, husbands, and lovers because such things recall life's passions in this place that memorializes the dead whose passions are so long gone. But then this is not just a place for remembering the dead. It is also a place to recall passion, love, intimacy, lost lovers, and to remember in the most elemental and most powerful way possible—emotionally. Our emotions remember in ways that our intellects never will.

The Vietnam memorial wall achieves its power through the names, both in the enormous totality of that list and the poignant personal individuality enshrined there. Although not the stuff of history, names are among our most intimate possessions. They make people real. They are the *I* of all memories, the beginning of self, the central character in all of the stories of our lives. The mystical power of a name standing for the totality of an individual human is manifested in the naming rituals of all cultures. Instinctively we know this when we approach the wall. Just as baptism and formal naming gives each individual a specific identify and a separate existence, the wall calls all those lost warriors into the presence of those who stand before it. Because their names are present, we must acknowledge each as an individual with an existence, an identity, and a reality that transcends death. The wall is hallowed by the conjunction of the names of the dead and the memories of the living.

Explanations of what happens at the wall or Ellis Island or my family cemetery, or through the picture postcard of my home, or at any memory place, fall short of what really happens inside of us when we have such experiences. But I think that it is all right that explanations fall short. We do not need explanations because we all have had the same experiences. We share a common humanity. We know what it is to be human. We all understand that nostalgia is a profound longing to go home, an attempt to recover the past and our lost selves. We also know that except insofar as we can use our memories and imaginations to visit the past, to visit ourselves as we used to be, and to once again see others who are gone ahead of us, it is a forlorn hope. Remembering can be a source of comfort and confirmation, but it can also be a reinjuring. We all mourn time passages. We are mortal. No more explanation is needed.

There are multiple ways to activate the past in our minds. All rely to greater or lesser extent on what Dilthey described as historical imagination. We all possess personal memories that manipulate the past into a sense of self in the present. We incorporate into these personal memories the memories of others, like my grandmother's, whose stories of the past linked my own memories to people and places before I was born. Artifacts, such as the postcard of my home before I was born, extend my memory of my own place to a time before I was there. The picture postcard has added credibility to my memory because enough of what I can see in it was still there when I knew the place. Like my grandmother's life, the postcard overlaps with my memory. Such intersections and linkages give added integrity to knowledge about the past. But linkages can also be synthetically created. Thus, Ellis Island has profound meaning for me because through historical inquiry I can link it to knowledge acquired through diaries, historical descriptions, photographs, official records, and oral history. With this context, I am able to imagine and feel the immigrant experience at the site. But at the Vietnam Veterans Memorial my reimagining of the pathos of the Vietnam War is much more immediate, activated by the provocative and evocative symbolism of the place, by examining the gifts and letters left at the wall, and by feeling the poignancy of the memories stimulated by the place and the names that reflect the individual identities of the dead.

Collective Memory

Thus far I have discussed memory as a personal and individual experience. Memory is also collective or even communal, often referred to by scholars and others too as an entity distinct from the memories of individuals. Of course there is no such thing as collective or communal memory distinct from personal memory because only individuals have memories. When I returned home to the Upper Peninsula (UP) of Michigan to write about my own memories, I preferred to revisit my own places of memory with my sister Anne or my cousin Rhena or with old friends. Now, as I reflect on our excursions, I know that I needed the companionship because it was an opportunity to confirm or question my own memories of the place. In this effort to confirm my own memories with other people's, we mutually defined and reaffirmed some shared memories and implicitly questioned others. Everyone experiences this process of coremembering. Definition and creation of shared memory is how we develop and sustain relationships with other people and also how we define ourselves as distinct from others. In this instance in the UP, I found an affirmation of family ties and long-standing friendships.

But experiences at places like Ellis Island or the Vietnam Veterans Memorial are different from remembrance with family and friends. While we all have our own thoughts about such places and differing points of connection with them, they do provoke similar feelings in all of us. Thus, I talk with others who visit such places and discover that we have constructed similar narratives around them. So, while collective memory is a chimera, we do create shared memory to establish our self-identity in juxtaposition to the identities of others, but shared memory also creates family ties and friendships. The sharing of memory brings about not only self-knowledge but also mutual understanding and trust between people. Memories are the cords that bind individuals together as neighbors, communities, and even larger groups. Conversely, mutually exclusive or conflicting memories can create mistrust and divisions between people. It is this principle that informs my own professional work in a public history organization.

The year 2001 was the 75th anniversary of the birth of Miles Davis. I no longer remember when I acquired my first Miles recording, but it was sometime after I came to St. Louis in 1988. That is when I began to learn about St. Louis and about Miles. The place and the person are intrinsically associated in my mind. A St. Louis native, born and raised in Illinois on the east side of the Mississippi, he played his first professional music on the west bank of the river in St. Louis. When I think of St. Louis, I hear Miles, and when I hear Miles, I think of St. Louis. For me, those cool, haunting trumpet tones are the melodic intonations of the soul of the place. Before he died in 1991, Miles Davis was acknowledged in his own country and abroad as a giant musical genius of the twentieth century. But Miles has been regrettably ignored in his hometown. In 1991, the local St. Louis newspaper ran a small obituary on an inside page while one of our nation's largest dailies prominently covered his death and the world mourned his passing.

Miles was black. Miles was brash and proud. Miles was from East St. Louis on the "other" side of the river, and Miles did not cater to white folk. Miles was scarcely remembered by white people, other than jazz aficionados, in his hometown. Yet in East St. Louis, which is predominantly African American, people did remember him and named a school for him. Among African Americans in the St. Louis region, there is a high level of awareness that Miles Davis came from this place. And Miles Davis himself acknowledged his personal and musical roots in this place. The bifurcated memory of Miles Davis is symptomatic of St. Louis's burden of an unshared past and of parallel histories that confirm and contribute to the region's racist reputation and divided history.

Recently the Missouri Historical Society in St. Louis organized a stunning exhibition examining the legacy of Miles Davis and facilitated the development of a year-long regional festival celebrating the life and music of Miles Davis. The exhibition, entitled *Miles: A Miles Davis Retrospective,* was the product of a collaboration among museum and jazz professionals as well as family, friends, and associates of Miles. Nearly thirty collaborating groups sponsored scores of events highlighting St. Louis blues and jazz, poetry, art, and African American culture on both sides of the Mississippi River. The opening of the exhibition at the Missouri Historical Society embodied my aspirations for the project. Hundreds of St. Louisans gathered to celebrate: African American leaders from both sides of the river, heads of major corporations, family and friends of Miles Davis, musicians, jazz and blues fans, members of the society, interested citizens. They were not discussing diversity, nor were they focused on racism, nor were they huddled in corners segregated by race, as so often happens, especially in St. Louis. Instead everybody was focused on a grand celebration of the life of this creative genius with deep St. Louis roots.

I saw and heard many things that evening. I saw representatives of our community celebrating the genius of a man that they had never celebrated before and learning to appreciate their place in a new way. I heard St. Louisans, particularly St. Louisans who were not African American, expanding their story of St. Louis to encompass Miles Davis, and I heard black St. Louisans surprised that Miles Davis was celebrated in a major cultural institution. I saw personal memories of those who loved or knew Miles converge and contribute to a newly shared memory of St. Louis as Miles Davis's place. I witnessed reunions of family, musicians, and others who once were friends. I saw people confront the ambiguities of Miles Davis's life and accept them as evidence of the common humanity that we all share. I detected a new intersection in our previously parallel histories, a new chapter of a new narrative that acknowledges the contributions of all the people who made this place. I felt another powerful confirmation of my conviction that how we remember the past matters now and has profound future consequences. I sensed a growing acknowledgment that if Miles's haunting, soulful music came from this place, then there is something marvelous and beautiful about this place, something worth celebrating indeed. I know that because of our efforts, in some small but important way, St. Louis will never be quite the same again.

I never knew Miles except through his music. Because of my role in the development of the exhibit, I now know his family, some of his musician friends, his biographer, and others who knew him well. In the exhibit gallery, I stand—as many others have—in front of the trumpet that Miles played to record his groundbreaking album "Kind of Blue." I imagine his fingers and lips on the instrument, and I can hear the clarion burst of "So What." I can almost see the breath blasting through the horn in staccato bursts. I remember Miles's words: "In music, I have such feeling for different phrases, and when I'm really enjoying something it's like I'm one with it. The phrase is me. . . . I see colors and things when I'm playing" (Davis 1989:399). I move on to the picture of Miles in Copenhagen. It is one of the few images I have seen in which he is obviously pleased. He has finished playing. He looks over his left shoulder. Sweat pours down his face. He cradles his trumpet in his arms. His usual haunted look is overshadowed with satisfaction. He is happy, I am sure, and I want to adopt that expression for this place of St. Louis. His music builds bridges between us and lightens the burdens that encumber us. His music is a shared space, and so is my place.

My memories are dead-bird handkerchief memories and home place memories, Ellis Island memories, Gettysburg memories, Evelyne's Comanche memories, Vietnam memories, and Miles Davis memories. Every memory has a referent, a place or a person that is at once a crucible and a confirmation. Some are remembered referents like the bedroom of my childhood. Others are artifacts like the Negaunee cemetery or Miles Davis's trumpet or the Vietnam memorial wall or Ellis Island. Out of all of this, I have dreamed myself, shaped my identity, established my values, and marked out my place in the world. Many of my memories are shared. Those of us who have visited Ellis Island, Gettysburg, or the Vietnam Veterans Memorial do not have identical memories of such places and the people and events associated with them, but rather we have memory outlines in common. Those memories do not just define a *me,* they also define an *us.*

When the past is not shared, when it lacks people or accessible places that confirm it, the past is less meaningful. If the past is entirely mediated by professionals and cannot be personally confirmed, it loses credibility. My experience in thirty years of work on behalf of the public's history convinces me that the history that matters to people is the past that they remember and have validated through emotional experience. A shared experience with the past, such as in the Miles Davis exhibition, has meaning because the visitor confronts objects that affirm that Miles did live and did play. The interplay with the object is emotional because it is a tangible link to Miles, just as the Negaunee Cemetery links me to Grandmother and others gone before. My reaction to Miles's red trumpet now in our exhibition case is to think something like: "Miles touched that very horn—that's where that beautiful music came from as he held that trumpet to his lips and pushed his streams of air through its convolutions." The past is knowable but not through words on printed pages so much as through emotional resonance, stimulated by places and objects of memory and the stories our whole community tells.

Remembering the Past, Re-Membering the Present

Elder's Constructions of Place and Self in a Philadelphia Neighborhood

4

MARIA G. CATTELL

THIS IS A STORY ABOUT THE WAY THINGS WERE in the year 1990 in a place called Olney. The story weaves together Olney's present of 1990 with its past, twining current happenings, history, and memory into stories about an anthropologist (me), the community of Olney, and some older white ethnics who were longtime residents of this section, or neighborhood, in the northeast quadrant of Philadelphia. I was carrying out an anthropological community study in Olney. But the story is not so much about me as about the community and, first and foremost, the older people who were the focus of the research. Many of them undoubtedly live now only in memory, in the memory of their friends and families, and in my accounts of them in conference presentations (e.g., Cattell 1992a, 1994, 1996, 1997a, 1997b), an unpublished research report (Cattell 1991a), and several other publications (Cattell 1991b, 1991c, 1992b, 1999).

Of course, the story continued after the research was completed. I learned that some of the participants in the research died or moved away from Olney, in spite of their determination to finish their days in their own homes. But I have not followed up on them in any systematic way, and so the story concerns a moment in time, the year 1990. It is a story of the past.

The Research Project: Aging-in-Place

Much gerontological research has focused on specialized and age-segregated communities such as nursing homes and retirement communities, marginal settings such as single-room occupancy (SRO) hotels, and the migration of elders, especially to the Sunbelt. The Olney research project complemented this kind of research by looking at the aging-in-place of community-dwellers, persons who continue to live in the same community in which they have lived for many years—which is what most older Americans say they want to do and what many in fact do. In Olney, which became a community of great cultural and ethnic diversity in the 1980s, this meant focusing on white ethnics because they were, for the most part, the people who were longtime residents. The neighborhood was examined as a source of meaning with multiple dimensions relating to competence, functioning, and physical health; independence; personal and family history; change and stability; and as an archive and a metaphor for one's own life.

One major construct guiding the research was "environmental insideness," or the experience of being physically, socially, and autobiographically within an environmental setting (Rowles 1978, 1983, 1984). The goal in this regard was to explore and understand the experience of aging-in-place from the perspective of older persons in an urban neighborhood that was undergoing many changes. The changes were likely to induce uneasy feelings of cognitive dissonance arising from disparities between objective and subjective evaluations of a person's living environment (Lawton 1986), or what might be called person-environment dissonance.

The second major construct was the "anthropology of the self," in which individuals are seen as reflexive persons who construct their own experience and whose behavior is proactive (Marsella, DeVos, and Hsu 1985; Shweder and LeVine 1984; Singer 1984; Turner and Bruner 1986). The goal in this regard was to explore the continuous interactions between persons and their environment (Lawton 1986), especially attachment to place and the personal meanings of place as aspects of identity and selfhood and, specifically, to investigate elders' perceptions of resources in the community and their importance in meeting their own needs. Thus Olney was considered as a resource environment seen, as much as possible, from the perspectives of community-dwelling white ethnic elders.

The field experience began in September 1989, on a warm sunny day with puffy white clouds floating across the high blue sky, with a self-guided tour of Olney. First I drove around Olney, from east to west, from north to south. Then I walked up and down Fifth Street's shopping district, several blocks dense with stores and eateries, alive with pedestrian traffic and noisy with motor traffic. Finally, I walked behind Fifth Street's shops, to both east and west. These are the residential areas, many with the brick row houses only two or three stories high that characterize Philadelphia, in contrast to high-rise cities such as Chicago and New York.

As a country girl who grew up on a farm in south-central Pennsylvania and, much later in life, as an anthropologist who spent two years in rural western Kenya researching the lives of old people (Cattell 1989), I felt some qualms about doing research in a big city like Philadelphia. How do you even get people to notice you? Won't they be suspicious of a stranger, refuse to talk with me, slam doors in my face? After all, this is the city. I was used to Lancaster (a small Pennsylvania city about seventy miles west of Philadelphia), but thought: "this big city stuff won't be easy." I could not have been more wrong!

It turned out that Olney was, in fact, much more like Lancaster than like a big city. The resemblance was partly physical, since Lancaster too is a city of brick row houses and tree-lined streets. People who live in Olney refer to themselves as Olneyites and regard their community as a small town. And most people were friendly. When I went to public meetings such as civic associations and special interest groups like the Olney Garden Club, there was no big city anonymity. I was always noticed. People approached me to find out who I was. When I told them about my research project, some invited me to visit them in their homes and introduced me to their friends and neighbors. I encouraged everyone to talk about what Olney was like in the past for them, how Olney had changed, how they were meeting their daily needs in the present. We went on neighborhood walks and shopping trips together and to senior group meetings. Occasionally I was asked to give a talk about my research in Olney; one senior group even asked me to talk about my research in Kenya. I soon felt right at home in Olney.

Seven older Olneyites became key informants or coresearchers. These relationships involved frequent home visits, observation of daily routines and social contacts, informal and focused interviews, collection of life history materials, and participation in activities outside the home such as shopping and attending meetings. About three dozen other elders and a few younger persons were interviewed on a less intense basis. I continued to observe public behavior and attend public meetings and events throughout the research period. Although I did not live in Olney, I sometimes stayed in one woman's home overnight. I shopped in Olney. Altogether, I felt that in many ways I was socially integrated into the community and developed an experiential sense of living in Olney as a newcomer. Vicariously, through the memories of older Olneyites, I also gained a sense of Olney's past.

Re-Membering the Past

An important assumption in the research is that meaning is fundamental in human lives and that anthropological fieldwork (also known as participant observation—see Keith 1986) is a good way to get at meanings in the lives of others (Rubinstein 1992). Another assumption is that meanings associated with objects, places, events, and persons accumulate over time, and that for older longtime residents, the community of Olney is a palimpsest, overwritten many times with meanings that affect present experiences. Thus, for each individual, Olney is a place that is presently lived in but is also remembered, reconstructed, imagined, and—above all—is a place of meaning.

Of particular interest here is the idea of "re-membering," a term Barbara Myerhoff took from Victor Turner (Kaminsky 1992:66) and explored with elderly Jewish members of a California senior center (Myerhoff 1978). Re-membering is an intense form of remembering that calls attention "to the reaggregation of members, the figures who belong to one's life story, one's own prior selves, as well as significant others who are part of the story. Re-membering . . . is a purposive, significant unification. . . . [that is] requisite to sense and ordering" (Myerhoff 1992:240). Re-membering creates links between storyteller and listener, between one's present self and past selves, between one's present self and important others in the past. Re-membering in a sense reconstitutes the past, brings it vividly to mind for the rememberer, as if places and people were really there. By this means, the past invests the present with emotion and meaning.

Olney: A Brief History

We begin with history, a history constituted from the mingling of material from published sources and information given to me by older Olneyites as they recalled Olney's past. In particular, much information on the built environment and community celebrations was shared with me by Olney's unofficial historian, Alpheus P. McCloskey, who was in his early 80s at the time of the research.

In the seventeenth and eighteenth centuries, the neighborhood now known as Olney was farmland. In the early nineteenth century two textile mills were built, along with workers' houses, a school, and a church. By mid-century, a railroad had been built along 7th and 8th Streets (the railroad is still Olney's western boundary). In the late-nineteenth century, wealthy Philadelphia businessmen and politicians built summer estates in the area, and more factories went up as part of the industrialization of the city. Philadelphia was then the second largest industrial center in the United States and a major port of entry, second only to New York. It was also the textile capital of America, with one-third of all wage earners employed in the textile and clothing industry, an industry that required only skilled labor and thus influenced which immigrant groups were likely to settle in Philadelphia (Golab 1973).

By the early twentieth century, trolley (streetcar) tracks were laid from Philadelphia's city center to lower Olney. As industry and the trolleys moved north, so did real estate development, and Olney became one of Philadelphia's streetcar suburbs. The farms and large estates were gradually replaced by the row houses for which Philadelphia is famous (75 percent of Philadelphia homes are row houses. Miller, Vogel, and Davis 1988:194). Among American cities, Philadelphia is known as the City of Homes because of its high rate of home ownership (Sutherland 1973). Immigrant groups often set up building and loan associations to help factory workers purchase homes (Clark 1973). During Olney's years of building, factory workers flocked to Olney for jobs and homes. One person recalled that an entire German village of textile workers was recruited to come live and work in Olney. Buying homes gave people a stake in the community and contributed to neighborhood stability (Miller, Vogel, and Davis 1988). That home purchase was a clear commitment to staying in the community was symbolized in one 84-year-old man's display, on his living room wall, of the check with which his father paid for the house in one lump sum. The check, for $3,500, was dated 1917.

People in their 70s and 80s at the time of the research recalled that when they were children in Olney, "there was a farm out our back door." They remembered pumping water at a farm well and emptying coal ashes into dirt streets. They remembered how the outhouses at Olney El (elementary school) were knocked over every Halloween. In 1924, Jake—Olney's last cow—died, and a 2,500-seat movie theater was built on what had been her pasture. By then, most of Olney had the basic amenities of sewer, water, and electricity. By 1940, it was pretty well filled up. As one man told me: "When I was six, in 1914, Olney was the country. By the time I got married in 1937, Olney was pretty well built up to what it is today." Today, lower Olney, the older southern portion, is almost entirely small row houses on narrow streets. Further north, the houses are larger, with front porches and yards, more twin and single homes, and wider streets lined with sycamores and other trees. Many of these houses have special features such as columns, porches, bay windows, and garages.

By 1910, there was a strong enough sense of community for Olney to hold its first Fourth of July celebration. One man in his early 80s (in 1990) recalled how "the streets in Olney would decorate up: string Japanese lanterns across the street with candles in them that lit up the Fourth of July night." In time, other community rituals developed; they included a big Memorial Day celebration, various small local events such as street fairs and block parties with races and games, and an annual doll show. A local newspaper, the *Olney Times,* began publication in a farmhouse in 1909; in 1990, its weekly circulation was 25,000. It was widely read by English speakers, and people often mentioned having "seen it in the *Olney Times.*"

Many local organizations developed, including ethnic clubs such as the German Society; recreational and sports groups; churches, service groups, and senior groups; the Olney Symphony Orchestra, Friends of the Olney Library, Friends of Fisher Park, Friends of Tacony Creek Park, and others. In the mid-1940s, the Greater Olney Community Council and the Olney Civic Association were established. Many of these groups had overlapping memberships and thus helped create dense social networks throughout Olney.

In the twentieth century, up until about 1980, Olney's population was predominantly white, first- or second-generation Germans and Irish Catholics, with a few other ethnic minorities such as Ukrainians, Portuguese, and Greeks. The Catholics created their own social infrastructure with two churches, two elementary schools, and a high school in Olney. Many shopkeepers spoke German and many Protestant churches had services in German. "You heard a lot of German around here," said one man (not himself German) who had lived in the same house for seventy-three years.

Olney in 1990

Olney is one of Philadelphia's forty-five neighborhoods, each with its own name, more or less distinct (but unofficial) boundaries, and varying characteristics regarding employment opportunities, quality of housing, socioeconomic status, predominant immigrant and ethnic groups, degree of ethnic diversity, and other factors. The neighborhoods are not separate municipalities; they are all part of the City of Philadelphia.

Because neighborhood boundaries are unofficial, they are subject to interpretation by residents. Responses to inquiries during the research indicated that Olney's western and eastern boundaries were agreed upon by everyone: to the west, the railroad running between 7th and 8th Streets, and to the east, the meandering Tacony (or Tookany) Creek. The southern and northern boundaries were open to interpretation. Some named Roosevelt Boulevard (U.S. route 1) as the southern boundary; others included the area known as Feltonville, making the southern boundary Wyoming Avenue. Similarly, to the north, some named Godfrey Avenue; others included the area known as East Oak Lane, with 65th Avenue as the northern boundary. For the research, I chose the larger area, including Feltonville and East Oak Lane, which corresponds to Greater Olney as defined by the Greater Olney Community Council. The Fifth Street Shopping District falls into the smaller area (with Roosevelt Boulevard and Godfrey Avenue as boundaries). The intersection of Fifth and Olney (Fifth Street and Olney Avenue) in the shopping district was generally agreed to be the heart of the community.

Following World War II, there were many changes in Olney, changes that occurred throughout Philadelphia, including deindustrialization and job loss as many industries went south or overseas. As the city, with its diminishing tax base, ran into severe financial constraints (it came close to bankruptcy in 1990), services such as policing, trash collection, and street cleaning declined. Crime, drugs, trash, and graffiti increased. In the 1970s and 1980s, there were rapid changes in the racial and ethnic composition of blocks and whole neighborhoods (Miller, Vogel, and Davis 1988:193–194, 294–296), including Olney, and many whites fled to the automobile suburbs ringing Philadelphia.

Olney's total population in 1980 was 57,243; by 1990, it had increased slightly to 58,820. Olney's population has consistently had a higher socioeconomic status than is found in most Philadelphia neighborhoods. In 1980 the proportion of those age sixty-five and over in Olney-Feltonville was about 18 percent, relatively high for the city (PHMC 1985:264).

In the 1980s, a dramatic shift toward ethnic diversity took place. There was a rapid increase in the proportions of African Americans, Asians, and Hispanics. In the 1980 census, 91.5 percent of Olney's population was white and 3.5 percent was black (Philadelphia City Planning Commission 1981). By 1990, whites constituted only 59 percent of Olney's population, with blacks being 16 percent and Asians, 13 percent (Borowski 1991). Hispanics (not a racial category in the census) also increased markedly. Within a period of only ten to fifteen years, Olney became a multiracial, multicultural community—the most diverse neighborhood in the city (Carvajal and Borowski 1991). In fact, some whites moved to Olney (or returned to it) because of the diversity (Goode and Schneider 1994). At the same time, and despite a high turnover of housing, Olney remained a neighborhood with many stable institutions largely controlled by established residents and many intergenerational families (Goode, Schneider, and Blanc 1992). In 1990, the new diversity was obvious on school playgrounds and in shopping and residential areas.

Dramatic changes also occurred along Fifth Street, in the shopping district, for many years Olney's central shopping area, catering to basic needs and desires for ethnic foods and other reminders of European homelands. Many people told me: "You used to be able to buy just about anything you needed on Fifth Street," a remark often followed by: "Things are so different today." What was different in 1990 was the rapid turnover of store ownership and merchandise and new signs, many written with Korean characters. Most buildings on this shopping strip are only two stories high, with stores on the ground floor and shopkeepers living on the second floor. Many stores had been family businesses, handed down from one generation to the next. Shopkeepers and customers knew each other. But in the 1980s, many businesses were bought by outsiders, especially Koreans. Some of these stores catered exclusively to Korean clientele; others meant to welcome all comers, but erected signs with Korean characters, which signified "not welcome" to many elders.

In 1986, the Korean community (with city permission) erected street signs in Korean. The signs became a focus of controversy. Established residents were angered because they had not been consulted through public meetings (Goode and Schneider 1994). People still talked about the Korean signs in 1990 as an indication of how Koreans (and other outsiders) were taking over Olney.

From my outsider's perspective, Olney in 1990 seemed a rich resource environment able to provide almost everything older residents (or residents of any age) might need. There were low-cost public and private transportation systems. At the corner of Fifth and Olney, seniors could catch a bus for a day trip to the Atlantic City casinos. Many formal health and social services were available to seniors, with a major medical center in Logan, a neighborhood bordering Olney. Olney has a public library, a post office, senior centers, churches, banks, supermarkets, bars, and a police ministation. Throughout the residential areas, there are corner groceries, doctors' and dentists' offices, and many services such as drycleaning, haircare, television repair, shoe repair, and travel agencies. In the Fifth Street shopping area, one can buy baked goods, fresh foods, groceries, gas, clothing, shoes, hardware, home furnishings, office supplies, wines and spirits, flowers, hearing aids, eyeglasses, and many other items. In other parts of Olney, there were newer stores, including three supermarkets and a big discounter. There were a number of restaurants, some of which—along with the public library—were regular meeting places for older people.

Olney looked good to me, but I was a newcomer. I had no sense of the changes that had taken place. Longtime residents of the community had different views. For them, Olney was a place of lifetimes of memories, memories implicated in their senses of self and personal identity. But there were deep gaps between memory and present reality. Though Olney was a place they knew and loved, a place they were proud to claim as their own in calling themselves Olneyites, in some ways they no longer felt at home.

Consequences for the Elders: Person-Environment Dissonance

Person-environment dissonance, or the feeling of unease between one's self and one's surroundings, was an everyday experience for many older white ethnics. "Sometimes I feel like an immigrant to another country," lamented a woman in her late 80s. For her, Olney was more alien in 1990 than it had been for her in 1933 when she arrived from Germany. "Sometimes it looks like a war zone; you even see Chinese mothers with babies on their backs," said a man, also in his 80s, whose family moved to Olney when he was 11. Such changes were unsettling for longtime residents. Many experienced a cognitive and emotional gulf between their concepts of self and neighborhood, and self and community.

The older white ethnics missed the days when Olney was mostly German and Irish. They admitted they would rather have "people like me" as neighbors. "Do you chat with your new neighbors when you meet outside?" I asked one man. Said he: "What's there to talk about with them?" Many had resigned themselves to having blacks, Cambodians, Thais, Hispanics, and others as neighbors but said: "It's just too bad we can't speak the same language," or, more bitterly, "They come here to make a better life and don't even bother to learn our language." Nevertheless, I almost never heard anyone use a racial epithet. People usually spoke precisely of Cambodian, Khmer, Puerto Rican, or black neighbors, or referred to different others as "them" or "those people," lamented that "they aren't like us," or used joking remarks to express their unease (cf. Goode and Schneider 1994).

Elders also regretted changes in neighborhood sociability. They recalled "when we sat on our porches and chatted while the children played." Porches (and front yards) were an attraction for people coming from further south in Philadelphia, where houses had only steps (called stoops) from front door to street. In the United States, porches were the center of leisure activities from the 1800s through the mid-1940s (Bowman and LaMarca 1997). Olneyites attributed the decline in porch-sitting and neighborliness to linguistic and cultural barriers, though the more likely culprits were automobiles, which took people away, and television and air conditioning, which shifted the social center to the living room (Bowman and LaMarca 1997; Miller, Vogel, and Davis 1988).

Some spoke of new and different neighbors in a positive way as teaching the old-timers about new foods and doing little things for them. Some said they placed their hope in the children, who could be seen playing together on school playgrounds and in residential blocks. "Everyone gets along in my block" was a recurrent theme. At the same time, there was constant monitoring of neighbors' behavior, especially negative behavior such as domestic fights and the ways the new people did or did not keep up their property.

Elders also encoded their distress about neighborhood changes in expressions of regret for the loss of community rituals, especially the Fourth of July celebrations, which in the past included a parade and fireworks but had been reduced by 1990 to "just the baby parade." The much newer Super Sunday in Olney, sponsored by Community Council and held in Fisher Park, features games, food, entertainment, and information. Those attending are primarily young people and families with children. For Olney's elders, Fisher Park was "a nice place" where they took their children for picnics and play on Sunday afternoons and where some of the Fourth of July ceremonies were held. The elders of 1990 were not so much interested in "that thing [Super Sunday] they do now in Fisher Park." The way Fisher Park used to be and the old Fourth of July ceremonies represented for them the Olney of their younger days and the way life ought to be.

For those who had lived in Olney and shopped on Fifth Street for thirty, fifty, even seventy years, the changes in the shopping district were, if anything, even more unsettling. Older residents made many comments about the Koreans taking over family businesses and favorite stores, not knowing their stock and not even speaking English. There were bitter jokes about being able to buy Cambodian pizza or Korean spaghetti and comments such as "It's not Fifth and Olney any more; it's Korean Plaza." Some complained about the closing (in early 1990) of the Schwarzwald Inn, a family-run German restaurant, which regularly served German dishes and specialties on occasion, such as hasenpfeffer every December.

In fact, as people became physically more frail, they became increasingly dependent on the Fifth Street stores. Because they could no longer carry heavy burdens, they made frequent or even daily expeditions to Fifth Street. Yet going shopping could be a frightening and confusing experience, with so many strangers on the sidewalks ("I never see anyone I know on Fifth Street any more") and so much rapid change in store ownership and merchandise along with a shift to chain-operated self-service stores. Shoppers were no longer greeted and helped by storeowners, which had been the old style of business relying on personal interaction and customer loyalty (cf. Goode and Schneider 1994).

Some older Olneyites responded to the ethnic influx and other changes by moving out of the community. I met some of them at senior centers in Olney, where they had returned to see their friends. They spoke of the reasons for their move: fears for personal safety, the "different people" moving in, how "dirty" the newcomers are, and how "dirty" Olney had become. But many stayed, and intended to stay "at least as long as I can manage." Their responses to the changes ranged from ambivalence and distrust to cautious acceptance. Some talked a lot about moving but stayed on, in spite of their unease. Others had no thought of leaving: "I love Olney," they said, "I'm staying right here."

Memory as Resource: Re-Membering the Past

An outsider's inventory of Olney as a resource environment was given earlier. But the chief research goal was to explore subjectively defined and personally meaningful resources that could be overlooked in formal assessments or, even if noticed, perhaps not understood by outsiders in the same ways as the older people understood them. Elders suggested a variety of such personally significant resources, including places to meet friends, bingo games, trips to casinos, other travel opportunities, convenience in shopping and transportation, formal groups (including some no longer in existence), community events and rituals, one's own home, friendly (or neighborly) neighbors and one's immediate neighborhood, and a sense of the wider Olney community developed from complex layers of memory and active contacts in the present. Many of these resources involved relationships and convenience, the latter referring to opportunities suited to the speaker's physical capabilities.

Resources began at home. Although this research focused on the neighborhood and community outside elders' homes, it was obvious that houses and the objects in them were foci for older Olneyites' feelings and memories: signs and symbols of the remembered past, anchors in the present, hope for the future (cf. Stafford 1996). Memories link a person's house and its contents with personal relationships, past and present, and with various aspects of self, including family and personal identity, important life events, and transgenerational responsibilities (Csikszentmihalyi and Rochberg-Halton 1981). For elders, the house lived in and the objects in the house are at the core of the process of re-membering, as individuals reexperience former selves and past and present relationships with others (Rubinstein 1987, 1989). Rubinstein (1987) argues that experiencing objects nonverbally (e.g., seeing and touching them) and talking about the memories associated with objects appear to reinforce older individuals' personal meaning systems, identities, and roles, much as rituals reinforce cultural premises. I would add that in Olney many older persons who felt uneasiness and estrangement outside their homes could still feel safe and at home in their own houses. This was the result not only of familiarity but also of the evocative powers of objects that enabled elders to re-member or reconstitute the past. Such re-membering provided a sense of comfort and safety for the re-memberer, probably because the re-memberer felt less lonely and more in control.

From home, individuals' orbits expanded to include next-door neighbors and their block (often called "my neighborhood") and, beyond that, the wider community of Olney. Older Olneyites shared a sense of neighborhood and community derived from the remembered past and culturally shaped ideals. Their attachment to place was a resource related to specific environmental features and to events and people, some re-membered, some active in the present.

Alfie, in his early 80s in 1990, had lived in Olney since he was six. He loved talking about the early days when Olney was the country, when the roads were dirt. Alfie told a little story: "One day I was crossing Tabor Road to Olney El [Elementary School], and it was raining hard. When I got to the other side, I looked back and saw my rubber sticking in the mud in the middle of the street." Alfie's image of leaving his footprint in a street long since paved over (and perhaps his rubber with it) speaks to Alfie's sense of his being, literally, a part of Olney. Alfie was so embedded in place, and place was so deep in him, that they seemed inseparable. He loved to roll the names of Olney places over his tongue: street names, trolley line numbers, the names of the owners of farms and estates that were displaced by row house construction. No doubt such recitations conjured up a host of related memories. But though Alfie loved to remember Olney the way it used to be, he was not stuck in the past. He kept up with current events in Olney, read the local newspaper, and attended public events such as the grand opening of the Olney police ministation, one of the early community policing efforts in the neighborhood. Alfie had Cambodian neighbors. Several times he said to me: "I just wish my neighbors and I spoke the same language." He always seemed sad when he said this. Once he went on to say: "Of course we could leave. But why should we? My wife and I have lived here almost all our lives. I grew up just four blocks from here. I don't want to leave."

Queried about the past, people usually brought up pleasant memories such as growing tomatoes across the street "where that store is now" or sitting on their porches or in their backyards and chatting with neighbors on summer evenings (the latter being a frequently mentioned feature of the old neighborhoods). Often they mentioned specific neighbors and the many little things people did for each other. They portrayed a generally harmonious and orderly world, in contrast to the present with so many "different people moving in . . . whose ways are not our ways." However, most older Olneyites stressed that "everyone gets along in my block," which was sometimes a euphemistic gloss on imperfect reality. Even occasional breaches of neighborliness did not divert people from insistence on neighborhood harmony as both practice and ideal. Surely it was more comforting to take that view! This fits with other research that indicates that older people are more likely than other age groups to express satisfaction with their situation, probably in large part because "to express satisfaction with what exists is effective in reducing 'cognitive dissonance'" (Lawton 1986:48).

By contrast, in the wider community beyond their own block, elders portrayed a more negative picture of civic deterioration, dirt, and cultural clash. They saw the community as being at risk and themselves at risk with it. Perhaps the greater negativity of comments about Fifth Street and other areas away from their own block provided a release for frustrations about their own immediate neighborhoods. But their comments often were right on target. Many businesses had been bought by Koreans and had signs in Korean, and stores changed hands often (even during the period of the research). Fifth Street and the areas around railroad bridges were visibly dirtier, even filthy, compared to residential areas. People often mentioned the dirt, recalling the days when Olney was clean, when people swept their sidewalks, and the city cleaned the streets. Dirt was a key metaphor for expressing discomfort about many other changes in Olney. As one woman said, "We can't say those ethnic words any more." But they could, and did, talk about dirt. Dirt was seen as the antithesis of community.

Anna, a seventy-four-year-old widow who had lived most of her adult life in Olney, told me that she was "scared to death someone will snatch my purse" on Fifth Street, where she did most of her everyday shopping. For her, Fifth Street had become a place of strangers and dirt—and the very real possibility of having her purse snatched. "When I came to Olney," she said, "it was lovely: spotless clean and people were friendly. It was a lovely place. . . . We used to be all the same sort of people. We lived the same way. Our children were going to school together. And in the summer we sat out and talked, or went down the street and talked. If you could help one another, you did it." Anna thought her own block was still nice, though she no longer left her doors unlocked as she used to. Her block had important memories for her of neighbors helping each other out, the flowers people grew, and neighborly sociability. She often thought about leaving Olney, but for now, "I'll stay, at least as long as I have good neighbors." When I visited Anna's block, it was indeed a pleasant, quiet, and very clean place.

Clearly these elders had a sense of Olney as a community existing over time. Their memories of Olney past were involved in their construction of Olney present. This was not a matter of living in the past. Rather, their past lived in them. Their personhood and self-identity were bound up with place and with their immediate experiences of Olney, as well as, and simultaneously with, their remembered community. Nor was the past static and unchanging. It was continually redefined and reinterpreted—in conversations, in the *Olney Times,* at community meetings, and in other settings.

Sometimes, I wondered if I was leading people to talk about the past. Gradually, I realized that they recalled old Olney and the past and compared past with present, not just because I was asking them about it, but because they did it anyway. Olney today and Olney past came up in conversations in which I was a mere listener or minor participant. Past and present were twin themes in the *Olney Times* and at meetings where I was simply a silent attendee. Discussion of these issues arose from the tensions they created in people, not as an artifact of the research. Mutti, for instance, gave me many glimpses into this reality.

In 1990, Mutti was a widow in her late 80s. She had come from Germany as a bride in the 1930s. When her husband died about 1960, Mutti's son urged her to move. "But I couldn't move. I told my son, 'I have my roots here. I have to stay here.' So I stayed." Her roots included neighbors on her block, other old-timers like her, several Olney organizations in which she was active, her house full of memories and memorabilia of her family, and her garden. "I've gardened here for half a century," said she. "I know my garden. And a garden club where my daughter lives wouldn't be the same as the one in Olney. I've been a member of the Olney Garden Club since it started." During the period in which I knew her, Mutti had many thoughts about whether she should continue to stay in Olney. Often she reminisced about the past, about gardens that no longer existed, about neighborliness that had diminished, friends who had gone. In the end, she decided to stay. "Olney is my home."

Conclusion

Thus it was, in 1990, that these elders demonstrated their creative adaptations to their changed community and changed selves, in part through remembering and in part through the more intense process of re-membering personal, family, and community history. Their memories were a resource evoking a sense of continuity and stability of both self and place. They called themselves Olneyites, not Philadelphians, because Olney had become a part of themselves, part of their identities. It seemed that many of them, like Alfie, had left their rubbers sticking in the mud; that, like Mutti, they had their roots in Olney—or Olney had its roots in them. Some former Olneyites who returned for visits said things such as "I feel as if I belong in Olney." Nevertheless, for everyone there were tensions between their feelings about the Olney they loved, the remembered community, and the Olney of present experience, which was often perceived as dirty and dangerous.

The remembered and re-membered community of Olney represented a time and place in which elders such as Mutti and Anna were young and strong, living busy, useful, fulfilling lives. It was good to remember their younger selves as competent parents, employees, gardeners, and so on. Their daily encounters as older persons caused them to see Olney in 1990 as dangerous and threatening, in contrast to the remembered community, which was safer, more close-knit, more neighborly. Though the contrast between memories and present experiences could be disturbing, the remembered community gave elders a sense of continuity, an enduring sense of Olney as a good place to live in spite of everything, a place where they belonged as competent persons, a place where life had been and continued to be full of meaning.

Acknowledgments

I am most grateful to the many Olneyites who welcomed me to their community, especially the many senior citizens who allowed me to visit in their homes and to attend, as a "junior citizen," their senior group meetings. Special thanks to Erna Rath, who regarded me as a daughter; Helena Chepy, Elsie Ewald, Fred Funk, Alpheus and Clarissa McCloskey, Bea Worthington, and Jack Weinbeck; Amy Zoniriw and her family; and the Greater Olney Community Council, which welcomed me as a member though I was only an honorary Olneyite. The research was funded by The Retirement Research Foundation in a grant to Robert L. Rubinstein and Mark R. Luborsky, Co-Principal Investigators, then at the Philadelphia Geriatric Center (PGC). It was my privilege not only to work with Bob and Mark but also to know the late M. Powell Lawton, Director of Research at PGC, dean of American gerontology and a warm human being who was keenly interested in person-environment relationships. Discussions about Olney and related matters with Baine Alexander, Helen Black, Judith Goode, Marcene Goodman, Marilyn McArthur, and Miriam Moss were helpful. My thanks to them all.

The Cemetery
A Site for the Construction of Memory, Identity, and Ethnicity

5

DORIS FRANCIS, LEONIE KELLAHER, AND GEORGINA NEOPHYTOU

THE MULTICULTURAL NATURE of British society, along with a renewed interest in the spiritual meaning of existence, generates new models of bereavement and more open, accepting attitudes toward death. This chapter examines the English cemetery as the unexplored locus for the linked constructions of identity, ethnicity, and memory. At life crises, particularly at times of death, issues of identity and community take center stage and may be renegotiated and reconstituted through cemetery memorial rituals.

Through the use of a symbolic repertoire of stones, flowers, words, and actions, mourning rites provide material manifestation of complex psychological and sociological processes that are not easily approached in discursive language. These rituals for the dead occur in a "commemorative time domain, where a mythic past, present and future coexist and sometimes coalesce" (Hart 1992:227). Historic and present-day cemeteries, as liminal places, bridge notions of self and other, time and space, individuals and community, and past and present homeland. Such landscapes encode, reproduce, and initiate constructions of memory at individual, familial, and collective levels. "The entrance to the Cemetery is a gate to memory and to who we are" (Herman 1996:51).

The data on which this paper is based were collected during a two-year study of mourning behaviour and ritual practices of bereavement in six London cemetery sites. The physical landscapes of these burial grounds—Greek Orthodox, Bangladeshi and Gujurati Muslim, Catholic, and Orthodox Jewish cemeteries, and municipal cemeteries serving Christian churched and unchurched populations—register different religious and vernacular traditions. With the consent of users, we made observations and conducted interviews directly at the graveside (the newly bereaved were rarely approached) to obtain detailed understanding of visitors' behavior and their feelings, dispositions, and reflections on the meanings and cultural significance of cemetery visiting. Observation and survey methods were also used to record demographic profiles and statistics of visiting patterns on ritual and ordinary occasions.

A number of arguments underscore the significance of the cemetery as a site appropriate for research on memory and ethnic identity. First, with the increased medicalization of death in England (four out of five deaths take place in institutional settings), life-tending activities are being symbolically transposed following death from the home to the cemetery. In some cases, newly evolving rites of mourning are being substituted for domestic caring behavior, as well as for terminal care, now often appropriated by hospital and mortuary professionals. Our data reveal the continuation and cultural elaboration of the municipal cemetery as the site of more idiosyncratic, collective, and eclectic expressions of grief, infused with both secular and spiritual meanings and symbols.

Second, current bereavement research is challenging the modern, orthodox paradigm where death in Western society is perceived as a loss from which the mourner is expected to recover, severing attachment and moving on to form new relationships (Klass, Silverman, and Nickman 1996; Walter 1996). Our cross-cultural cemetery data document the life span and intergenerational nature of grief bonds and the maintenance of ongoing contact with the deceased as a significant dimension of bereavement behavior in the several communities studied (Francis, Kellaher, and Neophytou 2001). Integral to this expanded model are the intertwined processes of memorialization and identity construction of both self and other.

Third, the processes of globalization and synchronicity are focusing anthropological attention on contemporary negotiations of identity formation and memory construction in a world where traditional conceptions of individuals as members of fixed and separate societies and cultures have become redundant (Baumann 2000; Rapport and Dawson 1998). The cognitive, social, and material search for identity within and between conceptual spaces and times raises intriguing associated questions about the "remapping" of memory (Boyarin 1994). Cemeteries, as liminal places where geography and chronology are reshaped and history is spatially spread out, offer diverse and relatively unexplored localities for examining the processes involved in the contemporary reconstitution of memory of self, family, and group.

Renegotiation of Self-Identity

After death, the deceased no longer provides a mirror in which mourners view their own reflections and realize themselves as social beings (Warner 1959). For survivors to continue to see themselves still living with and related to the other, they must reconstruct the image of the deceased and, in so doing, rethink their own identity. The choice of stone and wording on the memorial allows the living to rework the deceased's identity, possibly appropriating attributes of the departed for themselves. Traditionally, the grave is the material expression of rights and obligations between generations (Kenna 1976:21). Religion, ethnic culture, and local custom support and shape this iteratively evolving relationship between self and other. For example, English Jews traditionally visit the graves of their dead kin during the ritual month of *Elul*, preceding the Jewish New Year. This is a period of self-reflection, repentance, and forgiveness. In addition to set prayers, this annual autumn visit provides a ritualized time and space for personal recollection and reconciliation with the deceased: "The custom encourages you once a year to make an effort, to focus and to take that journey about your parents who are no longer there. You get in touch with the previous generations. It is their feelings of you and your feelings of them that you can re-evaluate."

While Roman Catholics are urged to remember and pray for and to their dead within the "communion of saints," the Bangladeshi and Gujurati Muslim community say that they remember their dead but have to acknowledge that they are in another realm. To pray to them, to memorialize them as if still closely attached to the survivors within kinship networks, would be inappropriate: "Allah hears these prayers [from the *Koran*] and then raises the dead person closer to him. The dead person cannot hear the prayers, but they go to Allah so that Allah helps them and the sins are deducted. Allah forgives all the sin." The Muslim individual is thus formally remembered in the context of all deceased kin and indeed, with all the dead, everywhere. Outside this religiously structured frame, however, personal sentiment is also expressed towards the deceased.

Memory is also at the core of Greek Orthodox theology. Memory and its ritual enactment transcend the separation between the living and the dead. Theologically there is no divide between the dead and the living among the Orthodox. As Ware (1995:29) states: "Death [is] . . . a separation that is no separation. This is the point to which Orthodox tradition attaches the utmost importance. The living and the departed belong to a single family." "Death is not seen as a final end to the relationship that preceded it. In conversations and dreams, and in all rituals associated with death, living and dead continue to communicate, though now separated into different worlds for a time. The force that transcends that separation is memory and its ritual enactment. Acts that commemorate the deceased have therefore an intrinsic value and are believed to confer grace" (Hirschon 1989:16). "To remember is a symbolic equivalent to reinstating life" (Hart 1992).

For some, the experience of death may lead to idealized memories of the deceased: "When they are gone, you put things into focus and forget about the bad. Now it is only the nice things I remember." For others, time brings a change in perspective. Such cemetery visits may foster renegotiation, enabling the survivor to transform the relationship and to link more positively with the past: "As I am getting older, I have a great appreciation of her abilities. She had many fine qualities and plenty of flaws. Now I accept both, but in the early days, I only saw the flaws." For others, there is a positive incorporation of traits of the other to oneself: "As I grow older, I am aware of her memory in me—I see myself more and more to be like my mother. As you age and grow older yourself, you take on so much of who they are."

For many, cemetery visits also allow the continuation of the unfinished conversation between generations and so may encourage growth, healing, and a reformulation of self: "Death is so final. There is no more contact. That's why you go to the cemetery. To say things you did not say or couldn't say, because they were too difficult or too painful. Now when I go to the cemetery, I go with a sense of triumph. I've overcome so much and become a person in my own right, instead of trying to please everybody, and being a disappointment."

Cemeteries are central, important spaces for socialization; they instruct and re-instruct the individual on how to mourn in ethnically and culturally specific ways, channelling the expression of emotion. Cemetery rituals also teach and disclose signs of assimilation and acculturation of the self. Among the Greek Orthodox community in London, believers are expected to visit the dead on All Souls Days, but hardly any second-generation members (and very few of the first) visit, or even know when these days fall. Similarly, there are very few visits to the burial ground on name-days,[1] but many people now visit the cemetery on Mother's Day and also on the birthday of the deceased. Easter, with its association of victory over death and resurrection, is considered a time that the Orthodox should commemorate their dead and visit their graves. Although Easter is still a time for large numbers of Greek Cypriots to attend to cemetery rituals, following the customs of other Londoners, it is Christmas that sees the largest number of visitors. However, Greek Orthodox memorial services enable and encourage the participation of the second and third generations as they are brought back into the ethnic community through generational obligations for their parents and grandparents. These ritual occasions are the main times when boys and men attend church and so learn to be both Greek and Orthodox in Britain. For the individual, ethnicity and an ethnic identity may come to provide a vital sense of continuity of self, a self that rests not only on assumptions about the past but also on hopes for the future.

Family Identity

Religious tenets and social pressure further reinforce the duty of family members to visit the cemetery. Among the Greek Orthodox, the anniversary of death is the occasion when all the family generations participate together in the public sharing of *Kollyva*,[2] a plate of wheat, raisins, and nuts. On such occasions, the priests are brought from the church to the cemetery to pray for the memory of the deceased. The prayer, repeated over and over at the gravesite, is for the departed's memory to remain forever: "They don't die as long as you recall their memory. If there is no one to light the *kandili* and to burn incense over the grave, it's as though you never existed." At such times, familial ties and blood ties, as well as duty, bind the living to the dead and secure both to the ethnic group. "It's because of her that we all come together as a family and keep the extended group in touch as she did when she was alive. She kept the family around her and taught the children Greek—now because of her, the little ones, our children, will know what to do when our turn comes to move into our final residence." "By visiting we remember, that is where the family is important. Who will remember you, if not your family? You will dissolve and disappear without a trace, if your kin are not there."

When close relatives visit the cemetery together, such occasions assist the renegotiation of familial relationships, forge family identity (or disharmony), and encourage conversations about the deceased that reconstruct their image and place within the family unit. Ritual visits also transmit traditional cultural ideals to younger generations through these constructed images of family ancestors. As one woman remarked about the annual cemetery visit at the Jewish New Year: "When we go to the cemetery, we reminisce and make contact with our past. This is a 'family day' to share thoughts, feelings, reminiscences. We talk of old times, and my children learn the history of the family, about who they were, and who was what. . . . The time in the cemetery is an important time. It draws you together as a family. You move away from the day-to-day rush, and you share the time together."

For study participants—themselves "now at the top of the family tree"—such occasions may also provide a new perspective on difficult family issues. As one particularly articulate informant noted: "In the cemetery, you can think through something with your ancestors. Solutions are not locked into time and place. People and family relationships are the same, no matter when the people lived. History can illuminate our lives: how they would have dealt with a situation, how I deal with it, and the adjustment between the two to get an alternative way of thinking about and to look at it."

Cemetery visits can also be a source of family tension and displays of disharmony, as when self-selected siblings or offspring assume sole responsibility for the upkeep of the grave of the deceased and reject the unwelcome flowers and plants brought by other grieving kin: "We went to the cemetery, but we found we were not welcome; our plants had been tossed out and were just left lying there, near the edge of the plot." In other families, a cemetery visit can provide a way to foster increased closeness, as when a Jewish daughter feels empowered by the liminal space of the burial ground to speak openly about intimate feelings with her mother and brother when they visit the grave of their father-husband together.

Collective Identity

Cemeteries are constructed as special sites of memory by groups whose sources of cultural identity may lie at a distance, geographically and or temporally. Here, by linking the bereavement and globalization literature, we examine the symbolic role of the cemetery in fostering and sustaining group identity and the ways the dead become a surrogate community for the living. We also try to identify the processes whereby individual and family identity become ethnic, communal identity and to examine how group history is linked to larger historical processes.

In England, the nature of cemetery ownership and grave tenure reveals trajectories of exclusion, assimilation, and inclusion, which impact the collective experiences of the different cultural groups studied. In the seventeenth century, when the Jews returned to England, land for burial was among the first property purchased by the immigrant community. Similarly, with the Catholics, many of whom were Irish immigrants, land for burial could only be acquired and consecrated subsequent to the relaxation of the penal code that had barred Catholics from owning property since the Reformation. In making provision for their own cemeteries, Jews and Catholics avoided burial on consecrated Anglican soil where they would be required to conform to the rites of interment mandated for members of the Church of England.

In the 1920s and 1930s, Orthodox Greek Cypriots chose burial in a specially designated section of a private cemetery. Today, this pattern is continued in other privately owned cemeteries. The more recently arrived Muslim population has been forced—because of exclusion from municipal cemeteries where they would have been required to abandon many of their special burial rites—to accept provision within privately owned burial grounds.

Significantly, in examining the meaning and construction of "homeland" as a dimension of communal and ethnic identity,[3] Barth's (1969) argument about the permeability and contextual definition of all ethnic boundaries is supported by evidence offered here. Our data reveal that both Jewish and Greek study participants stress the primacy of personal links and actions toward deceased kin. Thus the meaning of homeland and roots is kinship and ancestors, the continuity of generational connections, and the links between the family of the past and the family of the future. Members of the Greek Orthodox and United Synagogue communities characterize their behaviors as a continuous link in a chain forged by their parents, who acted in similar ways toward their parents: "I'm just a link in a long, long chain that goes back to my great-great grandparents in Cyprus." "It's traditional to come [to the cemetery]; we're doing what our parents, grandparents, and great-grandparents did." "I do not have the courage to say 'I won't go.' I just don't want to be the person who stops."

On ritual days, when thousands of people visit the cemetery and perform memorial rites, many emphasize their personal focus on family relationships as well as their shared communal heritage and or identification with coreligionists. However, although certain basic formulas are followed, there are variations in the ways in which these are performed and individually expressed.

For the Irish Catholics, while individual sentiment is important, the homeland is evoked much more materially, through reference to the land, the earth, and the turf of Ireland. Until very recently the ideal, and the numerical norm, was repatriation for burial in the parish of origin. Only when families come to include third and fourth generations does burial in England appear to be fully legitimate. An elderly man, for example, visiting the grave of his first wife who died three decades earlier said that her death had been such a shock that he had not been able to think, and because there were young children, their mother had been buried in London. He would also be buried in London, with this first wife, though he really preferred the idea of burial in Ireland: "When I go there, everyone knows who I am." He also said that there were now grandchildren who, as Irish Londoners, would need to visit their grandparents' grave.

Similarly for the Muslims, community entails membership in a greatly extended kinship group, established through birth, though changed and consolidated through the selective processes of migration and subsequent settlement. For the first generation of immigrant Bangladeshis or Gujuratis, now in their seventies, retired from work and speaking little English, the kinship network is spread very widely. It encompasses kin, alive and dead, on the subcontinent as well as family established and growing up in London and other parts of England. For many of these old people, especially the men, the path between the local mosque and the cemetery is well worn. Many visit the cemetery at least daily, sometimes alone, sometimes with peers who might be family members but who certainly attend the mosque. One of these men explained his reasons for coming to the cemetery: "I am here today to pray for myself and for all those who are buried here." He did not have a particular grave to visit in this cemetery since his brother's grave was in the north of England. But, along with others, he claimed that it was easier to reflect on the deceased and pray for oneself in a cemetery: "We pray at home . . . and at the mosque, but when you come to the cemetery, you get a direct line, so that is better."

A middle-aged man visited the grave of his sons: "I do not believe in praying for them . . . but it is necessary to pay respects. . . . We all come along and do the same thing." He says that visiting makes him feel "part of the community, the living community, because all Muslims come here to pay their respects." Another middle-aged man, who was also visiting the cemetery rather than a particular grave, said: "I come just to pray for them all and to remind myself of mortality." Pointing to his car, he added: "This could be a Rolls Royce, but it's not. Why? Because I come to the cemetery. If I didn't come here then I would probably cheat and steal, and then I could afford a Rolls Royce. If I steal from people and I die, then what will happen?"

Such expressions of connectedness, resonant with theories of social capital (Halpern 1998), suggest boundaries that extend beyond the Bangladeshi and Gujurati communities. At the same time, however, these Muslims explain how their principles, especially in relation to burial and expenditure, differentiate them from the Christian community, which also has graves in the same cemetery. They especially abhor as extravagant and wasteful the ornate memorials on Victorian graves. Apart from these considerations, the weight of the monument is an anathema to these Muslims, who go to considerable lengths to prevent the grave from being walked over or otherwise weighted down. "*Haram* is evil. And it is Haram to have something on the grave because it disturbs the dead. . . . Muslims believe that if there is something on the grave, then the angels cannot ask the questions to the dead."

On special ritual days, such as *Eyd* at the end of Ramadan, the very large numbers of visitors include many young children and babies. The implication is that they should be exposed to their cultural tradition. "It is important to remember our past, and if we come here, it will remind us to lead good lives. . . . This is a very strong feeling, and I feel it when I come here."

The middle-aged male spokesman for a three-generational family gave an account for their visit, which—while characterized by family sentiment—also makes links to wider collective contexts: "We've come to see their grandfather [speaker's father]. We don't bring flowers, we praise Allah. We come with the children because they love their grandfather and they must know their family is here as well as at home."

The notion of religious duty overrides any more personal motivation for visiting, at least in the accounts offered by these male visitors, who are of all generations. The explanations are generally formulaic as the men justify their visiting and praying through reference to Koranic script and Islamic law. Younger men, many in their late teens, tend to visit in small groups after the mosque and, particularly for this generation, on Fridays. They are more likely than the senior generation to wear ordinary apparel, not the prayer dress and headgear of the older men. While the cemetery is only one of the places where these young men will become socialized in the ways of Islam, it is arguable that, unlike clubs, school, and shops, the cemetery is particularly powerful, perhaps more so even than the mosque, in permitting acculturation to a collective past with kinship and extended group affiliation.

The few Muslim women encountered in the cemetery tend to conform in their explanations of visiting to the men's ideas of duty, remembrance of the dead, and reminders of mortality. At the same time, it is among the women that the strongest divergence from the "party line" is likely to be encountered, as in the case of a young Bangladeshi woman, dressed casually in jeans, who says that she usually comes here every week to attend to the grave of her father. She lives with her mother in an area of London where many Bangladeshi Muslims have settled.

> I am a Muslim—sort of. But I don't really believe now, I don't know really. Some people do hold to all the rigorous rules and all that, but I don't. . . . I did go to my father's funeral when all my relatives, mainly the extended family, were trying to tell me not to. But it's really up to the individual. It was my aunties who were telling me that I shouldn't go, but some were saying that it's okay for the closest relatives to go even if they are women. I just said, 'I'm going, and that's it.' I mean he was my dad, and I loved him, and I just said no one's going to keep me away. So they let me go. And I haven't got any brothers either. . . . It's up to individual families. . . . Sometimes I bring my sister's children because she won't come down here—she's a bit scared of graveyards—but she wants her kids to come, so I bring them here for her. And they can see the grave of their grandfather.

It is interesting to note here that resistance to custom is also accompanied by a strong sense of the collectivity to which this woman and her family, especially her sister's children, belong. In writing about the Irish in Britain, Halpern (1998) suggests that identity through reference to ethnic origins can be manipulated. Depending upon a range of conditions and circumstances, she argues that ethnicity can be played up or played down. Such flexibility is less possible for black and Asian immigrants, and the decision to bury rather than repatriate the deceased becomes an unequivocal statement about shifting connections, as well as an assertion of origins and ethnic identity. Nonetheless, it is clear that some latitude is possible for playing up or playing down Muslim identity.

In contrast, with increasing secularism and a general weakening of Church of England rites of bereavement, visitors to the municipal cemetery are creating new mourning customs—a *bricolage* of older romantic rites of grave tending and newly affordable gardening practices. In the 1950s, the municipal cemetery made available a new burial option at an affordable price: a smaller-sized memorial to replace the larger Victorian-style monument surrounded by a curb. In this new lawn cemetery landscape, uniformly sized gravestones are laid out in straight, back-to-back rows, with grass between each double row of memorials. Instead of a full grave to tend, mourners are allotted a small plot in front of each stone where they can create their own unique memorial garden, thereby making each grave personal and special.

Garden historian John Dixon Hunt (1997) has suggested that the bounded, liminal space of the cemetery and the tending of the grave garden become a privileged site for the recreation of the identity of both the deceased and the bereaved. In creating a singular memorial garden, each mourner projects his or her self-image while also selectively reworking the identity of the deceased. The routine tending of this garden offers an exceptional space and place where mourners can reflexively recount their past life with the deceased and at the same time review, rehearse, and reconceptualize their own untold life narrative. The grave garden becomes the encoded material expression of this identity of self and the memory of other and is read, witnessed, and validated by other members of the cemetery community. Here the processes of individual identity construction are appropriated by others and so become emblematic of communal identity. These evolving customs of memorialization link personal memories with a recreated sense of community consciousness.

At Christmas, these memorial grave gardens are festooned with seasonal decorations, and the gravestones are adorned with wreaths and cards demonstrating that the deceased are still considered to be members of the family group. In a parallel process of remembering and community creation, mourners whose family members were cremated place their Christmas bouquets one next to the other to create a large communal cross in the paved area in front of the crematorium. While adding her special Christmas arrangement, one study participant noted: "Here we join with others, all the people who come here feel as we do, a loss for their loved ones; we feel community with others."

Christmas is the ritual time when the dominant cultural community visits the municipal cemetery and thinks about the past. "Christmas is the time you think about them. We have a big family; we are all together at Christmas, and now they're missing. On Christmas Day, we toast to absent friends."

In the municipal cemetery that was the major research site for this study, many users come from the East End, a cultural and geographic community described in the classic studies of Townsend (1957) and Young and Willmott (1957). Over the past fifty years, this area has experienced wartime disruption, economic dislocation, and population change. The cemetery, now becoming more multicultural, is perceived symbolically as a physical and temporal extension of the old East End community. "Our roots are around here. The cemetery is like remembering the old way of life. It's like coming home."

As he stood in front of his parents' grave at Christmas, one middle-aged East Ender revealed his process of memory recreation in language reminiscent of both

Dickens and the rhetoric of the war years, language which obscures the difficult realities of those times:

> When I come to the cemetery at Christmas, I think of the times gone by. I think of my childhood. They were good times, we didn't have no money, we were working people. The people all down the street, we was all the same, we shared more then. After the war, we all helped each other. Life was better then, now we all have cars and better houses. But we did not have them then, we shared money, we would lend to each other. If someone were ill, the neighbours would get their shopping. Now the Old England is gone.

For these East Enders, home is the once homogeneous community group and its ancestors are now symbolically represented by the cemetery. This landscape of memory is used for cultural transmission and to reinforce generational obligations, past, present, and future: "We bring our grandchildren to the cemetery to teach them not to forget. We tell them all we can about their grandfather—the work he did as head of the family and how we all respected him. We pass this on, and so that they respect us, too, in the same way. We teach them also not to forget, and no matter how far away we go, we're from the East End and we're used to staying close."

Although these East Enders use the cemetery to reconstruct family and community identity—"All my family are buried here, and my mother's neighbour and her friend"—few choose or are able to trace their ancestors' graves back through time. Their inability to afford the price of burial in a marked family grave excluded many East Enders from contact with their ancestors. "Before they only had communal graves for six people, and strangers were buried on top of each other. We couldn't afford stones then. We do not go to see our grandfather; we would not know where to look." For many of these individuals, a plot on the lawn section was the first private grave the family was able to afford. It is often these same individuals who have now gained enfranchisement and are empowered to construct a new culture of memory shared among the community of mourners. This collective culture of remembrance provides an overlay to the reconstructed homogeneous community, now also symbolized by the cemetery.

For other communities whose ethnic identities lie at a distance, the cemetery is also a memoryscape, a reflection of their homeland and an expression of collective experience. Here, too, the cemetery is a culturally constructed place used by the community for the re-creation, renegotiation, and transmission of collective memory. The community shapes the cemetery, which in turn, shapes the community. "The dead must be near the living. To buy the plot gives you security." When communal ethnic identity is viewed as a form of membership in a greatly extended kinship group, then burial at a specific burial site is ascribed for members of the ethnic group. "After all, that's what it's all about, closeness; we are one blood." "There is no separation between the dead and the living; we are all part of the Orthodox [Greek] community." Here, ethnicity, lineage, and ancestry are united. People may also choose to relocate their homes closer to the cemetery where the deceased is buried, thereby further aligning neighbourhood with cultural and religious identity. "To be buried in a community cemetery makes me feel that we are with our own people; here where the Cypriots are buried, there is a small part of Cyprus." "The cemetery has people from my religious community; they are at home there; they're related to it. It's an extension of the way it is in life, so it is in death."

When a member of their local group dies, the tight-knit community rallies. They attend the funeral and accompany the body to its final resting place. In Greek funeral rituals, for example, the assembled community forgives the deceased by its presence and prayers and effects the passage of the soul. With death, the social fabric has been disrupted, but the community is reformed through their collective participation in these rites. Mourners seeking to make sense of their personal loss often rejoin the fold and return to traditional religious practices. The Church uses this life crisis to reinculcate and reinforce traditional religious rituals and customs. Each death strengthens the identification between the community, ethnic culture, and the cemetery.

Death rituals and cemeteries also express and re-create culturally constructed differences of class, gender, and generation, thereby dividing the community. While Muslim and Jewish religious rites attempt to materially represent the equality of all in death, the size of the specially purchased family plot and its location (near or far from the hall) exhibit status distinctions (monetary, or religious or lay leadership) within the community of the bereaved. Also, in Greek and municipal cemeteries, "front row" and "dress circle" placements give ready automobile access and display the more elaborate monuments to all who drive or walk past. Further social distinctions surface at Greek Cypriot cemeteries through the abundance of floral displays, garden furniture, and fencing around some graves. "We as Greeks go over the top in the things we do for our loved ones when they die, but it's the Greek way, that's how it's always been." This conspicuous consumption and status competition is further encouraged by the ways in which mourning and funeral observances are connected with the family's good name and standing within the community. A neglected or plain grave is often perceived to be indicative of diminished feeling and emotional indifference. "What would people say if the flowers are left dying in the vase and the stone turns grey? I would not feel comfortable; they would be talking about us and our family."

While gender and generational distinctions are also carried over from traditional practices, with acculturation these distinctions are gradually changing.

Muslim women, as discussed in the above example, are discouraged from visiting the cemetery, but some who are longer in residence in England do come as an act of resistance and emotional need. In contrast, older Greek women, dressed in black, have been depicted as dominating the public space of the cemetery, but today the Greek cemetery sees almost equal numbers of men and women. On most visits, it is family groups that dominate the landscape, particularly on Sundays. Directly after the church liturgy, groups of two or three generations of Cypriots weave their way through the graves, often stopping at more than one grave to perform the various rituals: lighting the kandili, incensing the grave, or placing flowers. Also, younger Jews are choosing to come to the cemetery at personal times, not just at the Jewish New Year and anniversary of the day of death. The twenty to thirty-five age category is overrepresented on ritual occasions at all cemetery sites, and more visitors of all ages are bringing flowers. Such emerging practices utilize the cemetery as a site for reworking the dialectic between assimilation and resistance to it.

Ethnic cemeteries thus record communal change through accommodation and assimilation to the host society. Many burial grounds have sections of war graves and memorials to servicemen with no known graves, who fell in active duty to the crown. Such national war memorials link ethnic group sacrifice to British and Commonwealth history. In Jewish cemeteries, for example, synchronistic remembrance services are held annually and combine Hebrew memorial prayers and the Israeli national anthem with the British traditions of lowering the standards, placing the memorial poppy wreath, and singing "God Save the Queen." Such occasions articulate an Anglo-Jewish identity and honour all those who fought, both living and dead. Significantly, descendants of the fallen rarely attend, but rather their aged comrades constitute this community of remembrance.

Thus, over time, such cemeteries record change in the group's culture: acculturation and permeability, resistance and boundary maintenance, and the oscillation between these poles. After visiting the graves of kin in an older cemetery, Jewish relatives often walk together through the grounds, noting the inscriptions, commenting on the stones, and telling stories about the people whom they knew, occasionally relating life crisis events in their own lives to the date of death of the deceased. Such journeys, which encourage social comment on the values of the past in terms of the present, articulate, reinforce, and also modify traditional cultural ideals.

The landscaping of the grounds, the style and languages (Hebrew, Greek, Arabic, or English) used on the monument, and the information detailed (such as place of birth in Cyprus or Gujurat) similarly encode the ethos of the times and reveal how familial obligations were honored by specific kin in the past and are being maintained by their descendants in the present. Over time, the meaning of these ethnic cemeteries changes further as they become full and are no longer used for active burial. There is consensus among all groups that for the deceased, "[t]heir roles end with their children's children—the past is over by the grandchildren."

There is a sloughing off of the obligation to visit the graves of kin after two or three generations. One middle-age man articulated his dilemma:

> I have this oscillation between my emotional feelings that even your great-grandparents are part of you and you should visit their graves and the practical part of me, that you visit and care for only the ones that you knew personally. I knew my grandparents, but not my father's grandparents. How far back are you expected to go? I love my children and my grandchildren, but do I or should I love my great-grandchildren? and my great-great-grandchildren? How far does the obligation of love to the family go? How far back? How far down? The idea of obligations of love to family arose when our own parents died. This link to past generations and to the future—that's here in the cemetery.

Thus with the death of the connecting relative, who visited his or her own parents and grandparents in an already closed cemetery, the link to this old graveyard is broken, and younger family members do not usually visit. The cemetery recedes further in time, the physical distance needed to travel to the burial ground being paralleled by the social distance of the ancestral generation.

In community rituals surrounding the memorial stone, sentiment and practicality dictate visits mainly by those relatives known personally. In the other diasporic groups studied, this disposition to curtail grave visits after two or three generations and to follow religious obligations only to deceased parents and other close kin advances the transplantation of the concept of homeland to a new societal context and privileges the cemetery in the reconstruction of ethnic identity.

For example, many among the first generation of Greek Cypriots, themselves born in Cyprus, expressed the preference for burial with their own immediate ancestors in Cyprus, rather than with their present descendants living in London. Here the primary objective of the immigrant group was to return home when they made an improvement in their economic situation. Their self-identity is much more likely to be grounded and rooted in the territory of the homeland. This generation is the source of memories about the Cypriot homeland. However, with the second generation, who themselves may return annually to visit the graves of their own repatriated parents in Cyprus, their choice of burial place is often less clear-cut. Their children may make the decision to bury them in the Cypriot section of their nearby cemetery, where they can fulfill their traditional obligations to visit the grave regularly to perform Orthodox rituals. "Although he was born in Cyprus, this is where he lived. . . . This is where I live; why take him back?" This decision is guided by religious orthodoxy and sentiment rather than economics, as the cost of repatriation and interment are approximately the same, which is also the case for the Muslim and Irish group studied. The choice to bury and carry out traditional practices in London further commits the group, making them more settled and rooted. This was graphically demonstrated when two study participants, who did return to Cyprus and attempted to resettle there, found it very difficult: "Our daughter is buried here; we could not be away from her. We tried, but this is our home now where her grave is. So we sold up again and came to London to be near her." This loosening of ties with the homeland and generational distance from the immigrant experience is widely shown by the reluctance to repatriate the deceased when close family and kin are settled here. "I will not go back; my wife is here; this is where I belong."

With three generations settled in London, there is a reconstructed and redefined memory of self and homeland, memory no longer derived from direct experience. Thus, in London, Orthodox Greek cemeteries are surrogate communities for the homeland, their memorial landscapes bridging idealized memories of Cyprus with new, evolving constructions of self and communal identity, "[a]t once deterritorialized and reterritorialized" (Fortier 2000:157).

Today, English Victorian cemeteries and monuments such as the Albert Memorial are being restored as valued repositories of the nation's history, architecture, and craftsmanship. With this impetus from the dominant culture, ethnic cemeteries are being similarly reevaluated and researched to document a group's collective past and publicize its contributions to the host society. Two recent occasions mark the increasing communal and national significance of older ethnic cemeteries. In 1997, the London Orthodox Jewish community commemorated the three-hundredth anniversary of the first Anglo-Jewish cemetery, which was consecrated in 1679. The ceremony, held in the cemetery grounds, was attended by religious and lay community leaders. They acknowledged the significance of this historic site "containing the mortal remains and memory of the architects of the Anglo-Jewish community." The memorial stones of the cemetery were metaphorically described as the "living stones of the original Temple," the bones of the community's ancestors as "memory and reverence for the past," and the cemetery as the "symbolic re-creation of the original cave purchased by Abraham to bury Sarah when he was a sojourner in Israel."

Similar descriptions were also used by a group of Hasidic (a sect of Orthodox Jewry) men and their sons, who assembled at this same cemetery on the ritual day of mourning marking the destruction of the Second Temple. The group's aim, as the present living generation, was to visit the graves of the community's ancestors, who are no longer visited by their own family descendants and to insure that these old cemeteries are maintained as cultural legacies of the past and as a link to the future. Their activities signify that the bodies of the past, marked or unmarked by stones, visited or unvisited, provide habitus for the present and the future. For them, the cemetery acts as the bridge between two worlds, the world of origin and that of settlement, the material world of here with the spiritual and metaphysical world of there.

In conclusion, this paper takes issue with W. Lloyd Warner who, in his classic study of Yankee City cemeteries (1959), states that disused burial grounds become historical monuments. This paper has argued, instead, that old closed cemeteries continue as liminal spaces providing a template of dimensional memory, which bridges the boundaries of space and time, the personal and the collective, and sentiment and obligation, and finally merges ethnic and indigenous cultures with all humanity.

Acknowledgments

The researchers wish to acknowledge the support received from the Economic and Social Research Council to the University of North London for "Cemetery as Garden" Award No. R 000 23 6493.

Notes

1. Traditionally it is one's name-day, falling on the annual festival of the relevant saint's day and not one's birthday, which is of importance.

2. *Kollyva* is boiled wheat handed out at funerals and memorials to be eaten in memory of the deceased. It is said that the wheat symbolizes the resurrection of the dead as a plant is created from a seed in the earth (Vassiliadis 1993).

3. Communal ethnic identities are multiple and neither discrete nor bounded. There is a crosscutting of social cleavages and solidarities, which are contested, that characterize plural societies (Baumann 1996; Fortier 2000).

Memories of the American Jewish *Aliyah* Connecting Individual and Collective Experience

6

JACOB J. CLIMO

FOR SOME TIME, scholars concerned with the ethnography of memory have grappled with the relationship between individual experience and collective experience. How can we understand our individual experience without also understanding our communal experience? How can we understand our communal experience without also understanding the place of individual experience within it? I recently came across two examples of a dynamic dissonance between individual experience and its larger social and historical context. The first is a book by Alison Owings (1993), *Frauen: German Women Recall the Third Reich*; it presents the narratives of a group of wives of Nazi SS guards. Now in their elder years, their narratives suggest that they remember the war years very differently from most other accounts. Their concerns, during World War II, were with housekeeping, childcare, and mundane matters. They were strangely ignorant of or oblivious to the larger horrors and daily events of the nearby death camps where their husbands went every morning for duty.

The second example of dynamic dissonance is found in a book by Martin Goldsmith (2000), *The Inextinguishable Symphony: A True Story of Music and Love in Nazi Germany*. Goldsmith writes of his parents' lives in Berlin just before World War II. Both were Jewish musicians. They met in a FolksKultur orchestra, formed under the Nazis to channel the time and energy of Jewish musicians, all of whom had been fired or denied gainful employment. His mother's and father's memories of those years of young adulthood are filled, ironically, with the sweetness of their personal relationship—their meeting, their playing together in concerts, the flowering of their romance—rather than with the foul, stifling, oppressive political environment of prewar Berlin. According to Goldsmith, even their final exit from Germany takes place through a series of surreal, serendipitous events in which they are only partially conscious and engaged. Their orchestra plays at an American diplomatic mission where the wife of an American diplomat enjoys their music, takes a personal interest in them, urges them to apply for emigration, and then facilitates their immigration to America.

A number of pressing questions emerge from these two books. How can an individual be involved in his or her personal life to the exclusion of surrounding dramatic social events and political turmoil, especially when their own lives and the lives of many others are clearly at stake? Translating this question for ethnography involves explaining or at least addressing the dissonance felt when individual experience appears to have little or no direct connection to history or social memory. How can an ethnographer of memory interpret the meaning of an individual's experiences within the larger context of collective memory when the individual offers no connection between them?

In this chapter, I suggest that the lack of connection between individual and collective experience can be explored productively when the ethnographer uses a multilayered view of memory. An approach that considers memory as complex and labyrinthine (Teski and Climo 1995) rather than unidimensional permits me to show that memory can be expressed in a highly individualized cultural repertoire or idiom, yet it can, at the same time, represent an individual's link to larger generational, ideological, and historical contexts. To make such connections, the ethnographer must not only consider the surface level expression of an individual's experience, that is, memory as expressed in the idiom of the moment, but also a deeper level of experience that includes ritual and symbolic relationships.

Research on Migration to Israel

In 1998, I began an ethnographic study of American Jewish migrants in Israel and their parents who remain in the United States. Initially, I hoped to focus attention on how parents and children from these dispersed families communicate with each other in order to maintain family bonds across long distances and over many years. I was also interested in observing the adaptations of American Jewish migrants to life in Israel and especially the changes and continuities in their ethnic identities as a result of their migration. In intensive, tape-recorded interviews in America and Israel, I encouraged parents and children to talk about their subjective experiences of family separation in their own way. I also listened carefully as the migrants recalled their experiences of *aliyah* (migration to Israel) and especially their own and their parents' memories of why they decided to migrate and live in Israel.

In analyzing the narratives of both generations, I was surprised to find that a single major idiom characterized the content and tone of their experiences. Both parents and their migrant children expressed almost all of their memories in an idiom of individualism. As an American Jew who seriously considered migrating to Israel over a period of many years, I believe I would have given very different answers to questions concerning my memory of the motives behind my aliyah experience. For example, I would situate the American migration to Israel within the larger context of Jewish culture, history, and ideology. I recall, for example, Melford Spiro's (1964) account of Polish and Russian Jews who immigrated to Palestine in the 1920s to establish kibbutzim. At that time, very few Jews from European shtetls supported their Zionist ideology. Yet, in the immediate aftermath of the Holocaust, that migration appeared to represent an important vanguard of Jewish survival. Coming from this perspective, I would need to ask: What does the American migration represent in light of changing ties between the American Jewish community and Israel? What does it say about change and the persistence of Jewish identity in Israel and in America? What impact will these immigrants and their children have on Israeli society? I would provide an overview of the migration of American Jews to Israel as a post-Holocaust event, but clearly within the larger context of Zionist, that is Jewish nationalist, ideology. Moreover, I would place the American aliyah within recent anthropological literature that examines nations as "imagined communities" (Anderson 1983) that construct national ideologies and memories and their constituent racial and ethnic categories (Balibar and Wallerstein 1991).

American Jewish Aliyah in Zionist Memory, Ideology, and History

Since nationalist ideologies produce nations, we need to learn how constructions of peoplehood in ethnic and national memory gain sufficient power over people's imaginations to create a sense of common identity capable of moving people to migrate and thereby form new identities based on relationships with a remembered primordial or ethnic group (Fox 1990; Williams 1989). It is important to learn how migrants adjust to new situations and specifically the role of national ideology and memory in recruiting and absorbing new immigrants (Zerubavel 1995).

For Jameson (1981), ideology is an attempt to come to terms with and transcend the unbearable relationships of social life. In doing so, all ideologies include both a mystical and a utopian moment of collective imagination, of choosing a past in order to open opportunities for the future. White (1987:150) conceptualized ideology as "narratological" because it takes the form of agents acting as if they were characters in a story whose plot links the beginning of a process to its conclusion. In ideology as in memory, the meaning of every present is the completion of what had been prefigured in the past.

Originally conceived in the European Jewish diaspora, Zionism emerged as a utopian ideology linking Jews throughout the world to their biblical homeland. For religious Jews, the call to return represented a spiritual fulfillment, a necessary preamble to the miraculous days of the Messiah. For secular Jews, it was seen as an opportunity to participate in building a Jewish homeland and nation. Zionist ideology proposed returning to the land and the Jewish community as the only remedy to religious persecution, political oppression, marginality, and poverty experienced by Jews in the diaspora. The ingathering of Jews throughout the world would result in the construction of a national identity, political sovereignty, and religious freedom. The program of extreme Zionism in the early twentieth century proposed a total revolution, "a complete break with the entire career of the Jew in favor of purely secular national life ('let us be like all the gentiles')" (Hertzberg 1960:16). The inclusion of aliyah in Zionism arose shortly after the establishment of Israel, when Israeli Prime Minister David Ben Gurion declared formally that all diaspora Jews should return to live in Israel as part of their commitment to Jewish nationalism (Avruch 1981).

The concept of aliyah translates only loosely as "migration to Israel" because the English word *migration* is ideologically neutral whereas *aliyah* carries great ideological significance. For example, Jews who leave Israel are frequently referred to with disdain as *Yordim,* meaning those who go down, while Jews who *make aliyah* and return to Israel are called *Olim,* those who go up.

Clearly the motives for American migration to Israel are found in ethnic and religious identity as Jews and in nationalist and Zionist memory. In fact, unlike most Jewish immigrants to Israel, who come as refugees out of economic and or political necessity, the American Jewish migration is completely voluntary, and its underlying motivations are ideological.

Perhaps because American Jews feel politically insecure, the major American Jewish institutions have never made aliyah a pillar of their political platforms or a guiding principle for their directions. The major platform has always been to respond first to American Jewish domestic issues, then for American Jews to provide material and political support to Israel to ensure its survival and development, but for other needy and less fortunate Jews from other diasporas to actually live there. In spite of such institutional ambivalence, some American Jews continue to feel and express nostalgia for the homeland. Such feelings are reinforced by many local Jewish educational programs and religious organizations. Yet very few American Jews make aliyah, perhaps 3,000 per year for the last thirty years (Avruch 1981; Waxman 1989).

Also reflecting its ideological foundations, one of the most outstanding features of the American migration to Israel is its ambivalent nature. It is a migration characterized by a high rate of return to America (some estimate 40 percent) and many people whose going and coming over a period of many years marks them as a population without clear roots in either country (Guarinzo 1994), yet with identities in both (Rapport 1998).

Aliyah Memories in an Idiom of Individualism

The participants in my study did not explicitly connect their memories of aliyah to these larger cultural, ideological, or religious movements. Instead, both generations expressed themes of individualism, featuring the unique, highly personalized set of motives underlying their decisions to migrate and live in Israel. Possibly their great attention to personal experience represents a cultural mode of expression, namely, American individualism. In any event, though their memories include several examples of their ideological attachment to Zionism and aliyah, all of them are expressed in an idiom of highly individualistic experiences.

Before I can interpret the significance of this individualistic mode of memory expression, it seems valuable to explore its parameters. First, parents' memories of their children's motives for aliyah are frequently expressed in a language that stresses the child's self-reliance and independence. A mother recalls her daughter's aliyah:

> She got married and has lived in Israel since 1977, about twenty years. After high school, she could go to Europe or Israel. Cheryl went to Europe, not Israel, and Joan went to Israel. She liked it. She was going to stay, then the Yom Kippur War, and she stayed till February after the war in Golan, on a kibbutz. Now she lives in the Negev. . . . She went to U. of M. for a year and a half, then joined Habonim [a leftist, nonreligious Zionist youth movement], I think with a group of friends, all very idealistic. She decided to go; those kids from her group all went. I wasn't happy about it. But my husband and I admired her. Listen, it took a lot of guts. We gave her a lot of credit. . . . They've accomplished a lot, expanded the business, my son-in-law went to the university and became an agronomist; cactuses, that's his field. He raises them from seed, then raises and sells them. I think my daughter here needs me more than my daughter in Israel.

Many parents admire their child's courage and respect their child's life choices as individual choices. At the same time parents place value on the independence of generations. Even when they are not particularly happy that their child has chosen to live so far away from them, most parents emphasize their support for their child's decisions, like this mother:

> During college, he took a semester at Haifa U. and got credit because I said you are not going anywhere unless you get credit for it. So he went and was gone about eight or ten weeks, loved it, loved the school. . . . Three or four times he went back, and the last time I took a look at him, and I knew he wasn't coming back. And he

> didn't. I felt that if he had that strong a calling to go, then there was no choice. And today it is his life, he has got to live it his way. I can't live it for him and I'm not a mother that's going to say no, no, no you can't go. And I'm not going to hang on and cry . . . there is too much that I want to do myself. I let my children live their lives and they have.

A second theme of individualism in both parent and migrant memories explains the external social and economic reasons underlying aliyah in terms of self-realization of the migrant child. Education is a key motive for aliyah as self-realization. Such education may begin early in the child's life and continue well into adulthood. Ideological training often begins with private day schools and attendance at Zionist and Jewish summer camps, followed in adolescence by tours or study abroad programs and visits to Israel. Later, many Olim attend yeshivas, colleges, and graduate schools in Israel. Eventually they migrate to work and live in Israel. Speaking of her daughter's aliyah, Sheila remembers:

> The first time she went to Israel was in the USY program [conservative United Synagogue Youth]. When she came back, she said she thought that's where she wanted to be, she came back definitely involved. She was always more involved with her Judaism than most of us. At the U. of M., she took junior year at Hebrew U. When she came back, she observed kashrut. I always and still have a kosher home. When she went, the one promise I asked her is that she would come back to complete her studies. . . . At that time [when we visited her], she said she'd like to stay on and finish her school there and . . . she'd come back. And ah, before she went to Hebrew University, she started to study her Hebrew. You never walked by her room that she didn't have a tape on.

Self-realization commonly involves falling in love and marrying someone who wants to live in Israel or agrees to live in Israel. A retired mother remembers her daughter's aliyah, clearly indicating her own preference that her daughter should not have made aliyah:

> She met her husband at a reformed Jewish camp in Wisconsin. She made aliyah 16 years ago. . . . They met at age fourteen or fifteen and he was nineteen, twenty. He was a counselor and she was a camper. . . . They kept up the relationship. She would visit in Chicago and see him. He came here a few times. He came here for a Mysty group [reformed Jewish youth organization] she arranged, and he stayed with us. He went to Israel and got his degree, and she went to visit him. We sent her off to Israel for the summer because we thought she'd change her mind if she lived there . . . she'd see what it was like and decide that wasn't for her . . . we were not encouraging. I've never considered myself a Zionist—it was a shock and depressing when she announced she was going to marry him and that's where she was going to live. . . . The first time she'd gone to Israel when she was 16 she came

back and said, "not for me." So love does strange things. She wasn't even being a Zionist so much.

Aliyah as self-realization characterizes many of the memories of the migrants as well. In stressing her own self-reliance and initiative, Irene claims it was difficult for her to find a job in her field. She needed land for her horses, and almost all the land in Israel is held by communities, rather than individuals. Communities that allow private ownership of land within a cooperative arrangement were suspicious of single women; "they saw them as family wreckers in a society that sees itself as consisting of families with children." Despite the stereotypes of innovations in Israel, Irene also found "some pessimism about innovations and people creating obstacles to trying new things." Irene's story is about a woman who put together several elements she loves in order to make her life in Israel work: her love of Israel and Hebrew, her love of horses, and her desire to remain single. In her narrative, she prevailed in spite of many obstacles.

After college Jerome found himself working in his father's electrical contracting business. He describes himself during that period as

> not really unhappy. . . . Coming home tired, like a worker. And we went to dinner and they [his parents] said, "Let's talk *tachlis,* you know, the bottom line. You're unhappy and life is too short. What do you want to do?". . . . They encouraged me to think and be independent and self-sufficient. You know . . . my family and Judaism and my sisters made a huge impact on my life. You know, they made a well-rounded, self-sufficient person who is able to do things like move to Israel and know that I have a loving family.

A final theme in the idiom of highly individualized experience appears in both generations' memories of the childhood and adolescent development of the migrant's desire for aliyah. For migrants to Israel, memories of growing up in a particular family and community may reveal the sources of their love for Israel and their motives for aliyah. For parents, memories of American Jewish family and community life may reveal the source of their child's Zionist identity. The desire to make aliyah takes shape as a personalized sense of Jewish heritage that linked them spiritually to Israel, beckoning them to come home; it was a personal obligation to return to the land of their ancestors.

In American Jewish families where one or more child makes aliyah, the memories of adult children about themselves and the parents' memories of their children stress highly individualistic experiences in the dramatic psychological development of their son's or daughter's desire to live in Israel and the courage and pioneering spirit that enabled them to realize their dream. At the time of their Bar Mitzvah, for example, or after graduating from high school, or after a youth group or study abroad summer in Israel, they declared to their family and friends that they wanted to return to live in Israel. Alternatively, they may have declared a desire to become more religious and keep kosher, or begun to study Hebrew seriously, or joined a Zionist youth movement. A mother remembers the origins of her son's aliyah identity in adolescence:

> He designs batteries. . . . He's now forty-four . . . . At fifteen, he said in his confirmation speech, "I would love to live in Israel where everyone is Jewish, even the garbage man." We were shocked. We were never there before but contributed money to Zionist organizations. After a high school trip to an archaeological dig, he didn't want to come back. He went to a kibbutz and delayed college, then went to another dig in New Mexico. Then for his M.A., he went to Weitzman Institute. Then he met her and they came back to the U.S. for her education.

Often a particular child is characterized as the owner or keeper of that family's Zionist or aliyah identity. In many of these families the migrant's siblings also spent a year or more in Israel. But at some juncture the migrant child began to differentiate himself or herself from siblings and parents:

> My sons were there for six months and they all came back from Israel. I mean they just went to help out during the war. [But] that's where she wanted to live. I had some mixed feelings about it . . . she being my eldest daughter and we had a fairly close relationship. But I always had the philosophy that children have to be who they are and what they want to be . . . I know that mine was different from my parents' lifestyle.

Generational Continuities in Ideology

A major assumption underlying my research is that cultural constructions of the self, the collective, and generational memories are closely interwoven in relationships to significant others (Briggs 1987; Lutz and White 1986; Middleton 1989; Rosaldo 1993; Shweder and LeVine 1990). Ethnographic life historians often focus on an individual's embeddedness in social relationships over the life course and the interdependence of individuals with others (Gunhilde Hagestad, personal communication, 1999). In such biographies, a person's memory always involves a dynamic relationship between present and past generations.

The concept of vicarious memory can help explain the process of transmitting collective ethnic identity from one generation to the next. By vicarious memory, I mean a memory that an individual holds with great personal and emotional commitment, yet it is a memory of an event or experience that the individual has not experienced directly (Climo 1995; Ishino 1995). We derive much of our identity from our vicarious memories of the experiences of teachers, parents, and others. The key to understanding how vicarious memory is transmitted from one generation to the next lies in the emotional commitments we make to the collective identities they perpetuate. Memory, then, and the cultural creation of memory repertoires or patterns of remembering that are distinctive to particular groups become essential components in the persistence of both individual and collective identity.

Barbara Myerhoff (1978) noted that the saliency of American Jewish identity changed over the life cycle. Elderly immigrant Jews in Venice, California, spoke Yiddish in their early childhoods in the shtetls of Europe, then spoke English in their adult years in America, and in old age revived Yiddish in the senior citizen's center that became their final community. By remembering and embracing the language of their childhood, these elderly Jews found a path for the transmission of the culture of their parents and at the same time became crucial interpreters of their parents' culture. Their use of Yiddish in old age illuminates their changing and overlapping identification with their Jewish traditions as well as their relationships with their own parents and children. More recently, Rakhmiel Peltz (1998) discovered a strong persistence of Yiddish among American-born children of immigrants in South Philadelphia. In both instances, the Yiddish language plays a role in collective memory and Jewish identity.

The main exception to the theme of individualism among American migrants to Israel and their parents appears when the memory of aliyah is couched in terms of generational continuity in Zionist ideology. Both parents and migrants remember aliyah as a Zionist commitment that has been transmitted from one generation to the next; they evoke a picture of American Jewish families in which parents nurtured the child's love of Zionism. A mother explains her son's aliyah as a continuation of family and parental ideology:

> In high school, I introduced him to Israel, and he went there on a year course. No ear for languages [but] he is a very strong-willed person. He was influenced so much by Zionism that he became fluent in Hebrew. He decided he belonged in Israel. I was active in Hadassah, and all the members on the board had children or grandchildren in Israel. It was a natural outcome of our orientation. I wasn't hilariously happy about it per se but, on the other hand, I knew it was the natural result of the type of life that we led.

Several stories focus on family-related motives for aliyah. These include the family's Zionistic environment, particularly when the parents tried but failed to make aliyah when the child was still young. A mother of six remembers the aliyah of her two eldest sons as part of the ideological continuity of her family:

> When my eldest son got married, he said "We are getting married and we are moving to Israel." It was his choice. I didn't say he can't go because we brought

> them up to love Israel. He's been there twenty years and my second son is there eleven years. He met an Israeli here, whose mother comes from Detroit. My husband said, "If you marry an Israeli girl, you better plan on living there because Israeli girls are very attached to their families." I miss them, I wish they were closer. I have wonderful relations with my grandchildren and my daughter-in-law. My second husband had lived in Israel, his first wife was an Israeli. So we had common ground . . . we had in common our love for Israel.

Such family motives may be traced to a parent or grandparent who was born in Israel or lived there for some time before coming to America. Even without that family bond, however, some families promote a strong Zionist environment, and in a number of cases, a child's aliyah is clearly related in some way to his or her relationship to a brother or sister who had attempted to make aliyah. Many migrants recall the development of their love for Israel and desire to move there as a continuation of their family's and parents' ideological commitment to Zionism.

Jerome's story not only illustrates the continuity of Zionist ideology over generations but also illustrates a strong vicarious attachment between the generations. Jerome's aliyah represents a fulfillment of his father's desire to live in Israel. At age fourteen, Jerome qualified for a tenth-grade program in Israel, after which he claims he would have done anything, signed up for any program he could, to get back to Israel. His parents recently bought a home in Florida. Jerome says, "That's their new life." His father still attends synagogue but has gotten away from the religious aspect of his life and gotten into golf, Florida, and the country club.

> For a couple of years, I was left out, you know, dangling in Judaism. And my Dad had already, kind of, not wrapped it up, he's still a very observant man . . . but that part of his life is over. He loves Israel. My Zionism is from him, and uh, my grandfather. My Dad was here the first time when he was fifteen or sixteen in 1956 . . . my sisters were older; they didn't get into the whole religious kick when my Dad did. They were already in high school and parties and . . . I was my father's son. So when I moved here I was fifteen, you know, also the same thing . . . something that he [father] would have liked to have been able to do . . . whether or not he had the opportunity. . . . He looked at me and said, "This is the life that I would have loved to have had." . . . It was good for me. I was, yes, I was fulfilling, I guess, my father's dream. . . . He gave me too much. He gave me the desire. He gave me the opportunity. He gave me the love of Israel.

Memory as a Ritual of Return: Separation, Loss, and Reunification

In the midst of such persistence in Zionist ideology over the generations we must find striking the charge of historian Y. H. Yerushalmi (1982), who argues that Jewish historians—and I'm extending this to include ethnographers of memory—can no longer be limited to finding continuities in Jewish history: the time has come to look at ruptures and breaches. Yerushalmi is important here for at least two reasons. First, his view of history and memory differs from Western notions that understand history as if it unfolds chronologically. In contrast, Yerushalmi's view is that traditionally memories of key events in Jewish history were performed and transmitted through religious rituals; thus chronologies of events became less important than rituals. Second, Yerushalmi's view is important because transferring memory over time through ritual and performance—individual and collective—leads to focusing attention on relationships between generations over time.

When we look at memory over several generations, we are very likely to find both persistence and change in form and content; even the symbols of ethnicity may change from one generation to the next, while ethnic identity and loyalty may persist (Climo 1990, 1995; Teski and Climo 1995). Ishino (1995), for example, reminds us how the Nisei, first American-born generation Japanese Americans, experienced internment camps during the Second World War. They hid much of their memory of this terror from their children, the Sansei, who later created the political motives for recompense from the American government. Both generations retain their identity as Japanese Americans, but their memories and experiences, complementary in one sense, are different in another.

Underlying the idiom of individualism and embedded in the discourse of aliyah, lies a deeper symbolic attachment to Israel. American Olim experience a vicarious attachment to Israel that has important ritual implications for the meaning of their collective Jewish and aliyah identities. Instead of returning to their parents' or grandparents' villages, as is common among other American diaspora communities, American Jewish migrants return to the land of their biblical ancestors. Migrants go to Israel in search of their primordial and spiritual origins, historical and collective roots. But this leads to an important symbolic paradox. On the one hand, the return to Israel symbolizes reunification with the idealized lost community of biblical days, while on the other hand, in order to make aliyah, migrants must separate from their living relatives, leaving behind in America their parents, siblings, and grandparents.

I am struck by the dominance of a major collective memory that is both ritualized and at the same time expressed in the idiom of individualism: the experience of being separated, suffering some personal loss, and then being reunited or reincorporated with the remembered lost community. Significantly, while this theme dominates migrants, it is completely absent in their parents' memories. Memories that include a ritual of separation and reunification differentiate the migrant generation from the parental generation, marking an important generational change from the ethnic diaspora identity of the parent to an Israeli national identity of the migrant child. To understand the symbolic transformation of American Jewish diaspora identity into Israeli national identity, it is crucial to analyze these individualized narratives of separation and reunification, dismembering and re-membering, and reincorporation with the lost community.

Reuniting or reincorporating with the lost community also suggests that one key aspect of the return from diaspora involves a process of "re-membering" in the symbolic sense of peopling the lost community with the self, living relatives, ancestors, and images of bodily violence including illness, death, and dismemberment (cf. Myerhoff 1992). Such re-membering tends to blur surface distinctions between family and community, self and collective, past and present, and space and time. It also provides an immigrant with important community networks in the adopted country, although they are idealized networks, memories constructed from individual, family, and community experiences.

On the surface level, their quest is for an ongoing community, peopled by those who are ideologically close and share their visions of Zionism. But on a deeper, symbolic level the life histories of American Jewish migrants to Israel draw a direct connection between their personal losses and their reunification and reincorporation with an ancestral lost community. American Jewish life is portrayed as having been cut off from the larger body of world Jewish culture. Most reasons migrant adult children and their parents give for their migrations reinforce the "pull" theory that Waxman (1989) proposed, claiming that American Jews migrate to Israel because of its appeal rather than their desire to leave an unhappy situation in America. Nevertheless, many migrants contradict Waxman's pull theory in that they find America a spiritual wasteland. As Mark puts it: "American Jews are suffering from a spiritual Holocaust. . . . The Jewish people are being destroyed through religious freedom; you can be who you are, and there's no difference . . . lox and bagels, going to synagogue on Rosh Hashana and Yom Kippur, it's horrible." And Ruth, who likes Israeli society because it provides a good environment for bringing up children, is critical of American Jewish family life: "Americans are getting degrees, delaying marriage, delaying having children. Some are doing okay, but many are not. I don't know how to explain it. A lot of divorce, a lot are unhappy, many are not having children. . . . American Jews are frustrated people—people alone, frustrated, unfulfilled, something."

The act of aliyah carries an implicit criticism of the American way of life, yet the meaning of returning to the ancestral social body is expressed in stories of personal losses through divorce, sickness, death, and even bodily violence. Migration to Israel symbolizes their efforts to recapture a community life they have lost in the United States.

Such personal losses, of course, are mitigated by reunification in Israel and the formation of a new identity and new re-membered communities there. Ruth lives with her husband, four children, and her American niece, who is estranged from her family. She left for Israel twenty years ago when she was eighteen and had just graduated from high school. Her parents had just completed a contentious divorce. As the youngest child (she has three older brothers), Ruth was most vulnerable. Her family had been strongly Zionistic all through her childhood, but she was broken hearted following the divorce. Her father died about four years ago. Her mother and stepmother visit Israel regularly. After Ruth migrated, her brother and his wife moved to Israel. Betsy, Ruth's stepmother, claims Ruth's aliyah was a reaction to her parent's divorce:

> Ruth may have gone originally, I can't remember if it was a year or a summer, but her father encouraged her to take that year. It was good for her to get away . . . there had been a divorce and it had been very traumatic. Ruth's parents, I think that may have motivated her. . . . She came home and told her father she was in love with this sabra. . . . He was frightened . . . and went back with her to meet him and they were married shortly after that.

Significantly, Ruth's stories include no discussion of her childhood and family life in America. She consistently stresses her strong desire to connect with Israel and at the same time leave her American identity behind. Ruth claims she never spent much time with Americans in Israel but, almost as soon as she could, integrated into Israeli society, assuming an Israeli identity.

Migrant memories are filled with stories of personal losses relating to grandparents, parents, and siblings, along with dead relatives and ancestors. Several examples include memories of American family visits to Israel shortly after the death of a close family member. Jerome is twenty-three and has lived in Israel slightly more than a year. He served as a medic in the Israeli army and worked at several jobs as a hotel waiter in Tel Aviv. Jerome claims his love for Israel and his desire to live there began when he was ten years old. Shortly after his grandfather died, Jerome went on a family vacation to Israel. He describes his grandfather's death and his family's vacation as "the hugest event in my family's life . . . all our lives changed very much after that. . . . When my grandfather died, my father went to say Kaddish for eleven months, and he realized there were nice people there [at the synagogue]. He made some business contacts, got involved in the whole Jewish identity . . . it was a shift even to more observant . . . I knew pretty much from then that I was going to live here."

Terminal illness and death are relevant in searching for and eventually reuniting with the lost community because when a person or someone in a family becomes terminally ill, it frequently becomes a catalyst in the search for one's identity. In her last film *In Her Own Time,* Barbara Myerhoff (1985) documents her response to learning she has terminal lung cancer. Her film portrays her return to her primordial roots in the Hasidic Orthodox Jewish community of Los Angeles. Early in the film she is searching for a miracle, then as she gradually comes to accept her fate, she turns to the Hasidic community for comfort.

In several migrant memories, the terminal illness of a family member becomes the impetus for a visit to Israel and the backdrop for an individual's story of the development of a stronger Jewish identity that eventually leads to aliyah. Irene is a single woman in her forties. She went to Israel sixteen years ago to live. But her first trip to Israel was with her family for ten days shortly after her older sister died of multiple sclerosis. As a girl, Irene became involved in caring for her sister and comforting her mother who had the burden of her sister's care: "I was three years younger than Susan. We weren't really close or anything. She had her world, and I was into horses. I was nine when she got sick. Susan was home and my mother was dealing with her . . . it got difficult emotionally . . . and being the person there, I ended up helping."

Images of bodily violence also appear in many narratives of American migrants to Israel. At breakfast one morning, my friend Pesach agreed to explain why and how he became an artist in Israel. He began by telling me a story from the Vietnam war. It seems an American soldier's platoon was surrounded by the enemy. The soldier called for help from his backup, but he also made a rather strange request: that the backup attack his position. When the strike came on his position, his own platoon was prepared and hidden. But because of the massive firing and explosions coming from his position, the attackers were led to think his platoon was stronger than it really was. The enemy retreated, his platoon was saved, and the soldier became a decorated hero. Pesach sees this story as a metaphor for his own experience fighting cancer: "Cancer is a disease in which the cells of the body rebel against their central authority; they go wild . . . the only remedy is to do battle with one's own body. And so in my case, my arm was amputated. In other cases, other kinds of disfigurement are commonplace."

Part of the reason for Pesach's success as an American immigrant artist lies in his ability to identify with the battle-weary people of Israel, ranging from Holocaust survivors to people who have lost family members in the various wars since the state has existed. Pesach did not think of himself as a successful artist, but his friends tell him his career has been distinctive, that he is recognized as an important artist in Israel, even though he immigrated there as an adult. Pesach's art touches the Israeli public because his own disfigured body has been a battlefield in which he fought to save his own life.

Discussion: Connecting Individual and Collective Experience

At the beginning of this paper, I posed a question regarding the lack of connection between individual experience and collective memory. How can an ethnographer interpret the meaning of an individual's experiences within the larger context of collective experience when the participant offers no connection between them? I claimed that a productive approach to this question would include an ethnographic understanding of memory as multilayered and complex. Drawing on my research with American migrants to Israel and their parents in America, I illustrated the possibility that a cultural repertoire or idiom of individualism may underlie more significant linkages of individual, generational, and collective memory. Now I wish to return to the question of the relationship between individual and collective experience and to discuss the assumptions underlying my interpretation of the connection.

One part of the answer might be to simply accept that social memory is not always or necessarily situated historically. Narratives of the present self need to focus on personal concerns, but individuals can narrate stories about their lives with little or no reference to larger political and historical contexts. This implies that the question of the relationship between individual and collective experience mainly reflects a methodological problem, particularly in cultural anthropology, since ethnographers always select the lives of key individuals to represent communal experiences (e.g., Shostak 1993). From this perspective, the question of the ethnographer's task in addressing and possibly reconciling the dynamic dissonance between individual and collective experiences raises issues that emerge from ethnographic field research.

Recent efforts in ethnographic approaches to life history have stressed the creation of a dialogue fundamental to the nature of the encounter between the anthropologist and the participant (Crapanzano 1985; Fabian 1983; Gubrium and Holstein 1995). For example, in considering Myerhoff's innovative contributions to ethnographic research in life history, Marc Kaminsky (1992:7) claims that Myerhoff called the result of such a collaboration the "third voice" in order to emphasize the dynamic contribution of the dialogue between two persons in the telling of an integrated life history narrative. "[Myerhoff] read the transcripts of a number of stories that she had collected . . . wondered aloud about what one is to do with all that material, and then commented that the 'tales from Fairfax are to be written in the third voice, which is neither the voice of the informant nor the voice of the interviewer, but the voice of their collaboration.'"

Ethnographic research in life history allows us to understand the connection between personal biography and local history (Bertaux 1981; Mintz 1996). But frequently, it is the ethnographer rather than the participant who makes the connection explicit. Wolf (1984) claims that European institutional history systematically marginalized colonized peoples, portraying them as objects rather than subjects of history and thus making them "people without history." Wolf's work has been influential in exposing the marginalization of colonized peoples. Again, in what appears to be a logical and significant extension of the importance of the third voice, ethnographers often include elements from their own autobiographies in order to locate and interpret the resulting biographical narratives in a larger social and historical context (Behar 1996; Climo 1999). Yet, putting the total responsibility for making connections between individuals' personal experience and the larger collective experience on the shoulders of the ethnographer tends to disempower the subjects of ethnography, implying that their lack of an explicit connection to larger collective memories and history arises out of ignorance or incompetence rather than from a deliberate choice.

A second part of the answer to my question may involve the claim that some people experience denial, or fear and denial. The cognitive dissonance they experience may be too threatening and stressful for them to situate themselves overtly within a recognized historical or political context. So they focus their attention on personal acts and adjustments instead, acts that disassociate them and thereby protect them from larger collective experiences and memories. In so doing they remove themselves psychologically from the danger of larger events over which they have little or no control. A large literature concerned with the Holocaust confirms that for several decades after the war ended many survivors refused to discuss their experiences even with their family members. It is not coincidental that most public memorials to the Holocaust did not begin until long after the Holocaust (Climo 1995). An ethnographer should not assume that people lack awareness of their place in the larger historical and collective experience, even when they fail to make the connection explicit in their narratives.

Finally, a third part of the answer is adapted from critical theory in anthropology. It suggests that at least two levels of memory must be considered. In Wittgensteinian philosophy, the most obvious level of human behavior (in this case memory behavior) can be termed "practical consciousness," which implies that most of the time, if asked, people can explain their memory of what they did and why they did it (see Giddens 1991). This most obvious level of memory should be documented and understood in its own terms. But critical theory suggests the existence of a second level of memory, an underlying symbolic memory that in many cases is equally or more important to the ethnographer. On this deeper level of memory, people do not situate themselves by any direct reference to their collective experience and therefore neither explain what they did nor why they did it with reference to their collective memory or history. In this explanation, people are so embedded in their collective memory and identity that they fail to make the connections explicit in their narratives. In such a case, rather than an individualism characterized by a true lack of connection to collective experience, we may speak of an idiom of individualism. American migrants to Israel speak about their memories in a cultural repertoire or idiom of individualism. Yet their rituals of return to Israel, their separation, their personal losses, and their rein-corporations and reunifications with the larger social body ritualize their deep and continuing attachments to Jewish collective memory and history. Such ritual and symbolic memories must be examined and interpreted within their legitimate historical context if the ethnographer ever hopes to explain the lack of connection on the surface level and uncover the deeper connections between individual and collective experience.

Acknowledgments

The author wishes to acknowledge grants from The College of Social Science and The Pearl Aldrich Foundation of Michigan State University and from the Lucius Littauer Foundation that made this research possible.

CONTESTED MEMORY AND HISTORY 

Kiowa
On Song and Memory

LUKE ERIC LASSITER

7

IN JULY OF 1990, at a small family powwow in Apache, Oklahoma, Kiowa elder Billy Evans Horse (1990a) stood up to make a speech:

We should be *proud.*
As Comanches,
Kiowa-Apaches,
And Kiowas.
We have a rich history.
No one can ever take that away from you.
The government has tried over and over.
Congress has passed *laws.*
They're trying to *assimilate* us into the white
culture.
That's the goal of Congress.
They've taken our land.
They've taken everything they could.
And I'm going to tell you one thing.
I will never let them have my language—
That's for sure.
I'm going to take care of it the best I know how.

Listen to this song and listen to it well.
And remember,
when you hear it sung,
pay respect to it.
It belongs to your ancestor.
A *great* war leader of the Kiowas,
Satethieday.[1]

The Kiowas, Comanches, and Apaches

In the presentation above, Billy Evans Horse references a relationship between the Kiowas, Comanches, and Kiowa-Apaches that is over two hundred years old. In the early eighteenth century, the united Kiowa and Kiowa-Apaches first migrated onto the Plains from present-day Montana and the Comanches from the Rocky Mountains and surrounding area. All three groups had found their way to the southern Plains by the late eighteenth century. Initially, the Comanches and the Kiowas were bitter enemies. But around 1790, the three groups established peace at a Spanish settlement and initiated a long-lasting sociopolitical and cultural relationship—despite radical differences such as language. Together the KCAs—as they call themselves today—nearly dominated the southern Plains. Their fiercest enemies included the southern Cheyenne and Arapahos and, later, the Texans and Americans.

Not until the United States began to express an explicit interest in the region did the federal government seek to remove the KCAs and other groups from the southern Plains to make way for U.S. settlement. At the Treaty of Medicine Lodge in 1867, the KCAs met with United Sates commissioners and officially agreed to remove to a reservation in Indian Territory (present-day Oklahoma). The Medicine Lodge agreement had serious shortcomings, however, and the reservation system it established failed miserably. In 1901, the United States government dealt a final blow to the KCAs by allotting their lands by severalty and opening over two million acres to white settlement (see Hagan 1990; Mooney 1898; Nye 1969; Wallace and Hoebel 1952).

Historically, the unification of the KCAs was not just political and not employed only in warfare or dealings with other polities. The three groups intermarried and exchanged important sociocultural institutions like religious and warrior societies. Today most, if not all, contemporary KCAs trace their ancestry and their traditions through a complex web of Kiowa, Comanche, and Kiowa-Apache relationships, kin and otherwise (see Boyd 1981, 1983; Foster 1991; Kavanagh 1996).

Not until the Indian Reorganization Act of 1934 (IRA) were so-called Indian tribes encouraged to organize as independent political entities. And the KCAs were no exception. Today the Kiowa, Comanche, and Kiowa-Apache tribes are essentially organized as separate polities under the IRA and the Oklahoma Indian Welfare Act of 1936. In many ways, traditions like language and song reinforce these politically defined tribal distinctions. But in other ways, the power of language and song—as social constructs that engender experience and meaning—also helps to articulate a common KCA sociocultural identity and as Billy Evans Horse (1991a) would add, a common struggle. This KCA struggle exists separately from their identities assigned from the outside, both their politically defined identities as tribes and their racially derived identities as Native Americans (cf. Prucha 1985).

I have argued elsewhere that the power of song to articulate this KCA identity is probably strongest now (see Lassiter 1998, 1999). Song currently looms as a dominant symbol in the community, especially as Native language is being spoken less and less. For many community members, song enjoys equal footing with language as one of the most vital traditions for maintaining and transmitting a distinctive social memory, the "rich history" to which Billy Evans Horse alludes above. The man, Satethieday, and his song that Horse references are good examples for illustrating this point.

Satethieday: His Song and His Story, Past and Present

Satethieday (Satanta in much of the literature) was Billy Evans Horse's great-great-grandfather. He was among the most prominent Kiowa chiefs of the late nineteenth century. Kiowa people remember him as a tenacious war leader who led Kiowas to several victories against the United States and Texas. Horse and several others have in their homes a portrait of Satethieday wearing a general's uniform given to him by General Hancock in 1867. After receiving the uniform, Satethieday wore it in several battles against the United States (Mooney 1898:178, 210).

Among his enemies, Satethieday was well known for his eloquent speeches that secured him the title Orator of the Plains at the Treaty of Medicine Lodge in 1867. There he diligently defended the rights of his people to remain free on the Plains. "I don't want to settle," he is quoted as saying. "I love to roam over the prairies. There I feel free and happy, but when we settle down we grow pale and die" (cited in Mooney 1898:208).

Kiowa people of the nineteenth century greatly admired Satethieday; today, they still do. In 1871, the United States arrested and imprisoned Satethieday (along with Big Tree and Sitting Bear) for killing seven teamsters in Texas. After a brief parole from 1873 to 1874, the United States returned him to prison in Huntsville, Texas, where he reportedly committed suicide in 1878 (see, e.g., Mooney 1898:206–210; Nye 1969:127ff.).

To this day many of Satethieday's descendants have accepted neither the basis for his arrest nor the reports of his suicide. Billy Evans Horse (1990a) told the families gathered at Apache:

> He took the blame for the Warren wagon-train massacre.
> And he wasn't even *there*.
> As you may or may not know the story prior to that,
> that was told by—

in my case,
my great-grandmother—
Ahtonenah,
that her daddy was not
at the present site at the time that would
happen.
But because of the different things that were
happening at that moment,
Satethieday accepted the responsibility.
End result was that the United States government
convicted *him* of murder.
And they have a plaque at Fort Richardson
highlighting their so-called notorious event as that.
And we feel that was *wrong.*
And we're going to have to find the documents to
substantiate *our* facts.
There are many, many other things that you
may or may not be aware of.
And the documents that are on file in Washington, D.C.,
the government claims that Chief Satethieday
committed suicide at Huntsville, Texas,
where he was incarcerated up there.
Documents, again, that have been seen, clearly
state and show that he was forced into taking
medication.
End result was that—
the assumption is that he committed suicide.

So, those are enormous projects to undertake to
try to clear the record,
so to speak,
for the injustice that has been done.

Two organizations have actively worked to keep Satethieday's memory alive within the community: the Chief Satanta Descendants and Satethieday Khatgomebaugh (White Bear's people). The latter is a community service organization inspired by "the spirit of his service" (as cited in Satethieday Khatgomebaugh 1994). The former grouping of Satethieday's descendants incorporated to clear Satethieday's record and to find and repatriate his war paraphernalia and trophies, which include a lance, shield, rope, and a United States Army bugle.

The Taimpego Society and the Gourd Dance

Both organizations and the families they represent have a special connection to song sung in the KCA community. Satethieday was once a prominent leader of the Taimpego Society, one of six Kiowa men's warrior societies that were active in the nineteenth century. Each society had its own songs and dances, and each year at the Kiowas' annual *K'aw-tow* (The Gathering or, more commonly in English, Sun Dance), the Taimpego Society performed its Rattle Dance. In the Rattle Dance members stood in place, shaking a rattle to the rhythm and cadence of Taimpego songs, which in turn—along with speeches and other presentations—communicated the society's accomplishments in battle (Horse 1991a; see Lowie 1916).

Within a few decades after Satethieday, the Taimpego began losing its traditional significance as the warrior lifestyle was coming to an end on the KCA reservation, especially after the United States government forcibly ended the Kiowas' K'aw-tow in 1890 (Mooney 1898:221, 358–361). Yet as the United States government sought to categorically terminate all dances and songs associated with the old way of life, living Taimpego members continued society encampments off and on until 1938, putting the Rattle Dance to new purposes, especially to welcome home Kiowas who had served in the First World War. By the close of the Second World War—at the same time that government pressure against Indian dances began to decline—the Taimpego Society was helping to facilitate the renewed relevance of old warrior traditions. On Armistice Day 1946, for example, Kiowas held a Taimpego Rattle Dance (Horse 1991a).

Interestingly, while other warrior societies were also revived to recognize world war veterans, the Taimpego began to take another path in the years following World War II. In 1955, at the American Indian Exposition in Anadarko, Oklahoma, Fred Tsoodle, a Kiowa who wanted to present a distinctive Kiowa dance at the Expo, gathered singers and dancers to perform the Rattle Dance of the Taimpego. The performance was meant for entertainment only, but "this presentation brought back memories of our cultural heritage and there were tears and soft crying among the elder spectators" (Kiowa Gourd Clan 1976:22).

Apparently, the presentation created a vibrant community-wide interest in the dance of the Taimpego. In the two years following the 1955 performance, a few inspired men consulted Kiowa elders and on January 30, 1957, formed what they decided to call the Kiowa Gourd Clan. No longer a warrior society, the Gourd Clan opened its membership to all men and focused exclusively on the dance of the Taimpego, which they renamed in English the Gourd Dance. "The purpose and function of this organization," they said, "was to perpetuate our Indian Heritage and to revive the Kiowa dance as near as possible from the past original ceremonies" (Kiowa Gourd Clan 1976:22). Since the official revival of the Taimpego

Society's Rattle Dance by the Kiowa Gourd Clan in 1957, the organization has held a dance every Fourth of July in Carnegie, Oklahoma.

The Role of Song in the Revival of the Taimpego's Rattle Dance

The revival of the Taimpego's Rattle Dance as the Gourd Dance centered on Taimpego songs. Indeed, because no Kiowa dance can be performed without the proper songs, remembering songs was absolutely critical for the Taimpego's performances during the years surrounding the world wars, at the American Indian Exposition, and for the creation of the Kiowa Gourd Clan. Although Taimpego encampments had ceased by the 1955 Expo performance, many Kiowas—like Billy Evans Horse's own grandfather—continued to sing Taimpego songs at singings, meetings of singers hosted in homes (Horse 1991b).

With this in mind, Billy Evans Horse (1991b) argues that these singings centered the Rattle Dance's revival. "It began when the songs were brought back, or sung," he explains. "And then the old people that were here at that time, like my grandpa [Tsoodle and the others] were asking them questions:

> 'What is that? What song is that?' And they give a little history about it.
> 'Well that sounds good. How did they dance?'
> And so they said, 'They dance this way.'
> 'And how did they dress?'
> 'Well, you could dress this way since it's modern times,' and so forth.

And they began to meet at homes round here, and then they were singing the songs, and grandpa would sing it to them, and they would listen and pick them up, and help him sing. . . . They had singing sessions at so-and-so's home once a week and then it began to go [the revival]."

While Taimpego encampments completely ceased after 1938, the songs lived on, albeit in isolation from the dance. The dance's revival drew its lifeblood from these singers or, more precisely, from their songs. Without the songs, the revival would not have been possible. It was no mistake, then, that songs (that is, what could be heard) proved far more important than such factors as dress, toward which the attitude was "Well, you could dress this way since it's modern times."

The new Gourd Clan members had links to the old Kiowa lifestyle through their parents and grandparents. But their connection to Taimpego proceeded primarily through singers like Billy Evans Horse's grandfather and the songs they sang. At the core of this song tradition were the very songs that their grandfathers like Satethieday—many of whom had been members of the Taimpego Society in the previous century—had sung and danced to.

Each Taimpego member had his own songs. Satethieday had many that were revived for the new Gourd Dance, like the one that Billy Evans Horse references at the beginning of this chapter. In this new context, the songs of Satethieday and other prominent warriors had a renewed relevance for Satethieday's descendants (Horse 1990a). In the intervening years, these songs had passed through a generation of singers whose knowledge of song had made them cultural guardians for Kiowa people. Billy Evans Horse (1990b) says of this process: "[My grandfather, Cornbread] would call me and then say, 'This song, listen to it.' And he'd tell me the story of it. And then he says, 'This is a Gourd Dance song'. . . . My other grandfathers sang and told me stories about expeditions that they were on, and how the song was born from the expedition."

In the nineteenth century the original Taimpego Society had Rattle Dance songs as well as its own Brush Dance songs, War Expedition songs, Scalp Dance songs, Victory Dance songs, and other songs associated with warfare and the K'aw-tow. As the revival continued, singers consolidated the original Rattle Dance songs with Brush Dance songs, songs from now-defunct societies, sweat lodge songs, K'aw-tow Dance songs, Ghost Dance songs, and countless others to impart a new life to the Gourd Dance (Horse 1990a, 1991a). The Kiowa Gourd Dance thus became a conduit for Kiowa song revival, and its song repertoire became a storehouse of older Kiowa songs. Adding to this storehouse are the many Gourd Dance songs that singers continually compose today.

These songs became a symbolic way for Kiowa people to affirm their specific relationship to the Gourd Dance as its popularity grew outside its Kiowa center and eclipsed the intertribal powwow world of southwestern Oklahoma. The Gourd Dance spread from the Kiowa Gourd Clan's annual Fourth of July celebration throughout the KCA community and now almost completely dominates powwow programs. Today, several dozen Kiowa, Comanche, and Kiowa-Apache organizations host Gourd Dances, so many that a Gourd Dance takes place nearly every weekend of the year. The Chief Satanta Descendants and Satethieday Khatgomebaugh are two of those organizations. Although it is conventionally considered a men's dance, everyone—including women and children—now dances in the Gourd Dance's popular form, though only men carry rattles (most now made of wood and tin) (see Lassiter 1998:99ff. for a fuller description).

Remembering Satethieday at Gourd Dances

At each Gourd Dance, Satethieday descendants celebrate his memory through his Gourd Dance songs. One way they do so is by blowing a bugle during Satethieday's songs. This act commemorates Satethieday's custom of blowing his bugle during his own songs at Taimpego ceremonial dances. As the story goes, Satethieday obtained a bugle from a United States Army soldier, learned how to play it, and used it to confuse the United States cavalry in battle. When the cavalry blew the charge, Satethieday blew the retreat—and subsequently led his people to several victories.

The bugle (along with his other war trophies) accordingly became identified with Satethieday and his warrior sodality, the Taimpego Society. To this day, his descendants have continued the bugle-blowing tradition (though they do not have the original bugle) (Horse 1991a; cf. Mooney 1898:326–327).

Another way Satethieday descendants celebrate their connection to Satethieday is through story presented at KCA Gourd Dances. In his speech in Apache, Billy Evans Horse (1990a) tells those gathered: "There are *songs* that have words in the songs, and it tells a story." He then explained the words:

> This song I'll sing
>   belongs to Satethieday.
> You heard it sung many times.
> And the words in Kiowa say:
>   'I'm going to travel north,
>   where the grey wolf country is.
>   The grey wolf might eat me up.
>   They may kill me.
>   I may not come back.'
> He was telling his brothers that.
> He said,
>   'And brother,'
>   he said,
>   'I *know*,
>   if I don't come back,
>   you will cry for me.'
> And that's what this song says.
> I *really* respect these songs,
>   because I understand them.
> My grandfather said it *that* way.

Story and KCA Memory

Such stories are what Kiowa song evokes in its contemporary performance. But the sound of this song and the bugle heard by KCA Gourd Dance participants are not just mementos from the past. Coupled with the stories that surround Satethieday's memory, they are—as Marea Teski (1995:55) argued for the remembered consciousness of a Polish exile government—"a community process of using historical and cultural metaphors," metaphors that construct a community consciousness, an identity powerfully existing in the present. Satethieday's nineteenth century struggles to resist settlement continue to be relevant to current KCA struggles to remain ethnically distinct. "Because all consciousness is remembering consciousness," wrote Teski

(1995:56), "the past becomes part of the present and of the future, too." The song mentioned by Billy Evans Horse at the beginning of this chapter and its associated stories invoke this consciousness and foreground the sentiments of Satethieday as a *present* consciousness, fashioning KCA memory as an ongoing social construction that struggles within and against distanced and reduced identities, political, racial, or other.

In this particular community, then, both song and narrative help to transmit a social identity that is uniquely set within the boundaries of the historical relationships among and between KCAs. But because this social identity is formed by these particular relationships, it is also negotiated *within* those boundaries. Just as the KCA ethnicity struggles within and against larger political identities, on another level, Kiowa, Comanche, and Kiowa-Apache memories compete with each other. Some Comanches claim as their own the song about which Billy Evans Horse speaks and attribute equally powerful narratives to its performance. Some Kiowa-Apaches refute the importance of Satethieday and the Gourd Dance. Some Kiowas disagree about which songs are actually Satethieday's. While KCAs do share a deep sentimental connection to song, Comanche song or Kiowa song or Kiowa-Apache song also provides the forum for negotiating a multifarious social memory and consequently a multifaceted social identity. As song is performed in the present, it is engaged and mediated among people who each remember their pasts and construct their present and future in different ways.

For Kiowa elders like Billy Evans Horse, Kiowa song and memory secure a unique Kiowa relationship that perseveres within a larger KCA identity as an ongoing relationship with what Kiowas call *daw*. Daw literally translates as power. Power is gathered, amassed, and thrown by *Daw-Kee* (Throwing Power) that Kiowas today interpret in English as God. Only *daw-gyah* (song) captures the power thrown by Daw-Kee. Those like Billy Evans Horse argue that the long established Kiowa relationship with daw and Daw-Kee are most strongly articulated by song. Song, along with language, maintains this very particular relationship—a relationship that defines Kiowa experience specifically and uniquely within a larger KCA ethnicity and, in turn, within larger Indian and American identities. As Kiowa language faces tremendous challenges in the next few decades, Kiowa song is emerging as a powerful conduit for maintaining and communicating this Kiowa experience (see Lassiter 1998:187–220).

The relationship between daw, Daw-Kee, and daw-gyah is not just a conceptual or intellectual connection, however. Billy Evans Horse and others explain that it is a felt connection, one that is intimately sensory. To know song's power, they say, is also to *feel* song's power—that is, to sense daw's actual presence is to sense the past in the present, to participate through sound in a Kiowa continuity story of struggle and survival that is generations old. One individual says, for example: "It's a feeling of being transported back in time and being reunited with my people." From this perspective, one can hear a song and know the memories it invokes, but encountering, sensing, and feeling the agents of memory in the practice of song is quite another thing. To feel Satethieday's song, then, is to sense the presence of Satethieday shaping the present and, to some degree, the future (Lassiter 1998:187–220).

Much like Bourdieu's habitus—or more precisely, like Paul Connerton's (1989) "bodily social memory"—Kiowa song mediates structure, meaning, and individual experience. The ritual performance of song and memory is not merely an intersection of actors and action; it is a process of consciousness enacted, felt, and made real in the body. This is what most interests me about how Kiowa song achieves meaning within this particular American Indian community. Such a sensory approach, I believe, opens a window onto how memory is actually experienced on an individual level and then negotiated in a larger community-centered dialogue.

I have explored these and other issues on various levels before (Lassiter 1998, 1999). But what is most perplexing to me in the context of this chapter is how elaborating social memory by way of community dialogue continues to be neglected in some disciplinary circles. Indeed, Connerton (1989:4–5) argues that the study of social memory, particularly how it becomes enacted in the body, is badly neglected in social science. I am thinking here in particular of Native American studies, especially in regard to the wider concern with the question of history. Anthropologists have for quite some time argued that community esthetics like song do not just reflect culture but also shape experience, power, and identity. Nevertheless, Native American studies continue in large part to overlook this, relying instead on the mechanical construction of memory, that is, the recording of chronological events achieved largely through archival-based historical constructions.

Of course ethnohistorians and historians have long critiqued the differences between archivally constructed histories and community-constructed histories and their political implications. But this intellectual and political gap remains too wide to ignore (see Lassiter 2000 and 2001 for fuller discussion). Consider this, for example, from a relatively recent work entitled, ironically, *The American Indian Experience*: "As with so much of American Indian history since contact with Europeans and Americans, it can best be told from the framework of white history" (Weeks 1988:xi). When the social construction of memory is unimportant to authors such as this, who so strongly privilege the so-called written record (which is what Weeks means by "white history"), understanding the intersection of experience and memory becomes all the more relevant. It becomes especially pertinent to our task "to journey with our informants through time as *they* conceptualize it" (Teski and Climo 1995:1; emphasis added) and to understand Kiowa song, story, and identity as grounded in social relationships, in memory, and in experience.

Acknowledgments

This chapter was originally presented at the 1998 annual meeting of the American Anthropological Association in Philadelphia. Much of the essay also appears in Lassiter (1997, 1998); it is reproduced here by permission of UCLA's American Indian Studies Center and the University of Arizona Press, respectively. Thanks to Carole L. Crumley, Larry Nesper, and Marjorie M. Schweitzer for their helpful comments and suggestions. The essay's shortcomings, however, are entirely mine.

Notes

1. I use poetic transcription in this paper for quoting certain types of talk that do not render themselves to the written page easily. Sociolinguists such as Dennis Tedlock (1983) and Dell Hymes (1981) have demonstrated that in events like public presentations, storytelling, and lengthy narration, clear patterns of speech emerge. Translating this pattern together with content helps to illustrate the communicated intent that standard styles of writing gloss. For the poetic transcriptions in this essay, a few general rules apply: (1) breaks in lines represent breathing pauses; (2) breaks between stanzas represent a change in topics by the speaker; (3) italics denote greater emphasis than the presentation's average tone.

Symbolic Violence and Language
Mexico and Its Uses of Symbols

8

ADINA CIMET

THE NATIONAL AND INTERNATIONAL SURPRISE that ensued after the Zapatistas—Chiapas indigenous groups, radical students, and others—declared war on the government of Mexico in 1994 needs to be explained. Most people think of these groups as lacking in economic means; indigenous groups exist precariously in Mexico and their socioeconomic and political status in the country is very low. Yet, there has never been a lachrymose reaction on their behalf by the majority. The federal government suggests that it has addressed some of the pressing issues of these groups, seeking to mitigate some of the inequalities that plague their daily life. Clinics, roads, and makeshift schools have been constructed. While never enough, these efforts were undertaken to give some attention to the needs of the indigenous population.[1]

It was education that was expected to bring real change to the indigenous groups. Since 1926, a variety of experiments have been launched. These have reflected different ideologies and objectives, from total acculturation, which did not happen, to more effective participation in the economy of the country while acknowledging cultural differences. In the regions of Michoacán, Oaxaca, Guerrero, and Chiapas, schools were established to train teachers for the indigenous people. The first attempts failed; then, after other partially successful initiatives, the need for bilingual teachers was recognized.[2] During the past twenty-five years, bilingual teachers have been trained. Perhaps inadvertently, the process also trained leaders, leaders who brokered their way between the two cultural worlds that had previously lived in relative exile from one another.

Yet, there is another side to this history, one that is informed by other facts that do not stress development and accomplishment, but rather enormous frustration, poverty, distance from the dominant culture, and failure to achieve economic betterment for these minority groups.[3] There are about ten million indigenous people in Mexico, comprising more than one hundred linguistic groups and dispersed all over the country. Given this reality, the precarious survival for almost five hundred years of these identifiable cultures, different from the national one, suggests remarkable resilience and resistance. For them, there has not been acculturation, adaptation, or a merger of the two worlds into *mestizo* culture. While the ideology of *mestizaje* is part of the dominant nationalistic narrative for unification, the reality one observes differs (Bonfil Batalla 1981). From this perspective, the Zapatista war initiated in 1994 should come as no surprise. This is a story of survival against all odds, using group memory as a resource, but with no economic base to support it and no tradition of active political ideology to protect it. Drawing perhaps from the protests of some minorities in our globalizing world, the Chiapas Zapatistas have merged with the international processes of political change with an extraordinary dexterity that has placed them, to a measurable extent, at the forefront of political transformations. Given the fierceness of the Zapatistas' will, the only surprise about their declaration of war should be the surprised reaction of the dominant groups in the country.

Some scholars, reflecting the opinion of part of the population at large, protested the support and sympathy to the indigenous protest. After all, the cause of the conflict in this area of the world harks to a distant past, five hundred years ago, during the Spanish conquest. According to this view of history, much has changed and much has happened that cannot be accounted for. This viewpoint uses memory as a balm to assuage guilt and to create distance from any possible sociological links that past history may impose. According to this view, the governing elites today are Mexican, not Spanish; they face problems and new intentions, and the government has invested much effort to help economically and culturally validate the indigenous groups as deprived groups. If they have not integrated, they must pay the consequences of their choices. So how can they legitimately complain? And why should the economic complaint be combined with a cultural complaint now? And, most of all, how long will we, the mestizo population, need to feel guilty, responsible, and dissatisfied with the political efforts that Mexico has opted for, while the indigenous people magnify our share in their plight?

According to this view then, over the last two centuries Mexico has attempted to recast itself, taking into account the complex issues of the time, and nobody has intentionally left these groups out of anything. Nobody would dare to claim, so the logic of this argument continues, that Mexico's path of political and economic self-definition has been easy and successful; yet the problems that the country faces are enormous problems, complex ones. To center all or much on the indigenous groups seems simplistic, limited, and plain wrong. In the midst of new globalization, the Chiapas uprising seemed to some distracting, self-centered, myopic, and misguided.[4]

One can acknowledge the benevolence that the mestizo culture and the governments of this last century in Mexico have had towards the indigenous peoples. One cannot ignore the government's sporadic attempts to remedy the inequalities and hardships of the indigenous groups. One can recognize many examples of good intentions on the part of the government over the past twenty-five years; indeed, these have been noticed by most, including the indigenous groups.[5] But good intentions are not enough; they often fall short of their goals. Furthermore, the arguments now are not about the good or bad intentions of the dominant groups, but about the misplaced philosophical premises that guide the action and power in the interrelationship with these minorities. The never-changing situation of the minorities promotes inevitable questions, but these need not be about them and their culture; rather, these questions need to be directed to the dominant culture and its sociological product. This undergirds the protest of the Chiapas Zapatistas.[6]

Having devoted myself to the study of diverse facets of cultural minority life in Mexico and being a member of an ethnic minority there, I found a mechanism that hinders cultural minorities from maintaining their distinct identities. This mechanism of "incomplete allowance" (Cimet 1997) is implicit and unacknowledged, and it is activated by parts of the dominant society. I consider this a violation of human rights as well as a form of cultural destruction. In Mexico, indigenous groups have become, by the irony of history, cultural minorities. They are thus accorded the same status of incompleteness that the dominant groups impose on immigrants from other parts of the world. In the case of indigenous groups, however, these processes of subordination are obscured by layers of history going back to the Spanish conquest. Since I use language and symbols to find the mechanisms of control and am a Spanish-speaking member of Mexican society, I become, unwittingly, part of the dominant group. Making explicit some of these complexities can help us all understand the dominant group's unrecognized contribution to cultural ruination.

We need to explain the ongoing tensions between the cultural groups and the ongoing differences between cultures and their polities. The existence of indigenous groups today is the result of intense resistance at many levels; their open protests are examples. These are groups that have survived by virtue of their historic and cultural memory, a memory that articulates their plights and quiet successes and identifies the groups and behaviors that shaped their story (Gruzinski 1993; Todorov 1982). It is a constructed memory that is fed by the social situations that provide material to renew its meaning and activate it in the people (Foucault 1977). But where is this memory? Where or how can one see the reactivation of old thought? How can we address the ongoing activities that accompany cultural memory?

Language, Memory, and Power

I argue that the original clash of power groups, to be maintained as it is, is reenacted again and again as the old confrontation of the Spanish and the Indians. The characters that confront each other must still be polarized in a representational opposition that pictures the past, even when these are renewed actors at each point in time. We have a situation, a habitus, that prepares the reenactment of the same foes as agents of the old ideologies. This kind of argument and view of society and history, although a macro perspective, reduces the historical distance from the original clash and helps locate the activated psychocultural memory of a group in an ongoing quotidian structure that maintains difference.

One of the best areas to study this juncture of memory, confrontation, and power differentials is language. Language and cultural confrontation provide the locus for historical formations and meanings that are encoded and reenacted by the users in what turns out to be a naturalized structure. Thus, even though these historical meanings are activated, they are not apparent to many users. Many miss the historical message. Language and the many symbols encrusted in it work together in a process of contextualizing. Because Spanish language use in Mexico belongs to the historical formative period of the conquest, in Spanish we find codes and symbols that contain fossilized historical information that by virtue of its constant usage is repeated and reactivated into the present. Speaking or not speaking Spanish is a tool: for one group it is domination, for the other it is resistance.

The last fifteen years have displayed worldwide social triumphs of inclusion: regions have been economically globalized, politically linked, and culturally interconnected (Bauman 1998). In Europe, America, and intercontinentally, we have alliances that seem to call for a renaming of the definition of the groups involved. The old dreams for a common universal language (Burke 1991) (Esperanto for instance) or another pan-cultural dominant style took root precisely in a century characterized by the sharpest and most violent exclusionary ideologies, policies, and practices. But finally, the process of taking in rather than taking out (although one implies the other by definition) is being implemented even when we lack labels for these changes. But, as with all social processes, the erasing of boundaries has made people regain consciousness of other boundaries. Perhaps these boundaries serve as a defense against the anomic feelings that world changes unleash. We have a simultaneous worldwide attempt by many groups—cultural, ethnic, linguistic, religious, or combined—to protect their differences. Minorities of many kinds and numbers are demanding to be politically recognized. Language plays a special role in the changes studied. Distancing from the ethnic language, loss of the ethnic language, and taking on the majority language are all social phenomena addressed. Language is not only the barometer, the tool, and the window to these changes but the locus of much of what is going on. Language is then not only the symbol but also the means (Joyce 1991). It is with language, the choice of language and its use, that we can start noticing these redefinitions of identity within a society.

But language not only illuminates the inner individual struggles of the self with society, it also offers a perspective from which to examine society at large and the forces that mold individual choice. I attempt to analyze Mexican minority–majority relations from the perspective of indigenous groups and seek to show that the violent, unequal power between the groups dates to the Spanish conquest five hundred years ago and remains embedded in society and in the language of the society today. Language is an ideological marker that reinvents and reinstates violence within social relations in its everyday use. I will focus on communications between the two groups, in the persons of minority and majority representatives of the groups, at two moments in which signs and language played a key role.

In its ideological representation of itself, Mexico boasts to have attempted inclusion since its Independence War. After all, the mestizos, the group resulting from the mixture of Indian and Spanish culture, took over the reins of the country. It is through language and the elaboration of what it meant to be of one culture rather than another that this new hybrid identity was created. Spanish, the language of the original conquerors, became and has remained the dominant language of society (Kiernan 1991). Relations of power and domination could not have been established without certain discourses of socially established truth. Specific values, concepts, goals, norms, hierarchies, and divisions were taken from the arsenal of the Old World to reconstruct a social world that sought to separate politically from its intellectual root but never succeeded in being different. Other factors joined in this process, of course, leaving also their mark in language: religion, politics, technology, and extinction were all part of the process.

There is no doubt that the mediating role of language ideology in organizing power was exercised to perfection in this case. It also helped establish a tone in all ideological issues of the country. Within the boundaries of New Spain, the Spanish language became not only the territorial marker of conquered space, the deployer and facilitator of the imposed practices, but also the principal symbol of what it helped to create: the myth of belonging to a new nation, unified, homogeneous, and righteous.

Spanish language continued to rule with an ideology that defined as right what it was doing in the new territories and what it wanted the indigenous other to do as well. Some ideas came from religious behavior and belief while others were hidden in interaction within the day-to-day reenactment of accepted differential interrelationships among the people. Language was the historic vessel containing the ideologies that structured the renewed country.[7] Language was the repository of the ideas and values that were to constitute the new society, inherited from the old world. By retaining the language and many of the instituted values and norms that are set in the language even while so many social arrangements changed within the society, we have retained for five hundred years—albeit largely unconsciously—an inheritance that is based on the conquering mentality that reigned then. The War of Independence (1810), the Revolution (1910), and all the other upheavals that Mexico has experienced have not ruptured the continuity of a sustaining pattern of domination.[8] Language is therefore an embodied habitus of ideology that reinforces the dominant styles of dominant groups and legitimizes power differentials.

It would be useful, but impossible within the space of this essay, to examine how the boundaries of inclusion were established, that is, to summarize how in 1521 the Spanish gained absolute control of the conquered within three months.[9] For our purposes, the issue of the interrelation between groups and the making of new minorities can be approached by looking at the fossilized patterns that occur in language as tools to tell us who we are and how we behave. Much, of course, has been lost. For example, the exact name of the last Aztec emperor is not known to us: *Moctezuma, Motecuhzoma,* and other forms are variations of a name that has been so obliterated from the social memory as to be lost phonetically.[10] Even when we cannot recover the culture, we can recover knowledge of how some of that obliteration was accomplished and how, after many bloody fights, the conquerors continued to stamp their dominion in societal relations. The Spanish language can serve as the locus of multiple memories of dialogues that rediscover for us these historical struggles (Foucault 1977:203).

Language was the essential tool through which a new definition of the situation was established. Through the practices that language named and helped establish, the patterns of inclusion and exclusion—of what and who counts and what and who is expendable—were engraved, encoded, and turned into a habitus. The conquering language, the most basic and most grounding tool of the new society, became the new cultural capital, legitimizing further control of the local population. In the violence that did not disappear and achieved further regenerating patterns through reenactments, language is the catalyst for the process as it establishes a practice and its truth as rules by which groups must live. This specific language, Spanish, embodied the power asymmetry and social differential that was reproduced again and again in this society. Here, we find the ideologies that are deployed as a resource for the status quo.[11]

Reenacting Domination and Resistance

I will now describe two moments of interaction and analyze what they convey in terms of asymmetric power relations between the groups. Each example is a reenactment of domination and resistance.[12] The two historical moments are distant in time from each other, yet similar in their meaning. One took place in 1790; the other in 1994. The first moment, which I call a dialogue of one voice, is a kind of conversation between the authorities and two monolithic stones that were uncovered in 1790. The stones were remnants of the indigenous cultures, and the rediscoverers, the power elite of the time, were friars and educated laymen, representatives of both Catholic Church and Spanish Crown. I call it a dialogue in one voice because only one party spoke aloud; the Indians seemed to accept or tolerate the decisions and actions of the authorities, leaving what may be erroneously taken as evidence of their thinking. Yet however imbalanced the dialogue is, it is a dialogue in which the differential power of the interlocutors becomes very apparent.

The second moment, which I refer to as a voiceless dialogue, is another repetition of old arguments between the same two groups: the indigenous minority in Chiapas and the controlling government representatives from the local and national levels. It is a voiceless dialogue because the analysis is of the encounter of the two groups and the symbols they used to engage in a dialogue. Their material disputes are not described, not because they lack relevance or importance, but because it is in the language and the symbols used that we find the rules of the interaction between the minority and majority. The asymmetry is thus present at the very beginning of the encounter between the groups, and it signals the habitus that some would like to break.

Neither moment is a dialogue in the conventional sense of the term. In the first case, we have only the representatives of the dominant majority speaking, yet much of their communication renewed the terms of the old dialogue that was initiated in 1521. The remnants of the old cultures and the cultures they represent were treated as objects. No person of those cultures appeared to have a voice; nevertheless, some of the indigenous actions attempted to show defiance and resistance. In the second case, the extraordinary aggressive encounter of 1994 between indigenous groups (specifically the EZLN or Zapatista Army) and government representatives is a reenactment of similar previous representations. Here the dialogue takes place even prior to any party expressing itself with a voice. Even more than five hundred years from the first encounter, almost all of the same dialectical definitions that established the relationship seem to be at play.[13]

Dialogue in One Voice: The Commandment To Not See

Part of the prerogative exercised by the dominant groups was to achieve the greatest visibility for themselves while diminishing the visibility of the minorities. A demand that they imposed on themselves and on others was to not see, that is, not to acknowledge the existence, the value, or the importance of any element of the minority societies that could conflict with their ideology. In a way, it was a measure to harness all loyalty to the selected symbols, discharging any others that could possibly function as a challenge.

On August 13, 1790, during construction in an area of what is today Mexico City's Plaza Mayor, Viceroy Revillagigedo, who was heading the construction, was told that a strange, scary-looking sculptured stone had been found. In the next few months, there were quite a few other recoveries, and specialists came to assess their meaning. The first stone was established to be the *Coatlicue*, symbol of the mother of gods in Indian culture. Strange to western eyes, the stone depicted a decapitated head already a skull, hands like claws, and streams of blood on the sides.[14] On December 17 of the same year, a huge second stone was found, the well-known *Piedra del Sol* or Sun Stone. Within three months of the fall of Tlatelolco in 1521, the two main cities of antiquity were destroyed at a speed unimaginable, and all cultural items found to be venerated by Indians were deemed by the Spanish to be works of the devil. The reaction of the masses to the discovery of these pieces more than two hundred years later showed their old resistance and resilience but offered no direct challenge to the imposed definitions of the situation. Over two centuries after the conquest, a renewed symbolic encounter challenged the terms of their relationship.

Although the two stones fared differently, the message was consistent and similar. The Sun Stone, or Aztec Calendar as it is also known, seemed to the eyes of the people of the 1700s a fine technological instrument. Familiar in its esthetic form, it depicted a far less barbarous Other than that originally portrayed by the Europeans. After all, diminishing the efforts in conquering New Spain was not in their own interest. So by showing the conquered as more sophisticated than previously presented, the stone gave greater status to the conquerors. The stone was hung in one of the towers of the cathedral for all to see as a trophy of the old war and as an object brought under the dominant religious-philosophical worldview of the time. The unpleasant Coatlicue complex, unclear and awesome, was taken to the campus of the university to be seen by specialists who might decipher its inscrutability.

Although the stone was kept from the public for the use of specialists only, Indians nevertheless learned of its location. When large groups of Indians searched it out and visited it with lit candles, the friars became worried about a possible rebirth of a cult and ordered that the stone be buried again.[15] This unilateral decision clearly attained the quality of dialogue: one group talked, acted, and established dominance; the other reacted, resisted, and remained resolute in its apparent silence. Although the commandment to not see was enforced, the minority's memory had not been lost. While the dominant ideology and power groups controlled the speaking social environment, the dominated groups maintained their memory in silence.

The only conversation with the past spoke of conquest, dominance, and control. In its reenactment, hierarchy, status, and value were also reestablished. The visibility and knowledge of the ancient time, symbolized by the calendar stone, were superseded by exhibiting it as a trophy. It was not seen as emblematic of artistic and intellectual sophistication, but rather as an award for the winning side, proclaiming the message of the victor. Meanwhile, the inscrutability of the Coatlicue was used to negate it by denying its existence.[16] Before this emblem could be understood and the emotions it elicited could be constructed as symbolic loyalty, it was entombed.

Maintaining differentiations or oppositions in a society facilitates its reproduction. These define social boundaries without explicit elaboration. Again and again, the boundaries of the included and excluded, politically, economically, and philosophically, are determined and renewed by specific groups. This effort by the authorities to see the indigenous artifacts as nothing other than objects within the language and thought of the society they controlled, in practice had the effect of perpetuating the exclusion of particular groups (Bourdieu 1984:471).

Where this dialogue took place was and is significant. Both stones were exhibited in public areas that appeared to be nonpolitical territory: the cathedral and the university. Yet education has always been a tool for control and is therefore political by definition. Both the cathedral and the university are defined by their tutelage and instruction purposes. In each, acceptable behavior, thought, tradition, and etiquette are taught. Contentions over these issues are always political and represent philosophical power struggles for further control of the situation. In this conversation in the 1790s, the message was that the elites could govern without the need to obtain consent. Indigenous people were not included as subjects but only portrayed as passive objects within the new hybrid culture. By educating, delimiting, and absorbing selectively and calculatingly, definitions of time, space, and social power were reproduced. The fact that the Coatlicue was later exhumed again and buried again, sent a clear message concerning the place of the old cultures in the new world. The otherness of the Indian groups had to be recognized, but only minimally, in a form that could be accepted within the society. Any trespass beyond that was absolutely unacceptable. Here we see at work an official claim for inclusion of the indigenous cultures and people at the same time that they were subject to practices that rendered them inscrutable and invisible (Mehta 1997:73).

The Voiceless Dialogue: The Command To Not Be Seen

If one of the rules of the interaction between the minority and majority is for the majority to not see, then the next rule becomes for the minority to learn not to be seen. Minority members had to learn to be quiet and not too definite as they spoke their protests. In other words, they learned to adapt to the demands of the dominant society by finding innovative ways to express themselves within the parameters of what is allowed and understood by the dominant society. The asymmetry between indigenous groups and the governing elite has been a persistent feature of their relationship. However, it is apparent that much of it has been buried in the government proclamations of its achievements. Open dissatisfaction erupted in the struggle in Chiapas,[17] but it came packaged in socially acceptable terms.

The reencounter was different from the one described in the 1700s. Indeed, much has changed. In 1994, there was a rebellious group fighting openly. Indigenous groups had redefined themselves from peasants to Indians as they made their claims known. And they had managed to organize nationally in a variety of organizations and even linked up internationally with other indigenous minority groups.[18]

The last twenty-five years have represented a period of growth and consolidation for the indigenous groups as an organization with congresses that started in Chiapas's San Cristobal de las Casas in 1974, 1975, and 1977. By 1989, the shape of the indigenous organizations and the articulation of the specific issues they claimed had already crystallized. The legal status that Indians obtained with these organizations added to the legitimacy and awareness that accompanied the 500-year celebrations in 1992 and contributed to a reevaluation of their ethnicity. At the same time, the dominant society also redefined its own myths, merging with a variety of international groups and movements such as the International Pact for Political and Civil Rights and the Universal Declaration of Human Rights. All this contributed to the refining of the inner political rhetoric of homogenization-unification (mestizaje) that the PRI government used to mollify its population. Universal principles questioned the validity of the perpetual undermining of the local minorities, thus igniting the flammable tensions that existed in the polity. The surprise element caught the government off guard, unable to respond to a set of demands that had a ring of legitimacy and was now more difficult to deny.[19]

Here, I want to analyze the Chiapas reencounter itself. It represents the initiation of an aggressive dialogue, since it was a preparation for a bellicose confrontation between two distinct but very unequal parties. On one side was the government, with a military force that, even if not updated to the arsenal levels of a belligerent nation entering the new millennium, has a full active militia with modern arms, tanks, explosives, and planes; plus, the Mexican government is a partner in NAFTA with its northern neighbor, defined as the most powerful nation in the world. The opposing group, few in number and dressed in their usual folkloric attire, appeared on the scene wearing dark ski masks, some armed with rifles of another era and some with broomsticks, an infantry of women and men with no other military force to back them, even though they had received well over $8 million from abroad. Most of them were not able to speak the official language of the country. Those who did speak Spanish and were interviewed spoke as foreigners do, with interesting, unusual metaphors. Yet they often appeared powerless in arguing in the grand elaborate style of the country's political establishment. This encounter, voiceless still, is at the same time a synchronic and a diachronic moment. It has the potential for a fabulous metaphor to bring out the surreal contrasts and the abysmal distance of the contenders. How is this dialogue even possible?[20] How does the government respond in the end of the twentieth century to a threat to its legitimacy and domination from a group that looks so weak?

In defining some of the characteristics of Mexican society and specifically the governmental policy towards minorities, I have elsewhere used the term incomplete allowance to describe the mechanism used by the government to deal with the inclusion and exclusion of the minorities.[21] The government places emphasis on citizenship (inclusion), while it has no room for representation and no permissible practice within the decision-making apparatus for groups (exclusion). Incomplete allowance toward minority members of the society, who are citizens, allows the government to play with the definitions of inclusion and exclusion, which in the end are a definition of itself. There is a tension between its official representation and its misrepresentation. There are no political channels for a minority to exert political power as a group, even though the Mexican constitution was amended in 1996 to specifically recognize religious minorities.

How is it then that each of the two groups recognizes itself as the opposing Other? Do the indigenous groups pretend to hide behind their masks? Do they imagine themselves taking on the role as warriors challenging the basic tenets of this society? At the same time, why has the government started to pay attention to their speech and their symbolic army? Must the powerful government really respond to this strange, dissenting group? What made the government respond to the dialogue of the masked people and see them as a threat? Or are they just playing their part until the audience tires and abandons the theater? In other words, how is it that these two parties playing their respective roles have managed to engage the Other to be taken seriously?

We have two parties that are unequal (in more than one way). The government representatives are the known party. Their spokesmen are individuals whose names and curricula we know; that is important information even though some of the main negotiators have changed during the course of the dialogues. Yet, even when they seem to be individuals known to us, we can claim that they hide under the ideology of the ruling government, which pays lip service to the demands of the Indians. Although they are individuals, they represent socially defined positions that conceal themselves (Cahill 1998:131).

Over the years, in response to pressure, the government has created institutions to monitor the cultural and economic conditions of the indigenous groups. Yet, political redefinitions of their condition have been totally avoided. In the current intellectual climate of the country, however, the Chiapas uprising has touched a chord that has vibrated very deeply. Perhaps it has to do with the international awareness of cultures. Within the current international dialogue between minorities and majorities, their ability to engage the government is a dialogue that has opened up a space uncharted in Mexican history. The ability of the masked actors, the unknown participants, to remain unknown in terms of their individuality and self, while being transparent in terms of their socially defined personhood, has unexpectedly put both parties on an equal footing in this dialogue. And the dialogue itself has become an occasion for interaction, recreating and legitimizing ipso facto the two agents as valid contenders. The fight then was and is on, but most importantly for our argument, the language and the symbols of the contentions have been understood by both parties. They are not surprised; each side knows what the Other is saying.

It is in this process that the treatment of the Other has been aired and magnified. In its historical character, the parties mimicked the old positions. The mimicry of the indigenous groups, their posing as warriors, expresses the excesses of the structure as applied to them.[22] But by playing the part of equals, they unwittingly posed an imminent threat to the power structure. By appropriating the style of the Other, the power elite, they have exemplified for others the fact that the power structure strangles them and have challenged the structure that claims to be including them. The fact that this dialogue happened with such relative ease attests to the already ongoing normative debate that the groups engage in; the Chiapas Indians spoke, and the opposition understood.

The Indian groups had to speak the same language as the opposition to make their protest known, yet not all spoke Spanish fluently nor easily enough to undertake the national defense of their cause. They used an interpreter, Subcomandante Marcos, as their leader or spokesman (La Grange 1997). Marcos is a left-oriented former student who has spent more than ten years in their midst; he speaks with them and can speak for them. Historically, Indians may have adopted a new identity of sorts, while at the same time retaining their cultural legacy. Because the intertwining of religions, cultures, and old ethnic knowledge is so tight, language has remained at the center of their mythology: their own languages embody the cultural elements of distinction. Language for them is not just form but also substance. It contains the persisting elements of the old culture, while it offers a challenge to the new one. It is the base of the cultural, political memory that they deploy to maintain their diverse identities. It is a way to look back as they look forward. But it remains to be seen if their looking forward will be creative enough to change the opposite party. It is for them to forge that path, and while cultural memory nourishes the process, it can also thwart it if nothing else appears on the intellectual horizon.[23]

But why do they choose mimicry and evasion? Partly, it is an obvious military defense strategy; yet their desire to appear authentic within a society that has always buried them has allowed them only partial representation. Their chosen actions refract the terms under which they are defined. It also refracts the incomplete allowance into which they have been forced. That is why the power elite were ready to interact with the masked warriors immediately, never questioning this style. Unspoken rules had been masterfully recognized by both groups: the inexistent silent challenger emerged, coming without a face as the only way the power elite could recognize them. This partial presence is the counterpart to the partial vision that the power elite has of the Other. The mimicry then is by both groups, the challenger and the challenged. The partial representation and its recognition represent the old ideology in language anew. In the words of Bhabha (1997:156): "It is a form of colonial discourse that is uttered inter dicta: a discourse at the crossroads of what is known and what is permissible and that which is known and must be kept concealed; a discourse uttered between the lines and as such both against the rules and within them. The question of the representation of difference is always a problem of authority."

Yet as much as the Chiapas EZLN army has used metonymy as camouflage to enter the scene, the government has responded with its own. But in this case, the dialogue is not pure repetition. Indians have struggled to innovate their ideology, as the dominant groups have, for this dialogue. They have asked for completely new political arrangements in their regions; these translate into completely new ways of dealing with minorities democratically. They do not want a return to the past, neither mere tolerance nor a more sympathetic response to their precarious condition. They want no more false harmonization between the groups and no more silencing of their demands in exchange for benefits. What they seek is a completely new politics. This challenge is what has made the uprising so terrifying to the government and the society at large.[24] The Indians have articulated their demands in the language of the conquerors, but they have spoken from the legacy of the language of the conquered, which is a culture and experience of resistance. Incomplete allowance, the breach between what indigenous and other minorities can do in Mexico and what the powerful think Mexico's government and society is offering, has become (again) apparent. By enacting the play and mimicking the reality they want to avoid while keeping their identities alive, minority groups have unmasked the empty promises of the elite who depend on a reified structure. The Zapatistas of Chiapas expressed their goal very clearly: "a world where there is room for all the worlds."

Acknowledgements

I would like to express my appreciation and gratitude to Jacob Climo. A chance intellectual encounter opened the door to the opportunity for collaboration in this project. For the gracefulness with which he has welcomed me, I thank him.

Notes

1. Natives of other countries that have had colonizing experiences like Mexico's—for example, Canada and the United States—have also been bracketed and silenced. Nobody hears their claims, not internationally nor nationally (Coombe 1995:265).

2. For a review of the historical changes in government policy on indigenous education from 1926–1963 that led to bilingual and bicultural education in the 1980s, see Dietz (2000) and Perez Enriquez (1989).

3. Most Mexican historians agree today that the Indians' story has not yet been integrated into mainstream history, as is also the case for American historians (see Wood 1998). There is a group that works "to give voice to the historically silent" (Wood, 1998:41). Also see Bonfil Batalla (1989).

4. Heading the group of academics and intellectuals that argue in this fashion is the historian Enrique Krauze (1999); for the controversy it stirred, see Guerrero (1998); La Grange and Rico (1999); Lomniz (1998).

5. We refer to the National Plan for Bilingual and Bicultural Education, ANPIBAC (1980).

6. To get a more realistic and complex history of the actors involved (indigenous people, government representatives, paramilitary guards of wealthy landowners, student supporters, and Catholic and Protestant clergy), see the periodicals *Chiapas,* especially from 1996 to 1998, *Proceso,* especially for 1999, and Jímenez Ricardez (1997); for a pictorial representation, see Saramago (2000).

7. "Language has always been the companion of empire" is an aphorism attributed to the grammarian Nebrija in 1492.

8. See the parallelism in the latest argument of recent Nobel Prize winner Saramago (2000).

9. The work of Gruzinski (1993) and Todorov (1982) is basic to the understandings used here.

10. Two elegiac poems written by the *cuicapique* (surviving poets), along with other material from 1528 still in Nahuatl, and writing that used the Latin alphabet in Nahuatl still exist. See León Portilla (1992, 1997) and Bonfil Batalla (1989).

11. The possibility and hope for a different future, following Raymond Williams's words (1977), does open up. In searching the underlying ideologies of power found in language, we elaborate not only on issues of language and its use but also on recomposing the process by which the constant reaffirmation of interactions through language are making their mark, which can be changed or controlled in new directions. That knowledge may break the reified hold of these old ideologies within language and start up a process of elaboration for a new political and ethical change of that society.

12. Other examples of this exist, for example, the invectives that language adopted that came from signaling linkage to Indianness: Indians as lazy, stupid, polytheists, and valueless; the change of first name and last name from meanings in the local vernacular name style to European style (a change that was registered within five years of the Spanish conquest); and clothing as symbolic communication (see *Los Mexicanos Pintados por si Mismos,* originally published in Mexico in 1853).

13. The declining economy of the region, caused by falling coffee prices and elimination of coffee subsidies, played a great part in the decision of the Zapatistas to launch a war. Perhaps three other elements also played a part in this story: the end of the land redistributions that were seen as the end of the long-promised goals of the Mexican revolution; the privatization of communally held land that gave an advantage, again, to larger landholders; and the signing of NAFTA, the international treaty with the United States and Canada. Other elements that came to play a part in the story included leaders who were formed by governmental organizations as they prepared bilingual teachers, and other teachers trained by community deacons and catechists through the diocese of San Cristobal de Las Casas headed by Samuel Ruiz. Sindicalization also played a part, since it had organized its members, who eventually became an important source of the Zapatista base. For specifics of the confrontations, see Aguirre Beltrán (1992); Bonfil Batalla (1981); Harvey (1998).

14. For the first analysis of these discoveries, see De León y Gama (1990).

15. As another caveat to this story, in 1803 when Humboldt came to New Spain, he was granted permission to exhume the Coatlicue for study. He obtained the piece for three months, and then it was interred again.

16. Mehta (1997) makes an interesting distinction between the incomprehensible and the inscrutable. The first can be reversed because the object may be comprehended through studying the subject. Inscrutability is not the fault of the subject; it sends the message that, defying description, the object requires rejection.

17. Indigenous groups in Chiapas have had a long and uneven confrontation with the authorities over issues of work, economics, and development. Religious confrontations under Catholic and Protestant banners have added to the political fire. By 1993, after forty-five mostly non-Spanish-speaking Indians were arrested, the confrontation took a sharper turn. Since these Indians did not get proper representation and translation services during the judicial process, the outcome made the next confrontations clearer and the two groups' separation became inevitable; the new organized groups anticipated the EZLN (National Liberation Zapatista Army) as a rebellious army. Today the EZLN has thirty-eight autonomous municipalities under control from 111 that make up the area (García Canclini 1995). In 2001 they went to Mexico City to negotiate with the government in a march that has been compared to the civil right marches of the United States. The national congress did indeed receive them.

18. It is not only the first minority war fought with the support of internet observers, but by now, the groups get support money internationally from a variety of sympathizers.

19. Ernst Bloch used the term "surprise" and "astonishment" as concepts that betray the thought of the unexpected future that one may harbor. It certainly fits the situation here described.

20. Part of the theoretical argument to undertake this analysis is taken from Merleau-Ponty's (1973) work on language. He develops the notion of "silence" between language and speech, where silence enables language to occur as speech.

21. The term is useful not only to describe the limits imposed on a minority but to characterize the minority and the majority as they interrelate (Cimet 1997).

22. See the extremely suggestive article by Bhabha (1997). Although it is a very rich analysis of the action of the colonized, it leaves undeveloped the interaction between the colonized and the colonizer. I suggest that my concept of incomplete allowance (Cimet 1997) addresses the interaction as a double osmotic process between two parties, creating the possibility of not only addressing the effect the interaction has on the excluded but also on the exclusionist. This dialectic is crucial and has been noticed since Hegel and Nietschze, among others, but was also recently made essential in the work of Bourdieu and Foucault, for instance. There is no intent to diminish the integrity of any action when we label some actions mimicry; this is a term used to signal that much of any action is part of a learned repertoire, a habitus. That goes for all sides. It also does not imply that it cannot change. But change of consciousness and language as well as action require efforts and conscious intent that often involve a paradigmatic redirection.

23. Nobel laureate Octavio Paz (1998), who did not always maintain an unambiguous position towards indigenous cultures, has a poem that echoes some of what is said here (translation mine):

> *Mixcoac fue mi pueblo: tres silabas nocturnas*
> *Un antifaz de sombra sobre un rostro solar.*
> *Vino Nuestra Senora, la Tolvanera Madre.*
> *Vino y se lo comio. Yo andaba por el mundo.*
> *Mi casa fueron mis palabras, mi tumba el aire.*
> Mixcoac was my people: three night syllables
> A shadow mask over a solar face.
> Came our Lady, the Whirlwind's dust Mother.
> She came and she ate it. I walked through the world.
> My house was my words, my tomb the air.

24. Many intellectuals and individuals, even when they are not always active politically, have become sympathetic to the EZLN group. Others have used the moment to affirm the legacy of homogeneity. Trying to reject any guilt or shame because of the old process, recounting that it is an old battle and a settled battle, they do not see themselves as particularly contributing to the battle in any way directly, nor do they have any understanding of the reproductive nature of the ideology of the conqueror in which all citizens of the country are coparticipants.

RECONCILIATION AND REDRESS

Remembering and Forgetting: Creative Expression and Reconciliation in Post-Pinochet Chile

9

CHERYL NATZMER

TELLING THE STORY OF A NATION'S PAST is a highly political act involving struggles over whose stories will be remembered and preserved and whose memories will be repressed or forgotten. The ownership of memory is a question of power. Individuals and groups struggle over who has the right to represent the past and whose memories will become institutionalized. Creative expression is an arena where that struggle takes place and where it can be observed. Through the stories that people tell, the images they create, the social dramas they enact, and the institutions they embrace and resist, the events of the past are interpreted and transformed into social realities. Memories are given physical substance and become history. The struggle over memory is especially intense in societies recovering from periods of civil war, state terrorism, or ethnic conflict. In a society where the past is highly contested, the ability to create a social history or national narrative that can accommodate the memories of opposing groups may well determine the success of reconciliation efforts.

In the aftermath of seventeen years of military dictatorship and state terrorism, Chile is now in the process of working towards reconciliation as the forces of remembering and forgetting battle over how the story of the Pinochet years will be told. The task of reconciliation is to reestablish functional relationships between ideologically opposed groups and reconcile conflicting views of the past, in order to construct a history compatible with the memories of both sides. Reconciliation will be especially difficult in Chile. Unlike countries that have suffered under repressive, totalitarian governments and now have a consensus that the state was unjust in its actions, Chile has no such consensus. Some factions still argue that the violence and oppression in Chile were necessary to maintain the freedom and sovereignty of the state against the threat of communism. In contrast to

South Africa, where today few openly admit to being in favor of apartheid, in Chile there remain many supporters of Pinochet and his regime.

Chile is often likened to two nations sharing the same territory, but divided by an ideological chasm and opposing memories of the past. Pinochet supporters—rightwing conservatives composed primarily of Chilean elite, industrialists, and the military—view the 1973 coup that overthrew the socialist democratic government of Salvador Allende as inevitable and necessary to save Chile from communism and economic ruin. They remember the fear they felt for their lives and property when Allende was elected to office in 1970 in the heart of the Cold War. They recall the economic crisis, with inflation rates reaching 350 percent, and the political unrest of Allende's last months in office. They cite the miracle of Chilean economic growth as proof that the end product justifies the means. They are convinced that the economic austerity measures necessary for the economic recovery would not have been possible under a democracy. They believe atrocities were committed by both sides and that they are being exaggerated by the left. They contend that the best thing to do now is to forget about what may have happened in the past and to move on. As Pinochet expressed it in a speech on September 13, 1995, two days after the twenty-second anniversary of the military coup: "It is best to remain silent and to forget. It is the only thing to do: we must forget. And forgetting does not occur by opening cases, putting people in jail. FORGET, this is the word, and for this to occur, both sides have to forget and continue working" (Derechos Chile 1999, emphasis in original).

The opposition, comprised primarily of labor leaders, workers, leftist intellectuals, and families of the dead and "disappeared," remember the elation they felt when Salvador Allende became the first democratically elected Marxist president anywhere in the world. They remember the optimism of his early days when progressive programs such as labor reforms and land redistribution to indigenous peoples made the idea of a better life for the working class and minorities seem like a possibility. They remember the shock of the military coup and the image of *La Moneda* (the presidential palace) in flames as President Allende gave his life defending his democratically elected government. They remember the detention, torture, and execution of thousands of Allende supporters in the National Stadium. They remember living under enforced silence and the terror of seventeen years of state-conducted torture, disappearances, and death. They are calling for the truth about what happened to those who have disappeared. They demand a public admission of guilt and ask that those responsible be brought to justice. They contend that only through truth and justice can the healing process begin.

Chile's National Commission on Truth and Reconciliation—formed in 1990 by presidential decree just six weeks after Patricio Aylwin's inauguration as president of Chile—was an attempt to unveil the truth. The commission ideologically represented both sides. It consisted of four Pinochet supporters and four individuals who had been in opposition to the former government. It documented the cases of 2,920 disappearances, executions, and tortures leading to death by taking testimony from the families of the victims (Hayner 2001). The commission found that 95 percent of the violence could be attributed to state agents and only 4 percent to the armed left. This should have been enough to dispel Pinochet's claims that the continuing violence was necessary to put down leftist insurgents. Although the Rettig Report, which contained the results of the findings of the commission, was released to the public by President Aylwin on national television and published in an insert in a daily newspaper, it was not widely debated by the Chilean public. This contrasts sharply with the way the results of the Truth and Reconciliation Commission in South Africa were publicized. They were broadcast live over national radio each day and televised on Sunday evenings; stories were printed daily in the major newspapers during most of the two-and-a-half years of its operation. The people of Chile, however, did not feel comfortable or safe speaking about their truth commission's findings. At the time of the report's release, most Chileans did not believe that human rights issues had been resolved (Cleary 1997). Those in opposition to Pinochet still lived in silent fear of reprisals from the military. The Chilean media, which is considered to be—in theory—the watchdog of democracy, remained under control of the right.

Pinochet's arrest and the accusations for his crimes against humanity have opened up the possibility for a more public debate in Chile about those years. However, there remain differences of opinion as to the extent of torture, human rights abuses, and political executions carried out by the state from the time the democratically elected Allende government was overthrown in 1973 to 1990 when Pinochet stepped down as the totalitarian head of state. Part of this is because the National Commission on Truth and Reconciliation did not have a mandate to take testimony in cases of torture that did not result in death. This limit on the investigative powers of the commission silenced the voices of an estimated 50,000 to 200,000 torture survivors (Hayner 2001).

This chapter addresses the process of reconciling these various and often opposing memories to construct, reconstruct, and revise social history. It examines the social and psychological factors that contribute to the ideological struggle about how history will be told and contends that creative expression is a major arena where that struggle takes place and can be observed. It develops a model for the use of creative expression in the analysis of the struggle over social memory, followed by examples from the media, popular culture, and literature, as well as rituals in public spaces and personal narratives collected during fieldwork. Finally, the paper considers untold stories, the voices that remain silent. History is shaped not only by the stories that are told, but also by those that are silenced and or forgotten.

A Model for Constructing and Reconstructing the Past

In analyzing the struggle over how the story of the past will be told in post-Pinochet Chile, I draw on the model proposed by Teski and Climo for constructing and reconstructing the past through the memory repertoire (Teski and Climo 1995). Teski and Climo argue that memory is not a matter of simply recalling past experiences; rather, it is a complex and continuing process of selection, negotiation, and struggle over what will be remembered and what forgotten. The process involves remembering and forgetting, changing and restructuring one's perception of the past so that it both supports the needs of the present and projects a logical future. Individuals compose life narratives by picking through all the events of the past and selecting and highlighting those experiences that weave a cohesive story about where they have been and where they are headed (Bateson 1990). For a society, as well as for an individual, the past must be constructed, reconstructed, and continuously reinterpreted in light of present events and a vision of the future. According to the model, the past is almost as unknown to us as the future. Representations of past events, as written records, artifacts, and other forms, tend to stabilize memories, but at the same time open them up to new debates and interpretations about their meanings and significance. In order for reconciliation to take place in a divided society like Chile, a social history must be constructed that incorporates and makes sense of the memories of both sides. If the dominant side merely imposes its memory on the entire society, old conflicts will remain festering beneath the surface. But where and how does the struggle over memory take place? Where in society can the process be observed?

Thomas Abercrombie (1998) agrees that people make rather than inherit their past, and he suggests some interesting locations for the construction of memory. He argues, in *Pathways of Memory and Power,* that Western historians have tended to depend on oral narratives—which are linear like Western histories—when trying to reconstruct prehistoric Andean culture, while they exclude other forms of marking social memory specific to Andean culture. These Andean forms include ritualized singing, dancing, drinking, and sacrificing. Like Abercrombie, I believe that social memory is constructed and contested not only in oral narratives and written histories but also in a vast array of creative cultural expressions. I propose that the use of creative expression is not limited to Andean, Third World, or non-Western societies, but is a primary arena for the struggle over memory in all societies.

Creative expression encompasses a wide range of human behavior including speaking, writing, creating images, and performing, with the primary characteristic being the intention of communicating something to someone else. The communication can be in a form as simple as the stories told in everyday life or as complex as the stories communicated by museums, libraries, and educational institutions. Like Berger and Luckmann (1966), I view creative expression as a vehicle through which the subjective universe of individuals—their thoughts, memories, dreams, beliefs, and emotions—become part of the objective universe. Once objectified and made real, these representations from individual imagination can be observed, acted upon, reproduced, modified, debated, or passed on to the next generation. They can be adopted by groups or institutionalized by the state. As Garcia Canclini (1993) points out, the expression of creative artists is a prime site for discourse in response to change. Through stories, images, material representations, written texts, theatrical performances and demonstrations, dominant and subordinate groups struggle over what is to be remembered and what is to be forgotten (Castañeda 1997; Myerhoff 1992; Warren 1992, 1998). These stories of oppression and resistance, struggle and achievement, enter the public domain where they can be suppressed, transformed, or woven into the fabric of social reality.

Language, symbols, images, and actions reflect social identity and at the same time construct it. Creative expression provides an arena where cultural differences, social identities, and ideological values are produced and contested (Camnitzer 1994; Clifford 1988, 1997; Kleymeyer 1994; Marcus and Meyers 1995). It is a vehicle for materializing and giving form to cultural memory. The powerful try to institutionalize narratives that support their positions of dominance and power, while subordinate groups resist by finding ways to creatively express their own stories and insert them into the public consciousness. I view creative expression as a dynamic force for creating culture, resisting hegemony, and bringing about social change in all levels of society. If we accept that individuals and groups create social reality through the presentation and representation of themselves, then it follows, as Bourdieu and Wacquant (1992:14) state, that one can transform the world by transforming its representation.

This paper is based on representations of the Chilean situation in the media, popular culture, and literary works, as well as on my own observations and interviews conducted during an exploratory research project during the summer of 1997 in Temuco and Santiago and surrounding areas. The purpose of the research was to explore the manner in which material representations shape and are shaped by memory. Field methods included observations; informal interviews with a cross-section of Chilean society; visits to public sites that encompass memory including the General Cemetery, Pablo Neruda's home, and the Salvador Allende Solidarity Museum; and a pilot study on the material representation of memory. In the pilot study three participants were given a disposable camera and asked to photograph material objects that held particular meaning and significance in their lives. The participants were then interviewed and asked to construct a partial life narrative around these symbolic representations. Although the pilot study indicated that this particular research design needs to be modified and tested further, all three interviews yielded information about the thoughts, emotions, meanings, values, and beliefs of the participants—those subjective realities that are often difficult to elicit in the everyday process of fieldwork.

The Struggle over Memory Expressed in the Media, Popular Culture, and Literature

The arrest of General Augusto Pinochet in London in October of 1998 is a dramatic example of how present events can change memories of the past and cause a restructuring of the memory repertoire. It demonstrates how a change in representation can change the perception of reality, which then becomes a new reality. Regardless of whether he is brought to trial in Chile, the public accusations against Pinochet are potent symbolic acts. The charges that Pinochet is personally responsible for crimes against humanity—genocide, torture, and terrorism—committed under his dictatorship have started the debate about how the seventeen years under his authoritarian rule will be remembered out of the illicit shadows and onto the national and international stages. Although Chile returned to democracy in 1990, Pinochet remained a powerful figure. He was Commander-in-Chief of the Chilean army until March of 1998 and exerted tremendous control in the Senate through his self-appointed position as "Senator for Life."

Pinochet's detention by the British authorities and physical absence from Chile changed the power structure within Chile and its representation in acts of creative expression. Novelist Isabel Allende (1999), niece of Salvador Allende, noted a subtle but significant linguistic change: since his arrest, the Chilean media no longer refer to Pinochet as Senator for Life, but as "the former dictator." This signals a slippage of the state's power to impose and maintain its own version of history. It is especially significant since Chilean media, like those of most nations in the modern world (Fairclough 1989), are controlled by the right and express and reproduce the dominant ideology. This shift from Senator for Life, with its positive connotations of respectability and authority, to the negative connotations and implied loss of power embedded in the term former dictator, both reflects social reality and creates it through its transmission of a new representation to the audience.

The twenty-fifth anniversary of the military coup, September 11, 1998, stimulated the production of many new books. One of the most popular and influential in rewriting history is a book by Chilean journalist Patricia Verdugo, *Secret Interference*. It includes a CD of conversations secretly recorded by a ham radio operator between Pinochet and his fellow-officers during the bombing of the presidential palace. In the tape Pinochet is clearly heard saying in response to a question regarding the offer of safe passage to former president Salvador Allende, "The offer to take him out of the country is maintained . . . but the plane falls, old boy, when it's in flight" (Anderson 1998:50). This contradicts the dominant story imposed on history by Pinochet and his supporters, who contend that they intended to allow Allende to leave the country peacefully and that his suicide was an unnecessary act of cowardice.

It is not the authenticity or validity of the tape that interests us here, but that this alternative viewpoint has been allowed to surface now, twenty-five years after the coup. The fact that the book and tape were published and distributed in Chile and allowed to reach an international media audience shows that even before Pinochet's detention in London, the atmosphere in Chile was more open to the opposition voice. Pinochet's arrest and the publication of conflicting views of the confrontation between Pinochet and Allende have not changed the actual experiences of what happened, but the representation of events is changing. As the representation changes, the perception and understanding of the events is changing, which will ultimately affect the way the event is remembered historically.

Photographic representations are another location for the battle over how the past will be remembered. Photographs can serve as powerful tools to communicate a particular point of view, to create a mood or shape an opinion. Depictions of oppression, social unrest, protest demonstrations, and the victims of state torture and violence, as seen in the haunting images taken by human rights activist Marcelo Montecino (1994), give concrete form to memories otherwise subordinated to the state's will to forget. Montecino's artful images engage the viewer powerfully in confronting the universal horror of human rights abuses. A photograph is not, however, an objective documentation of reality. As Catherine Lutz and Jane Collins (1993) point out, a photograph is created by the person taking the photograph and, like other forms of creative expression, it reflects the perspective, values, and worldview of the creator. Photographers choose what to shoot and how to frame the image in order to communicate what they are trying to say. They direct the viewer to see the scene and respond to it emotionally in a directed and controlled way.

Lucia Pinochet, daughter of Augusto Pinochet, has published a large coffee-table book of photographs of her father. An example from Lucia Pinochet's book clearly demonstrates how a photograph can be manipulated to tell a particular story. One picture shows Pinochet on a visit to Madame Tussaud's Wax Museum in London. He wags his finger at a wax figure of Lenin as if to chastise him (Anderson 1998:47). The superposition of the image of the living Pinochet against that of a lifeless, powerless Lenin symbolically evokes the idea of Pinochet's victory and domination over communism. It idealizes Pinochet in his self-proclaimed role as the defender of Western civilization.

Media representations are usually carefully planned and orchestrated to maximize the drama of the moment and to appeal to national and international actors and audiences. But controlling the meaning of an image can be difficult. Creative expression sometimes communicates unintended messages. In a feature article on Pinochet in a London newspaper (Lawson 1999), a smiling Pinochet is pictured holding an infant in his lap and surrounded by six of his grandchildren. This large color photograph was obviously constructed to generate sympathy for Pinochet, the elderly grandfather whose arrest separated him from a loving family. However, three of the grandsons in the photograph wore Darth Maul T-shirts. Darth Maul, the villain from the most recent Star Wars film *The Phantom Menace*, was prominently displayed on the fronts of these children's shirts along with the words "The Dark Side." The irony of this contrast between good and evil, reality and fiction, could not have been lost on many viewers. This symbolic association between Pinochet's grandchildren and the dark side of American popular culture also reminds us consciously or unconsciously of the role that the U.S. played in the 1973 Chilean coup that brought Pinochet to power. Symbolic representations, whose power to communicate extends far beyond the boundaries of a particular event, can have a profound impact on social consciousness.

An important literary figure in the struggle over memory is Ariel Dorfman. Dorfman used symbolic representations effectively to oppose Pinochet's totalitarian regime and is now struggling with issues of reconciliation. Dorfman (1998:1) begins his memoir with the words "I should not be here to tell this story." An aide to Salvador Allende, Dorfman was scheduled for duty in La Moneda the day of the coup but had switched shifts with a fellow aide. He believes that he was spared from death so that he could tell his version of what happened that day and, through his writing, work towards truth and reconciliation. Dorfman's play, *la muerte y la doncella*, was made into the movie *Death and the Maiden*, directed by Roman Polanski and starring Sigourney Weaver and Ben Kingsley. It dramatizes the struggle between individuals over truth and meaning. In the film, a victim of torture thinks she recognizes the voice of her tormentor when a chance encounter brings a stranger into her home. Dorfman uses this situation to explore issues of reconciliation in praxis. He examines the psychological aspects of how individuals in their day-to-day activities intensify or resolve their hostilities. Dorfman raises a number of questions: How does one side live with the memories of atrocities committed and the other side justify their actions or live with the guilt? How do they learn to work together and interact in social situations? Can any true healing take place when people still live in fear and under the threat of military intervention? Is it legitimate to sacrifice the truth in order to preserve the peace and stability of the nation-state?

Books, plays, and films present the issues of reconciliation to a wide audience both within and outside of Chile. A question that needs further study is whether these representations actually help to resolve conflict. Do they encourage each side to better understand the experiences of the other and to empathize with their motivations? Or do reenactments and representations of conflict situations merely reinforce the ideology of the side responsible for producing the representation, while alienating the opposition?

The Struggle over Memory in Public Spaces

Spaces where events significant to a particular population have taken place can become depositories for memories. The spaces may become symbolic spaces where people go to gain a physical connection with important people and events from the past. Like other aspects of creative expression, these spaces can be manipulated to include some memories and exclude others and can become battlefields in the power struggle over memory.

The National Stadium in Santiago is such a contested space. It was the site of the largest detention camp in Santiago, holding an estimated 7,000 prisoners after the coup that overthrew the Allende government. It became a symbol of oppression, death, and despair, associated with memories of police interrogation, torture, and mock and real executions. Since that time there have been many attempts to impose other meanings and other memories on the space, to humanize it so that it can again play an active role in the social life of the people of Chile.

Patricio Aylwin, who was elected president of Chile after the plebiscite giving Pinochet a vote of no confidence in 1990, held his presidential victory celebration in the National Stadium, thus reclaiming the space for democracy. During the victory celebration, Chilean women whose husbands, sons, or other male relatives had been disappeared, danced the *cueca*, the national dance of Chile, *sola* or alone (Kleymeyer 1994:30). The cueca is always a couples dance, but for these women their only partner was a photograph of their disappeared relative pinned to their white blouses. This visual image, this dramatization of their social plight through the cueca sola, portrayed the pain and loss these women felt much more poignantly than words alone could have done. This poignant social protest by the women who refused to give up searching for their missing relatives was preserved and presented to an international audience by rock singer Sting in his song, "They Dance Alone."

Salvador Allende's daughter held a rock concert in the National Stadium to teach youth about her father's ideals of social justice and to counteract the misinformation about him propagated by the right (Anderson 1998). The concert attracted an estimated 70,000 people to the National Stadium in September 1997. A huge banner with a portrait of Allende hung over the stage. During a concert intermission, giant video screens showed the bombing of La Moneda by Pinochet forces on the day of the coup. Allende's last words, the words he used to speak to the people of Chile on the radio as the bombs were falling, were broadcast over the loudspeaker system:

> Surely Radio Magallanes will soon be silent and my quiet, metallic voice will no longer reach you. It does not matter because you will continue to hear me. I will always be with you. . . . Other patriots will overcome this bitter and gray moment. Always keep in mind that, sooner rather than later, the grand avenues through which the free man passes will open up, to build a better society. Long live Chile! Long live the people! Long live the workers!

The images, the sounds, and the social interaction of people created a theater of experience for the construction, reconstruction, and transformation of memory and for its embodiment in the personas of the participating actors. The staging of the memorial to Allende in the National Stadium also functioned to reclaim the space and its symbolic meaning for the living.

The ownership of memory is further objectified, contested, and preserved at the sites of public and private museums, memorials, and monuments. *La Chascona,* the private Santiago home of Chilean poet Pablo Neruda,[1] has become a symbol of resistance and of the power of ideas to withstand state repression. Neruda, a Nobel-prize-winning poet and Marxist spokesperson, died in 1973, just twelve days after the coup. He died of a broken heart, according to those who view his life and death as emblematic of socialistic ideals, and of prostate cancer, according to the medical records. After his death the state, in an effort to erase memories, destroyed many of Neruda's personal effects, rerouted a river to flood his home, and posted armed guards around the property to keep visitors away. Today Neruda's home has been restored by a private foundation and is open to the public. It is filled with fascinating objects that he collected in his travels around the world, ranging from delicate seashells to folk art, books, and paintings. Neruda's love of the sea is expressed in this town home through a dining room fitted out like a ship's galley. Neruda painted a blue line on the rocks outside the window to give the impression of a far horizon on the sea and ran a stream under the window so diners would get the feeling they were sailing along the water. The material objects, the spirit of playfulness embedded in the home's physical structure, and the stories related by tour guides now serve to remind visitors of the power of creative expression to nurture the human spirit and to resist oppression. As Neruda (1978:269) put it, "The child who doesn't play is not a child, but the man who doesn't play has lost forever the child who lived in him and he will certainly miss him." Neruda's home is a space for the mind and the spirit to play and to remember.

Possessing Pablo Neruda's work was strictly prohibited during Pinochet's dictatorship.[2] One of my informants described how she risked her life to smuggle a copy of Neruda's *Memoirs* into Chile for an older friend who had a burning desire to read it before he died. My informant narrated how her friend wept with joy when he saw the autobiography. He then tore the dust jacket off, burned it to ashes in the fireplace, carefully pasted the contents of the book inside the cover of another book, and replaced it on his bookshelf. To be discovered with a Neruda book in one's possession by the Chilean police would have been reason enough for severe reprisals, torture, and even death. Neruda, his writings, and his life itself symbolize resistance to the oppressive oligarchy of the right.

The General Cemetery in Santiago is another public site of struggle over memories. On September 11, 1997, the 24th anniversary of the coup, I was able to accompany a returned political exile and her two daughters, both students at the local university, to the General Cemetery to participate in this particular family's personal commemoration ceremony. For them, it was a day of sharing memories and ideologies, for demonstrating solidarity with the left, and for expressing resistance to national hegemony. They had been coming to the cemetery each year on September 11 since they returned from exile four years before, and the repetition of certain symbolic acts had given their actions the characteristics of ritual. The girls insisted that I accompany them to the cemetery. It was important to them that I, an outsider, witness their ritual and understand its significance to their family and the broader implications for the construction of memory in Chile. They described it beforehand in such detail that I could see before I experienced them the important symbolic aspects of each year's pilgrimage—red carnations, the mass graves, the graves of Salvador Allende and Victor Jara, the monument to the disappeared. The description that follows is colored by not only what I saw and heard on that September 11th visit, but also by the voices of the daughters talking in anticipation of the event.

I had made arrangements to attend a four o'clock memorial service for Salvador Allende at the General Cemetery with the exile family if the situation in the city did not appear to be too dangerous. The two o'clock television news showed images of a violent confrontation between protesters and the police at the General Cemetery, and the news commentator urged individuals to stay in their homes and avoid the streets. The violence had broken out after a peaceful morning memorial march of 4,500 Allende supporters from downtown Santiago to the cemetery in Recoleta. Many of the marchers carried placards with large black and white photographs of the disappeared and the words "*donde estan?*" (Where are they?). Television images showed protestors throwing rocks and molotov cocktails at tanklike vehicles that were firing water cannons at the crowds. *Carabineros* (police) were brandishing nightsticks and bulletproof shields as they struggled to arrest protestors. I was afraid that the violence would deter our visit to the cemetery, but I underestimated the determination of the exile family. They called soon after the news broadcast and said they would pick me up at the *Tobalaba* metro station at three o'clock for the drive to the cemetery.

We were met at the main cemetery entrance by armed guards who announced that the cemetery was closed for the remainder of the day. We parked the car and purchased red carnations from one of the flower venders lining the sidewalk along the main entrance. Then we walked around the periphery and entered the cemetery by a side entrance that was inexplicably unattended. We went first to the section where simple black iron crosses marked the mass graves of the unidentified, the *no nombre* or "no name" graves. Each gravesite held ten to twelve unidentified bodies. The young women, usually so talkative and animated, were solemn and subdued as we plowed through waist-high weeds and balanced on unidentifiable rubble to secure red carnations to several of the most desolate, the most forgotten graves. Next we walked to the National Memorial to the Dead and Disappeared[3] and placed a red carnation beneath the white marble wall. The wall lists the names and dates of birth and death of close to 3,000 individuals who were killed or executed by the Pinochet forces during the dictatorship. We observed that some of the victims had been children as young as three years old. On either side of the wall are rows and rows of empty drawers waiting for the remains of the disappeared and those bodies yet to be identified. The memorial serves as a physical space for coming together, remembering, and mourning for those families who have never learned what happened to their missing relatives nor recovered their bodies.

Carabineros on horseback blocked the path to Salvador Allende's grave, so we turned instead to the grave of Victor Jara, a folksinger who had been arrested in the middle of a concert soon after the coup. When he refused to stop singing, he was tortured, his hands were smashed, and he was executed in the National Stadium. Jara's songs became another symbol of the resistance. Even those songs without political content served as a signal among leftists during the years of repression. A few bars of a Jara song being hummed was enough to recognize others with like-minded political views.

We circled back again to the avenue that led to Salvador Allende's grave. It was strewn with the debris of the earlier confrontation between protesters and the police. Among the rubble from this confrontation, I was surprised to see hundreds of handbills with the face of a young Che Guevara, still a symbol of resistance in Chile, as well as many other parts of the world. The handbills, printed by FER, a leftist student group, contained the admonition "Study, Believe, Struggle, and Triumph." Finally, we placed the last of our red carnations next to thousands of others at the family crypt holding the remains of Salvador Allende. Small groups of people, perhaps two hundred in all, were gathered around the tomb talking reverently amongst themselves. A musician strummed a guitar and sang softly but melodiously.

People visit the Monument to the Dead and Disappeared in the National Cemetery in Santiago, Chile. Memory is embedded both in the monument with its names of over 3,000 individuals believed to have perished under the dictatorship of Augusto Pinochet and in the number of people who come together to remember. Courtesy of Cheryl Natzmer

For this family, as well as for thousands of others, commemorating the anniversary of the coup is a way to reconcile their emotions regarding the past. It is what Victor Turner (1982:12) calls a "social drama" that has "something of the investigative, judgmental, and even punitive character of law-in-action, and something of the sacred, mythic, numinous, even 'supernatural' character of religious action."

The Struggle over Memory in the Individual

The struggle over what will be remembered and what will be forgotten takes place not only on the national stage and in public confrontations but also in the day-to-day interactions of everyday life (Bourdieu 1977). The narratives that individuals relate in the home, at work, and in social spaces provide a vehicle for reflecting on and synthesizing experiences, ideals, and perceptions. The telling of a story involves the active participation of a teller and a listener and provides a platform for the intersubjective formation of new social realities. Sharing stories with children is a way of teaching and educating the child. The military coup that overthrew Salvador Allende occurred more than twenty-five years ago. The children of the opposing sides, the left and the right, the oppressors and the oppressed, are now young adults. The stories they have heard told and retold by their mothers and fathers, or alternatively the silences of stories not told, have shaped their own identities and their sense of place in history.

One of the participants in my pilot project on memory and material culture was a Chilean university student who had recently returned to Chile after having lived in political exile in Canada since he was three years old. I gave him a disposable camera and asked him to photograph material objects that represented important aspects of his life story or symbolized meaningful influences on his identity. After developing the photographs, I asked him to arrange the images in the order he would like to talk about them and to tell me why he had chosen each image. One of the photographs showed his parents, who had been social activists and supporters of Allende before the coup, sitting together on a couch. In response to their photograph, he told me the following narrative. It illustrates how the experiences of the parents have become a part of the shared histories, the vicarious memories of the children (Teski and Climo, N.d.):

> When my dad was arrested, the first thing they did was grab his wallet. Took everything out. He had a bunch of pictures of his sisters and one of my mum. The police said, "Who is this?" "That's my sister. That's my sister." And when he pointed to my mum's picture, he said, "That's my sister too." But the interrogator left all the pictures of the sisters on the right and separated the picture of my mum from the others and left it off to the side by itself. My father was afraid that they were looking for her and would find her from that photo. She was involved

> in the same activities that he was. When they interrogated women they raped them, they beat them, they tortured them. My father could not stand the thought that that would happen to my mother. 'I don't care if they kill me right now, they are not going to have a picture of her, they are not going to find her.' So when the police left the room, he leaned over, his hands were cuffed behind his back, but he leaned over, and he ate the picture, he ate the picture. He chewed it up and he swallowed it. He said, 'I don't care if they kill me right now, they are not going to find her.' They weren't even married yet. The things my mum did for my dad too. She waited for him. She could have found someone else, but she didn't. Then when he got out, my mum left everything to go with my dad. They left the country. I love them both for that. They have taught me so much. They taught me everything.

When I asked the young narrator about his own feelings regarding his father's experience of interrogation and torture, he responded:

> What was the terrible thing that my dad did that he had to die? Well, he didn't die, but he came close. The terrible thing my dad did, he gave poor people food, clothes. He taught poor children how to read and write. He helped them get organized and fight for their rights—the party of the popular. Some people say the country was in a bad state at that time. But I don't think it was in that bad a state that people had to die. It could have been done democratically if people weren't happy with the way things were.

The story that the student told me is not the same story that I relay above. It is not the same story that was told to the son by the father. The words may be exactly the same, but the context in which the story is told has changed. The reason for telling the story has changed. Nonverbal modes of communication such as gesture, timing, and inflection are absent from this representation of the narrative. The audience, whose reception of the story shapes its form and content, is different in all three cases. In the telling and retelling of a story, the narrative assumes social attributes and becomes an object itself quite apart from the experience, memories, and intentions of its originator.

Forgotten Memories

It is not only the memories expressed and contested that shape how history will be remembered but also those that are absent, ignored, or forgotten. Conceptualizing the struggle over memory in Chile as a left–right polarity ignores large segments of Chilean society whose stories are untold. For example, the *Mapuche,* an indigenous group that makes up approximately 10 percent of the Chilean population, was one of the most heavily repressed groups under the Pinochet dictatorship, yet the voice of the Mapuche is conspicuously absent from the reconciliation dialogue, as it is from most national discourse. Perhaps this is because the return to democracy has not brought an end to repression for the Mapuche (Ancan Jara 1997; Aylwin 1998).

Mapuche are engaged in an ongoing struggle to reclaim their ancestral lands. Under Pinochet, much of their land that was owned communally was divided and sold to private owners outside the Mapuche community. Land has traditionally been the basis of Mapuche economic, political, social, and religious institutions; to attack Mapuche landholdings is to attack the very essence of what it means to be Mapuche. Today many Mapuche live under conditions of extreme poverty in rural areas of southern Chile where they are battling the encroachment of corporate and state development projects. The lumbering activities of *Forestal Arauco* in Lumaco, the Ralco Dam project, and the proposed construction of coastal and inland highways through Mapuche territories are meeting active resistance from the Mapuche. An equal number of Mapuche have migrated to the cities,[4] especially to Santiago, where they have lost many of their cultural traditions and become almost invisible. Reconciliation for the Mapuche would entail not only truth and justice for past oppression but also economic justice and recognition and respect for their rights to their cultural autonomy in the present.

Others have learned silence from years of living in fear. They keep a low profile out of habit and their stories are unlikely to be told. A cab driver in the south of Chile overheard one of our party talking about having been active in the socialist movement and living in exile. He recounted his own experiences. He was a seventeen-year-old university student at the time of the coup. He was arrested, interrogated with a gun to his temple, and then for reasons he never knew, released. The school, which was known to be supportive of the socialist government of Allende, was destroyed, and most students and professors were killed. This man managed to flee with his wife and young children across the border into Argentina, where he got a job working for Exxon. In the mid-1980s, he was forced to return to Chile. The political oppression in Argentina made it more dangerous to remain there than to return home. Even though Chile has returned to democracy, he continues to live in fear. He is afraid to register to vote for fear that something will happen to his wife and children. He doesn't want to assume a position with any profile higher than that of a taxi driver. He wants to be invisible within the society. We do not hear the stories of countless other ordinary people whose lives, youthful dreams, and potential were disrupted by the military repression.

The Chilean middle class, with a vested interest in neoliberal economic expansion, is often more concerned with getting ahead or maintaining its lifestyle than with ideological conflict. I talked with a middle-aged woman who struggles to pay her monthly rent in an upper-income suburb of Santiago by peddling cheese from door to door. Although the economic status and political conservatism of her family allowed her to remain aloof from the political struggles of the Pinochet years, her cousin, who was a leftist agitator, is one of the disappeared. She has close ties to her aunt, the mother of the disappeared cousin, and often interacts through phone calls and visits. The aunt has never stopped searching for her son and has traveled internationally to draw on family political connections to try to gather information on his whereabouts. This story could be a part of the ongoing narrative that makes up the story of the cheese seller's life. But it is not. Her focus is on the intense struggle to maintain her middle-class status, and the present absorbs her energies. Like those who suffer guilt or remorse for the crimes they committed and those who by their inaction allowed atrocities to be committed, she avoids political discussions and believes it is best to forget the past.

Museums institutionalize, legitimize, and preserve memories of the past. The controlling oligarchy of the right has long held power over Chilean public spaces that might otherwise be locations for dialogue. These spaces need to be opened up if Chile is to become a participatory democracy. The wealthy elite has used its hegemonic powers to repress the voices of dissent in public institutions. Art museums in Chile favor the classical over the contemporary, the international over the local. Through this process of selection, they are able to effectively censor works with social or political content.

For example, where are the displays of *arpilleras* in Chilean museums? Arpilleras are patchwork pictures created from scraps of material by the mothers, sisters, and wives of the disappeared in the slums of Santiago. They depict stories of the everyday life of individuals under extreme oppression. At the same time, they demonstrate the power of ordinary individuals to resist the tyranny of the powerful and to bring about social change (Agosin 1996). The women of Chile sewed their personal stories and emotions into these wall hangings. They encompass images of police brutality, torture, executions, the abduction of loved ones, and the endless search for missing relatives, yet the tapestries are far from dour. They are brightly colored, imaginative, and filled with energy, emotion, and activity. They reflect the resilient spirit of these women who would not give up searching for their loved ones and who risked their very lives to tell their stories. Creating the tapestries within the solidarity of the collaborative tapestry workshops served as therapy and an emotional release from the fear, terror, and despair of their everyday lives. The sale of the tapestries provided income for families, many of whom had lost their primary breadwinner. The arpilleras were smuggled out of Chile and have been exhibited throughout the world. They were instrumental in raising international awareness of human rights violations under the Pinochet dictatorship. One would expect that with the return to democracy, these tapestries, which are so rich in memory, would be considered national treasures and that efforts would be made to preserve, celebrate, and exhibit them. However, the women's continuing demands for truth and justice—demands that those responsible be brought to trial—are viewed as a destabilizing threat to the young democracy and a hindrance to the reconciliation process (Agosin 1996). Instead of being honored and celebrated, the arpillera makers today are marginalized and isolated in Chilean society and have come to symbolize other silenced and forgotten voices.

Conclusion: Further Questions

This chapter has examined the ways individuals and groups use creative expression to construct, reconstruct, and transform memories, as they are embedded in particular people, places, objects, and events. As representations change, perceptions of the past as well as the future also change. A question that merits further study is whether creative expression in and of itself provides a healing experience for society. Do the telling of stories, the enacting of social dramas, the creation of images, and the recreation of events provide a psychological release? Do they provide experiences in self-expression to individuals who have lived under the threat of state censorship and military intervention and need to relearn how to express themselves in a participatory democracy? Does recreating and reimagining the past encourage dialogue across ideological gulfs and help each side to understand the other? Or does remembering merely fan the flames of controversy, increase hostilities, and intensify difference?

Some Chileans say it is time to forget the past and look to the future. Others say that only through remembering can the mistakes of the past be avoided and the healing process begin. The forces of remembering and forgetting continue to battle in Chile, and the praxis of their struggle will shape history as well as the future.

Acknowledgments

An earlier version of this paper was presented at the Central States Anthropology Conference in Chicago in 1999; the questions and comments received there were helpful in shaping its present form. I would like to thank the editors of this book, Maria Cattell and Jacob Climo, for their vision and guidance, and Kate O'Neill, Merrill Evans, Dewey Lawrence, and Charles Nicholson for exchanging ideas and comments on earlier drafts and or making suggestions for sources. Thanks also go to the Center for Latin American and Caribbean Studies (CLACS) and The Center for Advanced Study of International Development (CASID) at Michigan State University for funding the pilot project research in Santiago and Temuco, Chile, and to the informants and pilot project participants in Chile who were so generous with their time, their friendship, and their stories.

Notes

1. Pablo Neruda, born in Parral, Chile in 1904, is one of the best-known and best-loved poets of the twentieth century. He shared the World Peace Prize with Paul Robeson and Pablo Picasso in 1950 and was awarded the Nobel Prize for Literature in 1971.

2. Censorship was used as a means of social control by the state during the Pinochet years. Artwork that was modern and of an international style was supported by the state and allowed to be shown in public spaces—theaters, museums, concert halls. Local art and artists, as well as art forms with social content, were repressed.

3. The National Monument to the Dead and Disappeared in the General Cemetery in Santiago, Chile is the first monument in all of Latin America to commemorate the plight of the disappeared, those whose political deaths have never been confirmed and whose bodies have never been recovered.

4. The 1992 Chilean census revealed that close to one million individuals identified themselves as Mapuche and that of those individuals who claimed Mapuche heritage, over 50 percent now live in urban areas (Ancan Jara 1997).

The Meshingomesia Indian Village Schoolhouse in Memory and History

10

LARRY NESPER

> *[I]t is the spatial image alone that, by reason of its stability, gives us an illusion of not having changed through time and of retrieving the past in the present. But that's how memory is defined. Space alone is stable enough to endure without growing old or losing any of its parts.*
>
> —MAURICE HALBWACHS (1980:157)

IN 1998, 79-YEAR-OLD LORA SIDERS was the tribal historian of the Miami Indians of Indiana. It was an office created for her that honored the value of her memory among these no longer federally recognized indigenous people. As far as she or anyone else knew, she was the only living Miami Indian with personal memories of the schoolhouse:

> Otho Winger[1] was very close to my family because he was my father's teacher and he used to come to our house and visit us. That, possibly, is the beginning of my connection with the schoolhouse. . . . My father never went anyplace. About the only place he ever went was to one of my uncles and one of my aunts. Other than that, don't ask him to go anyplace because he wouldn't go. But, if there was a meeting up around Jalapa he would go, and we never went there and didn't go and visit the school.

I saw the Miami Indian Village Schoolhouse for the first time on a warm, rainy day in February of 1998. Earlier in the year, Elizabeth Glenn had offered to show me some of the sites in Miami Indian country in east central Indiana as I would be teaching Indians of the Great Lakes in the spring and might want to bring students out on a field trip. I succeeded Elizabeth in the anthropology department at Ball State University in the fall of 1997. For the last couple of decades she has worked with the tribe, a group of people of whom Charles Callendar (1978:687) wrote: "Very little is known about the Indiana Miami, who are usually assumed to be almost entirely acculturated." Known by whom, we might ask, and "entirely acculturated" by whose standards?

We had just visited the Meshingomesia Cemetery, the largest Indian cemetery in the state, where there are about forty marked graves of members of the community who lived on the state's last Indian reservation toward the end of the nineteenth century. The community of relatives and descendants of their chief Metocina had been living, by the good graces of the chief Meshingomesia, on a reserve granted to his father in the Treaty of 1840. Six miles east of Marion, the area is rural, and as it is within a quarter mile of the Mississinewa River, unlike most of the northern half of the state, the land rolls somewhat.

As we drove across a timber-floored one-lane bridge, at a *T* in the road, Elizabeth pointed to what I took to be a shack about twenty feet square, standing near a defunct concrete silo, and identified it as the schoolhouse. She said there would be a meeting, a gathering, there in a few days, as the Miami were trying to get it back from the descendants of someone who appropriated it fifty or sixty years ago.[2] It had deteriorated to the point that it was no longer useful as a corncrib. Across the road, a brick house with a brick porch on at least two sides distracted my attention for a moment. Elizabeth noticed my noticing it and said that it had belonged to Nelson Aw-taw-aw-taw, Meshingomesia's grandson, a hundred years ago. A non-Indian family now occupied it.

The wooden schoolhouse was covered with rusted corrugated iron on the sides I could see. It rested a bit precariously on three rows of concrete block that were listing distinctly to the east. The windows had been boarded up. I noted a Christmas wreath on the door. Perhaps it was the mist, or the slap of the windshield wipers, or the dreariness of February, but I found the schoolhouse to be rather pathetic. Then I remembered that a chemist cannot discover the value of gold, and that the meaning of an object inheres in the historical system of relationships within which it exists, not in the object itself.

We looked at the shack from the road, then went on to the Godfroy cemetery a few miles away, where about as many other Miamis were also buried, many of these more recently. At one time Frances Godfroy, last war chief of the Miami, held a 5,000-acre parcel of land near the confluence of the Mississinewa and Wabash Rivers. In the 1850s, he took in some of those Miamis who had returned after following their relatives to the West during the Removal Period. Called Mt. Pleasant at the time, his wooden frame house was across the road and also in the possession of non-Indians.[3] Elizabeth pointed out graves and told me who was who. She noted the black granite gravestone of Edward Siders and his wife, Lora Siders Marks, whose birthdate only was etched into the dark rock: 1919. We were on our way to visit Lora at the Tribal Center in Peru, Indiana, in a high school building the tribe bought from the city in 1990 because, in recently elected Chief Paul Strack's words, "It was cheaper to sell for a hundred dollars than it was to destroy."

Indian Village School, 1896–1897. This church and school were the center of many Indian activities for forty years

School house dedication. Courtesy of L. Nesper

Historical Realities

Miamis were first encountered by the French in the middle of the seventeenth century. They were in diaspora. A significant contingent was the dominating group in a massive multiethnic refugee village in the Fox River Valley near Lake Winnebago, in what would become Wisconsin. With the decline of Iroquois hegemony in the late eighteenth century, a part of that group returned to the Upper Wabash-Maumee River area and settled on the portage at Kekionga (now Fort Wayne), between the continent's interior Mississippi drainage basin and the Great Lakes (Wepler 1984:1–12). They grew a unique form of white corn and let the world come to them.[4] They allied with and married the French, then allied with the English against the Americans. In the century-long period that the United States regarded the indigenous inhabitants as fully sovereign, between 1795 and 1871, Miami chiefs ceded most of the tribal estate over the course of nineteen treaties. Enacting the benefits of an aristocratic multicultural disposition, highborn Miamis reserved lands for themselves and their families, thus escaping removal.

At midcentury after the 1846 removal and the return of over 100 Miamis who had spent some time in Kansas, the Miami men who could afford it wore scarves wrapped around their heads like turbans and frock coats and ruffled shirts over breechcloths, leggings, and moccasins. Women wore dark, full broadcloth ankle-length skirts and loose-fitting, brightly colored blouses, leggings with ribbon work, and—commonly—several pair of earrings (Rafert 1996:104). These were all local signs of distinction in a cosmopolitan idiom.[5]

There were about 250 people in seven exogamous, intermarrying, extended family groups led by a council of chiefs that had negotiated the individual reserves. The residential community living on a ten-square-mile tract on the north bank of the Mississinewa River in Grant County was led by Meshingomesia, who built the schoolhouse and the Miami Union Baptist Church in the early 1860s. Meshingomesia himself was baptized earlier "on a Sunday in June, 1861" (Rolland 1914:53; Winger 1943:74).

This putatively assimilative orientation represented a longtime Miami geopolitical strategy of effectively trading off certain surface cultural practices for social separation and distinction. This disposition was not unlike the equally hierarchical southeastern Cherokees, who also sought to maintain their integrity in a kind of reduplicative articulation with the encompassing non-Indian society. It is not insignificant that the Miamis regarded the Cherokees as their ancient enemies. It was in a conflict with the Cherokees that the Miamis received the name by which they know themselves (Trowbridge 1938:8). This accommodative strategy may be a general characteristic of indigenous groups with emergent classes. "Only among the Miamis did the French recognize leaders who seemed to possess power in the French sense" (White 1991:37). Indeed, George Hyde, using Nicholas Perrot's materials on

Major Miami Sites
circa 1847–1872

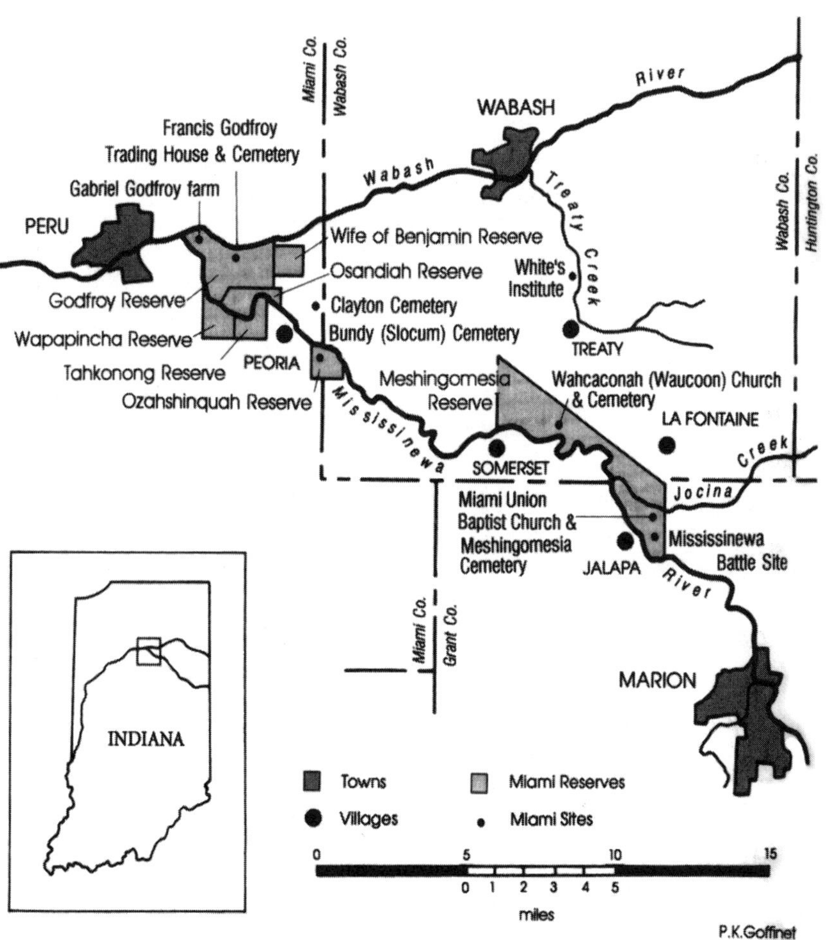

Major Miami sites, circa 1847–1872. Courtesy of Indiana Historical Society

the Miamis, suggested that the Miamis had "acquired a sun-king tradition from cultural contacts with either Mississippian mound builders or southwestern tribes, since all Miami chiefs wielded great power" (Anson 1970:14). Vernon Kinietz (1991:180) quotes Claude de la Potherie's seventeenth century history: "Among these latter was the head chief of the Miamis, named Tetinchoua, who, as if he had been the king, kept in his cabin day and night forty young men as a body guard. The Village that he governed was one of four to five thousand warriors: he was, in a word, feared and respected by all his neighbors."

The mound building reference is tantalizing. A people without "legends or myths of previous migrations" (Anson 1970:15), the Miamis were always well within the region designated by Robert Jeske's (1996) map of selected Mississippian and Upper Mississippian sites in the upper Midwest. They are clearly within the Cahokian sphere of influence or periphery, the site of the largest earthwork north of Mexico and a town more populous than London a thousand years ago. Whether affiliated with this ancient metropolis or not, the historic Miamis were a chiefly frontier people, clearly inclined to broker wealth between world systems.

Unlike many of their fellow Algonquians to the north, for whom leadership is a matter of acts, Miami leadership is a matter of being, that is, of descent. "Their chiefs are hereditary," Trowbridge (1938:13) wrote in 1824–25, his only named informants being the chiefs Le Gros and Richardville (vi). Later in the nineteenth century, Meshingomesia, eldest of the ten sons of Chief Metocina, "sometimes arranged marriages, performed marriage rites, removed children from parents who were neglectful or abusive, suggested adoptions, and ousted troublemakers from the village community . . . invited homeless Indians to the reservation . . . worked to maintain tribal rights, attended treaty negotiations . . . [and] . . . disbursed payments of annuities" (Rafert 1996:140–141). In the twentieth century, Miami leaders still compete for political legitimacy in the cultural idiom of genealogy. Though they are elected, it is, more often than not, a competition between members of the Richardville-LaFontaine and Meshingomesia clans or extended family groups—groups that exist by virtue of the memory of chiefs—who rise to candidacy on the basis of their distinction and whose personal projects are the life of the community.[6]

The Schoolhouse in Memory and History

How does this late-twentieth-century schoolhouse project relate to the longer cultural history? Lora Siders Marks remembered the schoolhouse:

> Well then, my mother died and I don't remember us going back. Probably the last time I visited that school was in the late twenties or early thirties. And then when I went back—I had lived away from here—doing different things. When I did go

back, there was a house there, and the school was gone. I assumed that the school had fallen in. Because, I think when I first started going there, the church was there, but it was in such bad repair we never bothered the church. Well, we would go to the door and look in, and I know there was practically no flooring so we stayed away from it. We would just go to the doorway and look in. Then of course, when we went back, there was nothing there, so I assumed that everything had fallen in. Until Chief Shoemaker[7] and his brother and I went to the attorneys in Marion and wanted to know why this house was built there. That was land that belonged to the cemetery, and then we found out that the school was not demolished, that it had been moved by a neighbor. When we approached Ray White [appointed chairman of the tribe in 1978 by Chief Shoemaker[8]] even though none of his folks ever went to that school, it still was the Miami Indian School and he was in favor of having Miami Indian things back in order. He was kind of a go-getter.

Lora Siders' personal memory motivated and mediated the chief repatriation project at a time when repatriation was becoming a symbol of autonomy. The Native American Graves Protection and Repatriation Act, passed by Congress in November of 1990, regulates archaeological excavations of Native American burial sites, prohibits their looting, and requires the return of culturally affiliated skeletal and burial goods in the possession of all federally funded museums to recognized federal Indian tribes. The law represents a sea change in federal policy with important implications for the country's native peoples. The private repatriation of a structure to a site of burials by a formerly federally recognized tribe represents an innovative transformation of the relationships between political communities in the context of this legislation. The repatriation of public architecture to the site of human burials is more than an accidental association. Pre- and protocontact chiefdoms associated the honored dead, the living elite, and the future in quite the same manner. This reimagining of the landscape along deeply traditional and ancient lines is the means of reconstituting a past in space that legitimates the present, the point made by Halbswach in the epigraph that opens this chapter. The project itself was a sign of the vitality of this community.

The schoolhouse was being remembered and repatriated. It was Lora Siders' honoring of Chief Shoemaker's desire to have the building back, returned to its original necropolitan location. Miamis visit the cemetery, a local *axis mundi,* as a kind of pilgrimage site. Wap Shing, the current spiritual leader at Peru, conducts healing ceremonies there. The schoolhouse itself was a site wherein the Miami people remembered and reimagined themselves as a people in the nineteenth century. From May 14 until July 7, 1873, scores of Miami people sat down with federal congressional commissioners in the schoolhouse, to make partition of the reserve, and spoke of their memories of their relatedness—who their parents, aunts, and uncles were, who their brothers and sisters, children, and grandchildren were, who they married and their children, the ages of all these people, whether they were living or dead, how they died, and when they came to live on the Meshingomesia reserve. It was a rehearsal for the General Allotment Act fourteen years later that divided up nearly all the tribal estates, distributed the land to individuals, and sold the surplus to non-Indians. Collectively, Indian people would lose 90 of 138 million acres between 1887 and 1934, when the policy was reversed. Sasaquaseah (quoted in Rafert and Marks 1991:156) testified: "I want to drop it here. I want to live here so when I die I will have a place prepared for me in the other world. I don't care how poor I am here. I want to be pure in heart so when I die I will have a place prepared for me."

With the reserve allotted to individuals, the landholdings were moved into the hands of the more capitalized non-Indian commercial farmers over the course of the last quarter of the nineteenth century. And in 1897, in response to a question as to how to litigate a case against the state of Indiana regarding taxation, the Assistant Attorney General of the United States informed the tribal leadership that they were no longer an Indian tribe under federal law.

This devastating event is remembered as the greatest of all possible betrayals and has motivated a series of undertakings that have transformed the historicity of this relatively socially distinct, superficially culturally assimilated group of communities over the course of the last century. They liquidated their mobile material patrimony in the early twentieth century, then later performed Indian pageants[9] in order to purchase the services of lawyers to speak on their behalf to the BIA and to Congress. Miami extended families—factionalized in response to the Indian Claims Commission—made, broke, and remade alliances with each other. They reconciled in the assembly of an exemplary application for federal recognition under the guidelines established by the Bureau of Indian Affairs in 1978, only to have it turned down in the early 1990s. All of these undertakings valorized memory,[10] even as the process of remembering strengthened the competing claims of family leaders for the leadership of the entire tribe. Lora's memory of her father's love for the school he attended before the termination personalized this repatriation of the landscape he was so disinclined to leave.

By the late 1990s, most of the 4,500 Eastern Miamis are working class and live in the small, declining rust-belt cities in the Upper Wabash River Valley. Socially and politically, the Miamis understand themselves to live in families or clans, named after the mid-nineteenth century chiefs and community leaders. These are transformations of the lineages that were so prominent in the Omaha kinship system they displayed in earlier centuries (Callendar 1978:611). This self-identification as descendants replicates the manner in which the tribal divisions in the eighteenth century came to be named. The Wea division of the Miamis was named for the Kekionga expatriate *Wuyoakeetonwau,* and the Piankeshaws were named for the Wea expatriate *Puyunkeeshau* (Trowbridge 1938:11). Representation on the tribal council today is by family or clan, as Miami people tellingly refer to them. And residence in these small cities of eastern Indiana reiterates this inclination. Today, 93 percent of the Miamis living in Peru are Godfroy descendants, 79 percent of the Miamis living in Huntington at the forks of the Wabash River are Richardville-LaFontaine, and in Marion, 72 percent of the Miamis are Meshingomesia (Rafert 1996:286). Over the course of the twentieth century, the Miamis came to trace descent bilaterally and marry non-Indians, the effect being to reinforce the boundaries between the groups that constitute the tribe (Greenbaum 1990:7).

Rehearsal for Repatriation: A Remembering Project

A decade and a half before it became a legal fact, the Miamis began the process of rehearsing provisions of the Native American Graves Protection and Repatriation Act, with the aforementioned Chief Shoemaker's announced desire "to put Miami things in order."

Lora Siders was the sole Miami with memories of the schoolhouse in its original location. It was by virtue of her memories of the schoolhouse and her now-passed sister Carmen that she was the tribe's historian in the 1990s. She had been a council member and knew she was a descendant of the nineteenth century polygamous chief Godfroy's second wife, Mary Mongosa. Mongosas have acted as mediators over the course of the century (Greenbaum 1990:11). Lora was not only located in the set of Miami historical relations, however. Chiefly in her own right, and acting chief for a short time in the early 1990s, she also mediated contemporary intercultural relations. Her personal memory honored Chief Shoemaker's desire. She shared that desire with the spiritual leader, Wap Shing, who wanted to draw some attention away from the land as significant only for its value as a War of 1812 battle site.[11] Wap Shing, in turn, shared this desire with non-tribal member Joan Calvert, who has worked very diligently to make repatriation possible by pursuing legal and social avenues for a number of years entirely at her own expense. Even this historical process is culturally structured.

The Miami people have always lived in a context of other societies, other peoples. The very location of their villages—for example, Kekionga, established on the portage between the headwaters of the Maumee and the Wabash, after their return from Iroquois-induced diaspora in Wisconsin in the seventeenth century—was motivated by a desire to mediate the French relationship with other tribes. Though Miami people made some of their living from growing that special white corn, they were also hunters, gatherers, and traders. Cosmologically, they are Algonquian hunters. As such, the social and cultural project was to cross social and conceptual boundaries for the purpose of procuring value and then to transform that into local social and spiritual wealth. This is as true for animal bodies, guardian spirits, and trade goods, as it is for monotheism and so-called non-Miami persons. Cultural icon Frances Slocum may be the paradigmatic case: a white child captive who would become a village chief's wife.[12] Shortly after a reunion with her brothers and sister, all in their sixties and seventies, her nephew George would come from the East to successfully bring the Miamis the Baptist faith but fail to teach them the skills and dispositions to be successful at commercial agriculture.

Wap Shing, the current spiritual leader at Peru, was raised in the Netherlands, and is a former Episcopal priest. His kinship ties are primarily adoptive. But, then again, more than three hundred years ago, LaSalle credibly and ceremonially presented himself to these Miamis' ancestors as the symbolically reincarnated *Ouabicolata* and was adopted as a relative (Hall 1997:10–13). Joan Calvert, the most active agent in the schoolhouse repatriation project to reconstitute a local Miami landscape of built form, was a nontribal member, though one who both imagined herself and was imagined to be somehow descended from Indiana's indigenous people. Indeed, Lora Siders would tell Joan that she felt that Chief Ray White's spirit was working through her.[13] This disposition to adopt, absorb, and assimilate people is widespread in the Great Lakes region and is a stark commentary on western ideas about race and ethnicity.

This valorization of history and built form is motivated in a dialogue of both internal and external social and cultural forces. Miamis struggled for recognition of their social and cultural distinction for the entire twentieth century. The non-Indian residents legitimize their own presence on the landscape by memorializing and temporalizing the idea of an Indian presence.[14] Warder Crow's letter to his nephew is exemplary in its nostalgia by referring to "the first owners of the land" (Crow 1936:2). Of the Meshingomesia cemetery itself he writes "their monuments and the ruined church are mute testimony of the extinction of a people once all powerful in our beloved Indiana" (Crow 1936:7). Miamis have had to show that they still exist and do it on terms that are recognizable to their local and potentially sympathetic non-Indian allies. They have had to demonstrate their historical existence and presence. This appropriation of exogenous concern for the past, however, converges with the endogenous valuing of the past, because of the role that descent has always played in the legitimization of political power, as is the case in any chieftainship.

This local dialectic resides in a larger context. The proliferation of emergent local identities, in many cases as revitalizations of historic ethnicities, represents the decline of Western hegemony. In Friedman's (1994) terms, dehegemonization and dehomogenization are aspects of the same process. The grand national narrative, the one we all learned in grammar and high school, the one that relegated people like the Miamis and other tribal people to a periphery in America's imagination, is on the decline. The form of this community's undertaking—the repatriation of an arguably colonialist institutional structure, a one-room schoolhouse—is not accidental either. It is a part of the global heritage movement Urry (1990:52) writes about. He situates it in "[t]he loss of trust of the future as it is undermined by . . . instantaneous time and the proliferation of incalculable risk; the view that contemporary social life is deeply disappointing and that there really was a golden age in the past; the increased aesthetic sensibility to signs or the patina of oldness, to old places, crafts, houses, countryside and so on."

Ray White, Miami chief in the early 1990s who transmitted the previous chief's desire to repatriate the schoolhouse, worked in the declining east central Indiana city of Muncie as an autoworker. He was active in the union leadership and spent his mature working years observing the signs of the deindustrialization of these small Midwestern cities. It could not have been lost on him that the strategy of migrating to the cities as factory workers that his people undertook in the twentieth century was losing viability.

The "loss of trust of the future" and the sense of "risk," "disappointment," and nostalgia for "a golden age" expressed by Urry (1990) have not only crossed social and cultural borders into peripheral sectors, they have become the basis of the possibility for a future for marginalized, peripheral regions. The schoolhouse project has this heritage dimension. Lora said that she would like to repatriate the Nelson Aw-taw-aw-taw house, where she remembers being told that the men played cards and socialized downstairs and the women sewed and talked upstairs. She would like to repatriate and restore the rest of the village near the old cemetery as well.

Intratribally, such remembering projects are part of the strategy of producing political legitimacy. The Huntington branch of the Miamis, mostly descendants of Richardville, sponsored tours of the Richardville-LaFontaine nineteenth-century brick house as part of the annual powwow in mid-August. The tribal council room at the Miami Tribal Center in Peru, with its tree stump reputedly from the site of the treaty signed in the early nineteenth century; the meeting house that was built at Seven Pillars on the Mississinewa River; the Chiefs' House in Huntington; the Bundy-Slocum, Godfroy, and Meshingomesia cemeteries; and now the Miami Indian Schoolhouse—all these are sites *of* memory but also sites *for* memory.[15] Marea Teski and Jacob Climo (1995:2) write that "Memory is not recall. Rather, it is a continuous process based on rumination by individuals and groups on the content and meaning of the recent and more distant past," and I would add, done in the service of constituting a present and a future and undertaken from a particular location.

Repatriation of the Schoolhouse

A few days after I saw the schoolhouse for the first time, we returned there to look at it with everyone who was involved in the process of its repatriation. It was a stunningly beautiful day—warm, bright, clear. This was the day that the recently constituted Schoolhouse Committee—tribal members Lora Siders, Carolyn Knauf, and Tom LeVonture—would visit the site as a group for the first time. It was anticipated to be significant, as it was an effort to motivate and enfranchise the committee members in the project Lora had inherited, as well as others who were interested in the schoolhouse project. These included Wap Shing, Joan Calvert, and former state senator Lauren Winger, son of Otho, who had procured funds for the tribe to purchase the building; the current owners of the schoolhouse; the prospective restoration specialist; and a representative of the Lions Club.

Lora gave the people who came a packet of the following photocopied documents:

1. the most recent correspondence from the tribe's attorney interpreting the most recent correspondence from the attorney representing Larry Stuber, current owner of the schoolhouse;
2. a one-page fragment of Peconga's autobiography typed in Miami with hand-written interlinear translation;
3. a document written on Miami Nation of Indians of the State of Indiana stationery entitled "School Cast" and identifying principals in the project;
4. a photo of the students in the second brick Indian Village School from 1906;
5. the Commissioner's Deed conveying the cemetery property to the Tribe, November 21, 1984; and
6. the Indiana Property Record Card for the cemetery.

Some part of enfranchisement was accomplished with these gifts. The dissemination of this order of information testifies to the past existence and significance of what Lora remembered. The group spent an hour looking at the building, then moved a quarter mile away to the cemetery to look at both its original site and to choose a site where the restored building would be placed.

Lora said she wanted to have a reunion of the people who came out to the schoolhouse that day, an example of the social and political dimensions of the repatriation process in shaping memory. The value of Lora's memory is altered by virtue of the quality of the social interaction on that day, by virtue of the sunshine, the warmth, the good feeling. I remember her leaning against the tombstone of Camillus Aw-taw-aw-taw, exhausted after hours of reminiscing, visiting, videotaping, dreaming about the future of this little necropolis, this life-giving land of the dead. Her memory of that day, now repeated more than once to the principals in this process, has enhanced the value of that day and this project.

The Ceremonial Transfer

In the bright, hot, and humid mid-afternoon of Saturday, September 19, 1998, nearly one hundred people, three-fourths of whom were tribal members, gathered at the schoolhouse for a Ceremony to Commemorate the Gift of the Miami School Building. Carolyn Knauf's husband, Harry, gave away copies of a postcard photograph depicting the extended Godfroy family at the turn of the twentieth century and marketed by the Eiteljorg Museum in Indianapolis. Al Harker, the tribe's attorney, presided over the transfer of the deed from Larry Stuber to Paul Strack, the recently elected chief of the Miami Tribe. Just as the principals were gathering outside the building, I asked Schoolhouse Committee member Tom Le Vonture, what he thought this meant:

> You see markers on the highways about where things *used to be,* now you are going to see a marker of where something *still is.* When you add that third dimension to history, it makes it more real and makes it easier to grasp. The man off the street, now he sees and thinks, "Well, this was reservation land." It would have been my great-great-great-great-grandfather who paid to build this school. It was on his land. He owned it, but he did it for them, for his people, for his grandchildren. *So* it helps to change that perception that Indians were isolationists. They embraced education. Education, at that time, was a fundamental tool for basic survival in this ever-changing society.

With Wap Shing in the hospital, Harker invited Darryl Baldwin, an heir apparent, to pray. First he greeted everyone in the Miami language, then spoke of his own ambivalence about his people's historical strategy of acquiescing in an assimilative articulation with the dominant society:

> It's really good to see everyone here. On the way out here we were kind of talking about the schoolhouse. One of the questions I asked was how much of the language do you think was spoken in and around the schoolhouse at the time a lot of our children, our ancestors were going to school here? It was a pretty general consensus that, at least at that time, still, a certain amount of language [was spoken] but it was probably also a beginning point for the loss of our language as well. It was the educational institutions at the time that started to begin to wipe the Indian off of many of the people. So it seems only fitting that here we are today to give an invocation, a prayer in the language.

After he finished praying, the Chief read the tribal council's resolution passed just that morning thanking the Stuber family for the gift of the schoolhouse. Then Lora Siders was invited to speak. She stepped forward and there was a long silence. It appeared that she was crying.

> I'm sorry. I am so happy for this day. People that know me know how happy I am for this day. So I guess, of necessity, I want you to go with me now. When he was

> a small child, my father went to this school. My father was a man who didn't go anyplace. He didn't want to leave home. And the only place he would go if anybody said they were coming to [was] Hog's Back, Jalapa, or this place. He was the first one ready to come. And so I started visiting this school when I was . . . my first memory was when I was three or four years old. My father and his brothers and sisters attended this school. There are a number of them here. Are any of Uncle Charlie's family here? Or my family, please raise your hand. [Four or five hands were raised.] Let it be known that we are descendants of this school. I just guess, I am just too happy to know that this is happening.

"My father was a man who didn't want to go anyplace. He didn't want to leave home . . . we are the descendants of this school"—this powerful public telling of memory, in the context of repatriation, produced the link between those hundred or so people and an imagined, emergent, historic Miami landscape. This was a version of Teski and Climo's (1995:9) vicarious memory, wherein "memories are passed from generation to generation to become the social and cultural memories of a group." Algonquian people throughout the Great Lakes and Ohio River Valley region regard public speech of this kind as a moment in a series of gift exchanges. Hearing certain things obliges the listener. Those present assumed the burden of Lora's memories and responsibility for social action that facilitates community redefinition and change.

Lora Siders reflected on her hopes for the future:

> In five years from now, I hope it [the schoolhouse] will be used, like so many times we have meetings with people from as far away as Lafayette and people from Fort Wayne. It's going to be a closer place. It's kind of midway. I look at it as that. But more important, I look at it, and the language committee, is real anxious to have language classes there. Now we have language classes once a year on our property. They stay for the week and they bring their kids. The exciting thing for me is that [they take] these little kids . . . out through the woods and they give them the Indian name for anything that happens to be growing, moving, anything that they see. They are learning the Indian words. . . . And these kids are growing up knowing our language. Well, they have an idea and I go right along with it that this is a school, this is the place where, say, every Saturday we could be having a language class there, every Sunday afternoon we could be having a language class there. They are getting the Cultural Committee together, what better place than at the school, for that cultural committee to meet? And a lot of those people are from the Fort Wayne-Huntington area, and some of them are from here, and what better place for them to meet? So I see that school continuing its teaching and learning abilities. I just see no end to it. I guess that's the most important thing.
>
> Being egotistical, or something, I would like to see a reunion there for the people who met, the day you and Elizabeth came down and Tom. I would like to see at least a reunion at least once a year of those people, and maybe people who are interested that didn't get to come that day, that didn't know about that day.

Remembering Lora

The reunion Lora hoped for took place in the fall of 2000 in the school's gymnasium, which the tribe had converted into a bingo hall. But this night the only sign of that function was the six TV monitors that rested on the rims of the basketball hoops. The space had been redecorated for the community celebration of Lora's life, now complete.

Lora lay facing the east in a purple dress with a feather fan in her hands. Her hair was grayer than I remembered it being. Her red dancing shawl lay draped over the side of the coffin, its fringe nearly touching the floor and barely moving in the slight breezes that wafted through the large room.

More than two dozen floral wreaths had been sent. They were interspersed with photos of Lora and her family, photos of the Miami reunion that has taken place for nearly one hundred years in Wabash, the schoolhouse, the framed Sagamore of the Wabash award from the governor, and the oil portrait painted by Evelyn Ritter. This portrait was reproduced along with thirty-nine other portraits of tribal leaders in *Always a People: Oral Histories of Contemporary Woodland Indians,* a book project undertaken at the behest of Ray White, Miami chief in the 1980s. Someone had taken the trouble of draping all the railings of the bleachers behind the bier with Mexican blankets.

Nick Clark, former director of the Minnetrista Council for Great Lakes Native American Studies in Muncie and, at the time, the director of the Prophetstown Museum and Cultural Center near Lafayette, took the role of emcee. He smudged some people with sage burning in a conch shell and directed the smoke with an eagle-wing fan toward others who drew the smoke to themselves with their hands, pulling it over their heads, faces, and torsos in what is becoming a pan-Indian act of purification. The *Twight Twee* drum sang with an Honor song. Lora named them ten years ago when this diffuse community of Wabash Miami began to feel the tug of the past and the future and expressed that in a variety of efforts to recreate their culture. On a blanket laid on the floor, people offered gifts for her passage: tobacco seeds, small bowls, sage, cedar, a favorite knife.

A man in his thirties addressed the assembly in the Miami language, gave a short translation, and placed his gift on the blanket.[16] Clarence White, of the recently recognized Pokegan Potawatomi, addressed those gathered in *Anishinabemowin,* then made fire with flint and steel and smoked a pipe for Lora.

The remembrance finished, Elizabeth Glenn and I walked out, visiting with Louise Hay and her niece. Louise is now the senior Miami elder, a woman in her mid-80s who owns the only piece of Miami land that has been continuously occupied by Miami people since they returned from the Iroquois diaspora in the 1680s.

Notes

1. Otho Winger taught at the Miami Indian Village School for three years beginning in 1895. Of the Indian students' ability to learn, he noted: "As a rule you might say they are better in subjects that require the use of memory, such as history, spelling and reading" (Winger 1943:75). He went on to the presidency of Manchester College and authored a number of local histories.

2. According to Warder Crow (1936:5) "east of the church about 150 feet a frame school house was still in use until 1897. It occupied land previously owned by the Indians for which they had been given no title—a sort of 'Squatter's Rights' arrangement given by common consent but not formally, only tacitly. It was not a new building in 1880, when Uncle Hamlin Crow saw it when he came from Ohio to visit his brother James. It was moved to the west side of the road . . . and probably is still used as a granary."

3. By the fall of 2000, Mt. Pleasant had burnt to the ground.

4. Rob Mann (1999) has pointed out that Little Turtle referred to the portage as "the glorious gate."

5. This aristocratic disposition had been noted earlier. Nathaniel West, in his investigation of claims made against the Miamis in January of 1839, noted that "indolence, extravagance and love of display pervade the whole nation; many of the young men wear clothes that cost at least $100, indeed, none but the finest goods will sell amongst them" (Poinsatte 1969:98). In somewhat the same way that eighteenth century Haitians and early nineteenth century Polynesians valorized American republican culture, and in so doing identified themselves as transnational politico-cultural avant garde, Miami War Chief Gabriel Godfroy named one of his many children George Washington (Glenn, Swartz, and Lewis, N.d.:11). And like the members of the chiefly family that governed Hawaii, who "signified the control of land, food and people" (Sahlins 1988:33) by their very bulk, Godfroy weighed between 300 and 350 pounds.

6. I draw here upon Sahlins' (1985:35–54) discussion of heroic history.

7. Lora's husband grew up with Chief Shoemaker in Wabash. The latter was a Meshingomesia descendant, and Edward Siders likely descended from the Godfroys, according to Lora Marks.

8. Stuart Rafert (1996:278) adds that the delegation of day-to-day management responsibilities to a *kapia* is a longstanding Miami political practice. The *Kaupeeau,* in Trowbridge's early nineteenth century orthography, is a "chief who holds the belts and other insignias of power." The belts were "illustrative of events in their history." I would add that Miami's Algonquoian-speaking "elder brothers" well to the north, the Ojibwe, are similarly inclined with Crane clan members delegating to Loons in the remembered political order of things.

9. Lora remembers the pageants being made up of fictional episodes of scalpings, kidnappings, chief's councils voting, hunting, dancing—"what the white people wanted to see." The city of Peru put on the Maconaquah pageant, the story of Frances Slocum who was kidnapped as a child by Delawares in 1778 from her home near the village of Wilkes-Barre in the Wyoming Valley of Pennsylvania and sold to the Miamis. As a fully enculturated mature Miami woman and wife of the war chief Deaf Man, she revealed her

original identity in 1835 and was visited by her long-lost and aging brothers. She also motivated the emigration of her nephew to Deaf Man's multiethnic village in 1846 (Winger 1943:1–20).

10. Rafert (1996:273–274) identifies groups in terms of the intensity of their involvement with Miami concerns: a core of twenty-five to thirty passionately committed Miamis, and five hundred to seven hundred who would work for the tribe, attended meetings and reunions, and "knew lots of tribal history."

11. At least two villages were destroyed in the Mississinewa Campaign (see Glenn, Swartz, and Lewis 1977).

12. See Chapter III, *Frances Slocum and Her Descendants: The Uses of an Indian Captivity* (Rafert 1982).

13. Though current practice is deeply rooted, it pervades Miami history. Meshingomesia's eldest son, Po-cong-yah, testified in 1873 that he was "acquainted with the customs of the Indians in their adoptions. When a person dies they go and bury him, but still they say his spirit is there at the house yet. They say that when they don't make an adoption, the spirit still stays there and all the rest of the family keep dying off" (Rafert and Marks 1991:411).

14. Muncie, Indiana, alone, for example, has four public monumental statues of Indians. None is Miami, though the oldest may be Woodland. Two are Plains Indians, and the most recent is either Southwest or Hallmark (as in greeting cards). The inclination on the part of the local non-Indian aristocracy to realize a fantastic indigenous past in public space is notable and a topic for future research in this region, a region that is known for its Indian hobbyism as well.

15. The exhibit "In the Presence of the Past: The Miami Indians of Indiana," was at the Eiteljorg Museum in Indianapolis for an eighteen-month run, closing in late 1998. It has played an important role in the ongoing revitalization of Miami Indian identity as well. A videotape entitled "Being Miami" and a CD-ROM bearing the same name as the exhibit remain as permanent repositories and continue to circulate.

16. The last person to have learned the language as a child, Ross Bundy, died in 1963.

Bibliography

Introduction

Abercrombie, Thomas A. 1998. *Pathways of Memory and Power: Ethnography and History among an Andean People.* Madison: University of Washington Press.

Adams, Cynthia, Malcolm C. Smith, Monisha Pasupathi, and Loretta Vitolo. 2002. Social Context Effects on Story Recall in Older and Younger Women: Does the Listener Make a Difference? *Journal of Gerontology* 57B(1):28–40.

Albert, Steven M., and Maria G. Cattell. 1994. *Old Age in Global Perspective: Cross-Cultural and Cross-National Views.* New York: G. K. Hall.

Allende, Isabel. 1995. *Paula.* M. S. Peden, tr. New York: HarperCollins.

Amoss, Pamela T. 1981. Coast Salish Elders. In *Other Ways of Growing Old: Anthropological Perspectives.* Pamela T. Amoss and Stevan Harrell, eds. 227–247. Stanford: Stanford University Press.

Antze, Paul, and Michael Lambek, eds. 1996. *Tense Past: Cultural Essays in Trauma and Memory.* New York: Routledge.

Archibald, Robert R. 1999. *A Place to Remember: Using History to Build Community.* Walnut Creek, CA: AltaMira Press.

Attfield, Judy. 2000. *Wild Things: The Material Culture of Everyday Lives.* New York: Berg.

Bailey, Garrick, and Roberta Glenn Bailey. 1986. *A History of the Navajos: The Reservation Years.* Santa Fe: School of American Research.

Baker, Michael. 2001. Lingering Distrust of Japan Extends Textbook Row. *Christian Science Monitor* July 20:7.

Bascom, William. 1980. *Sixteen Cowries: Yoruba Divination from Africa to the New World.* Bloomington: Indiana University Press.

Battaglia, Debbora. 1992. The Body in the Gift: Memory and Forgetting in Sabarl Mortuary Exchange. *American Ethnologist* 19(1):3–18.

Behar, Ruth, and Deborah A. Gordon, eds. 1995. *Women Writing Culture.* Berkeley: University of California Press.

Bellah, Robert N., Richard Madsen, William M. Sullivan, Ann Swidler, and Steven M. Tipton. 1985. *Habits of the Heart: Individualism and Commitment in American Life*. New York: Harper & Rowe.

Berger, Peter. 1963. *Invitation to Sociology: A Humanistic Perspective*. New York: Doubleday Anchor Book.

Bernard, H. Russell. 1988. *Research Methods in Cultural Anthropology*. Beverly Hills: Sage.

Black, Helen K., and Robert L. Rubinstein. 2000. *Old Souls: Aged Women, Poverty, and the Experience of God*. New York: Aldine de Gruyter.

Bluck, Susan. 2001. The Gift of a Lifetime. *Pathways to Aging* April:6–7.

Boris, Eileen, and Nupur Chaudhuri, eds. 1999. *Voices of Women Historians: The Personal, the Political, the Professional*. Bloomington: Indiana University Press.

Bourguignon, Erika. 1996. Vienna and Memory: Anthropology and Experience. *Ethos* 24(2):374–387.

Boyarin, Jonathan. 1991. *Polish Jews in Paris: The Ethnography of Memory*. Bloomington: Indiana University Press.

———, ed. 1994. *Remapping Memory: The Politics of TimeSpace*. Minneapolis: University of Minnesota Press.

Boyd, David R., ed. 2001. *Northern Wild: Best Contemporary Canadian Nature Writing*. Vancouver: Greystone.

Bozzoli, Belinda, with Mmantho Nkotsoe. 1991. *Women of Phokeng: Consciousness, Life Strategy, and Migrancy in South Africa, 1900–1983*. Social History of Africa Series. Portsmouth: Heinemann.

Bradbury, Ray. 1967 [1950]. *Fahrenheit 451*. New York: Simon & Schuster.

Brundage, W. Fitzhugh. 2000. Introduction: No Deed But Memory. In *Where These Memories Grow: History, Memory, and Southern Identity*. 1–28. Chapel Hill: University of North Carolina Press.

Bruner, Edward M. 1999. Return to Sumatra: 1957, 1997. *American Ethnologist* 26(2):461–477.

Bruner, J. S. 1987. Life as Narrative. *Social Research* 54:11–32.

Buruma, Ian. 1994. *The Wages of Guilt: Memories of War in Germany and Japan*. New York: Farrar, Straus & Giroux.

Carroll, Lewis. 1982. *The Complete Illustrated Works of Lewis Carroll*. Edward Guiliano, ed. New York: Avenel Books.

Casey, Edward S. 1987. *Remembering: A Phenomenological Study*. Bloomington: Indiana University Press.

Cattell, Maria G. 1992. Praise the Lord and Say No to Men: Older Samia Women Empowering Themselves. *Journal of Cross-Cultural Gerontology* 7(4):307–330.

Clifford, James, and George E. Marcus, eds. 1986. *Writing Culture: The Poetics and Politics of Ethnography*. Berkeley: University of California Press.

Climo, Jacob J. 1995. Prisoners of Silence: A Vicarious Holocaust Memory. In *The Labyrinth of Memory: Ethnographic Journeys*. Marea C. Teski and Jacob J. Climo, eds. 175–184. Westport, CT: Bergin & Garvey.

Climo, Jacob J., Marea C. Teski, and Philip B. Stafford, eds. N.d. *Memory Practices: Culture and the Creation of Memory Repertoires.* Unpublished manuscript.

Coetzee, Carli. 1998. Krotoä Remembered: A Mother of Unity, a Mother of Sorrows. In *Negotiating the Past: The Making of Memory in South Africa.* Sarah Nuttall and Carli Coetzee, eds. 112–119. Cape Town: Oxford University Press.

Collingwood, R. G. 1956. *The Idea of History.* London: Oxford University Press.

Connerton, Paul. 1989. *How Societies Remember.* Cambridge: Cambridge University Press.

Coser, Lewis A. 1992. Introduction: Maurice Halbwachs 1877–1945. In *On Collective Memory.* Lewis A. Coser, ed. and trans. Chicago: University of Chicago Press.

Csikszentmihalyi, Mihaly, and Eugene Rochberg-Halton. 1981. *The Meaning of Things: Domestic Symbols and the Self.* Cambridge: Cambridge University Press.

Csordas, Thomas J., ed. 1994. *Embodiment and Experience: The Existential Ground of Culture and Self.* Cambridge: Cambridge University Press.

Daniel, E. Valentine. 1996. *Charred Lullabies: Chapters in an Anthropography of Violence.* Princeton: Princeton University Press.

Davies, J., ed. 1994. *Ritual and Remembrance: Responses to Death in Human Societies.* Sheffield: Sheffield Academic Press.

Davison, Patricia. 1998. Museums and the Reshaping of Memory. In *Negotiating the Past: The Making of Memory in South Africa.* Sarah Nuttall and Carli Coetzee, eds. 143–160. Cape Town: Oxford University Press.

d'Azevedo, Warren L. 1962. Uses of the Past in Gola Discourse. *Journal of African History* 3(1):11–34.

De Boeck, Filip. 1998. Beyond the Grave: History, Memory and Death in Postcolonial Congo/Zaire. *Memory and the Postcolony: African Anthropology and the Critique of Power.* 21–57. London: Zed Books.

de Kok, Ingrid. 1998. Cracked Heirlooms: Memory on Exhibition. In *Negotiating the Past: The Making of Memory in South Africa.* Sarah Nuttall and Carli Coetzee, eds. 57–71. Cape Town: Oxford University Press.

Deacon, Harriet. 1998. Remembering Tragedy, Constructing Modernity: Robben Island as a National Monument. In *Negotiating the Past: The Making of Memory in South Africa.* Sarah Nuttall and Carli Coetzee, eds. 161–179. Cape Town: Oxford University Press.

Denzin, Norman K. 1989. *Interpretive Biography.* Qualitative Research Methods Series No. 17. Newbury Park, CA: Sage.

Durbin, Marshall. 1973. Cognitive Anthropology. *Handbook of Cultural and Social Anthropology.* John J. Honigmann, ed. 447–478. Chicago: Rand McNally.

Ember, Carol R., and David Levinson. 1991. The Substantive Contributions of Worldwide Cross-Cultural Studies Using Secondary Data. *Behavior Science Research* 25(1–4):79–140.

Feld, Steven, and Keith H. Basso, eds. 1996. *Senses of Place.* Santa Fe: School of American Research.

Fentress, James, and Chris Wickham. 1992. *Social Memory: New Perspectives on the Past.* Oxford: Blackwell.

Foner, Nancy. 1984. *Ages in Conflict: A Cross-Cultural Perspective on Inequality Between Old and Young*. New York: Columbia University Press.

Foster, George M., Thayer Scudder, Elizabeth Colson, and Robert V. Kemper, eds. 1979. *Long-term Field Research in Social Anthropology*. New York: Academic.

Frank, Gelya. 2000. Ethnography of Memory: An American Anthropologist's Family Story of Refuge from Nazism. *American Anthropologist* 102(4):899–903.

Friedrich, Paul. 1986. *The Princes of Naranja: An Essay in Anthrohistorical Method*. Austin: University of Texas Press.

Gazzaniga, Michael S. 1998. *The Mind's Past*. Berkeley: University of California Press.

Geertz, Clifford. 1973. *The Interpretation of Cultures*. New York: Basic.

Greenfield, Patricia M. 2000. What Psychology Can Do for Anthropology, or Why Anthropology Took Postmodernism on the Chin. *American Anthropologist* 102(3):564–576.

Gross, David L. 2000. *Lost Time: Remembering and Forgetting in Late Modern Culture*. Amherst: University of Massachusetts Press.

Gubrium, Jaber F. 1993. *Speaking of Life: Horizons of Meaning for Nursing Home Residents*. New York: Aldine de Gruyter.

Haight, Barbara K., and J. D. Webster, eds. 1995. *The Art and Science of Reminiscing: Theory, Research, Methods and Applications*. Washington, DC: Taylor & Francis.

Halbwachs, Maurice. 1992 [1950]. *On Collective Memory*. Lewis A. Coser, ed. and trans. Chicago: University of Chicago Press.

Harrison, Simon. 1999. Cultural Boundaries. *Anthropology Today* 15(5):10–13.

Hendricks, Jon, ed. 1995. *The Meaning of Reminiscence and Life Review*. Amityville, NY: Baywood.

Herzfeld, Michael. 1991. *A Place in History: Social and Monumental Time in a Cretan Town*. Princeton: Princeton University Press.

Hobsbawm, Eric, and Terence O. Ranger, eds. 1983. *The Invention of Tradition*. New York: Cambridge University Press.

Horowitz, Joy. 1996. *Tessie and Pearlie: A Granddaughter's Story*. New York: Touchstone.

Howe, Mark L., and Mary L. Courage. 1997. The Emergence and Early Development of Autobiographical Memory. *Psychological Review* 104(3):499–523.

Hudson, Charles. 1973. The Historical Approach in Anthropology. *Handbook of Social and Cultural Anthropology*. John Honigmann, ed. 111–141. New York: Rand McNally.

Ishino, Iwao. 1995. Memories and Their Unintended Consequences. In *The Labyrinth of Memory: Ethnographic Journeys*. Marea C. Teski and Jacob J. Climo, eds. 185–201. Westport, CT: Bergin & Garvey.

Jenkins, Janis, and Thomas J. Csordas, eds. 1997. Ethnography and Sociocultural Processes: A Symposium. Special issue, *Ethos* 25(2).

Kahn, Miriam. 1996. Your Place and Mine: Sharing Emotional Landscapes in Wamira, Papua New Guinea. In *Senses of Place*. Steven Feld and Keith H. Basso, eds. 167–196. Santa Fe: School of American Research.

Kammen, Michael G. 1991. *Mystic Chords of Memory: The Transformation of Tradition in American Culture*. New York: Knopf.

———. 1995. Some Patterns and Meanings of Memory Distortion in American History. In *Memory Distortion: How Minds, Brains, and Societies Reconstruct the Past*. Daniel L. Schacter, ed. 329–345. Cambridge: Harvard University Press.

———. 1997. *In the Past Lane: Historical Perspectives on American Culture*. New York: Oxford University Press.

Kaufman, Sharon R. 1986. *The Ageless Self: Sources of Meaning in Late Life*. Madison: University of Wisconsin Press.

Keith, Jennie. 1986. Participant Observation. In *New Methods for Old Age Research: Strategies for Studying Diversity*. Christine L. Fry and Jennie Keith, eds. 1–20. Westport, CT: Bergin & Garvey.

Kenyon, Gary, Phillip Clark, and Brian de Vries, eds. 2001. *Narrative Gerontology: Theory, Research, and Practice*. New York: Springer.

Kerner, Donna O. 1995. Chaptering the Narrative: The Material of Memory in Kilimanjaro, Tanzania. In *The Labyrinth of Memory: Ethnographic Journeys*. Marea C. Teski and Jacob J. Climo, eds. 113–127. Westport, CT: Bergin & Garvey.

Kirmayer, Laurence J. 1996. Landscapes of Memory: Trauma, Narrative, and Dissociation. In *Tense Past: Cultural Essays in Trauma and Memory*. Paul Antze and Michael Lambek, eds. 173–198. New York: Routledge.

Klein, Norman. 1997. *History of Forgetting: Los Angeles and the Erasure of Memory*. London/New York: Verso.

Kopytoff, Igor. 1995. Anthropology as History: Critiques by Our "Others." *Anthropology Newsletter* 36(5):12–13.

Korp, Maureen. 2000. *Sacred Art of the Earth: Ancient and Contemporary Earthworks*. New York: Continuum.

Kroeber, Alfred L., and Clyde Kluckhohn. 1952. *Culture: A Critical Review of Concepts and Definitions*. New York: Vintage.

Krog, Antjie. 1998. *Country of My Skull*. Johannesberg: Random House.

Kundera, Milan. 1969. *The Joke*. David Hamblyn and Oliver Stallybrass, tr. New York: Coward McCann.

———. 1980. *The Book of Laughter and Forgetting*. Michael Henry Hein, tr. New York: Knopf.

Laird, Carobeth. 1979. *Limbo: A Memoir about Life in a Nursing Home by a Survivor*. Novato, CA: Chandler & Sharp.

Lambek, Michael. 1996. The Past Imperfect: Remembering as Moral Practice. In *Tense Past: Cultural Essays in Trauma and Memory*. Paul Antze and Michael Lambek, eds. 235–254. New York: Routledge.

Lambek, Michael, and Paul Antze. 1996. Introduction: Forecasting Memory. In *Tense Past: Cultural Essays in Trauma and Memory*. Paul Antze and Michael Lambek, eds. xi–xxviii. New York: Routledge.

Langness, L. L., and Gelya Frank. 1981. *Lives: An Anthropological Approach to Biography*. Novato, CA: Chandler & Sharp.

Legesse, Asmarom. 1973. *Gada: Three Approaches to the Study of African Society*. New York: Free Press.

Lewis, Oscar. 1959. *Five Families: Mexican Case Studies in the Culture of Poverty*. New York: Basic Books.

———. 1961. *The Children of Sanchez: Autobiography of a Mexican Family*. New York: Random House.

Lyon, Thomas J., ed. 1989. *This Incomperable Lande: A Book of American Nature Writing*. Boston: Houghton Mifflin.

Makoni, Sinfree. 1998. African Languages as European Scripts: The Shaping of Communal Memory. In *Negotiating the Past: The Making of Memory in South Africa.* Sarah Nuttall and Carli Coetzee, eds. 242–248. Cape Town: Oxford University Press.

Mattingly, C. 1998. *Healing Dramas and Clinical Plots.* Cambridge: Cambridge University Press.

Meyer, Birgit. 1998. 'Make a Complete Break with the Past': Memory and Postcolonial Modernity in Ghanaian Pentecostal Discourse. In *Memory and the Postcolony: African Anthropology and the Critique of Power.* Richard Werbner, ed. 182–208. London: Zed Books.

Middleton, David, and Derek Edwards, eds. 1990. *Collective Remembering.* Newbury Park, CA: Sage.

Miller, Daniel. 2001. *Home Possessions: Material Culture Behind Closed Doors.* New York: Berg.

Moore, Sally Falk. 1993. Changing Perspectives on a Changing Africa: The Work of Anthropology. In *Africa and the Disciplines: The Contributions of Research in Africa to the Social Sciences and Humanities.* Robert H. Bates, V. Y. Mudimbe, and Jean O'Barr, eds. 3–57. Chicago: University of Chicago Press.

Munroe, Robert L., and Ruth H. Munroe. 1991. Results of Comparative Field Studies. *Behavior Science Research* 25(1–4):23–54.

Myerhoff, Barbara. 1980 [1978]. *Number Our Days.* New York: Touchstone.

———. 1992. Life History among the Elderly: Performance, Visibility, and Re-membering. In *Remembered Lives: The Work of Ritual, Storytelling, and Growing Older.* Marc Kaminsky, ed. 231–247. Ann Arbor: University of Michigan Press.

Myers, Fred R., ed. 2001. *The Empire of Things: Regimes of Value and Material Culture.* Santa Fe: School of American Research.

Nabhan, Gary Paul. 1992. Epilogue: Native Crops of the Americas: Passing Novelties or Lasting Contributions to Diversity? In *Chilies to Chocolate: Food the Americas Gave the World.* Nelson Foster and Linda S. Cordell, eds. 143–161. Tucson: University of Arizona Press.

Naroll, Raoul, and Ronald Cohen, eds. 1970. *A Handbook of Method in Cultural Anthropology.* New York/London: Columbia University Press.

Nazarea, Virginia D. 1998. *Cultural Memory and Biodiversity.* Tucson: University of Arizona Press.

Neisser, Ulric, and Robyn Fivush. 1993. *The Remembering Self: Construction and Accuracy in Self Narrative.* Sarah Nuttall and Carli Coetzee, eds. Cambridge: Cambridge University Press.

Nuttall, Sarah, and Carli Coetzee, eds. 1998. *Negotiating the Past: The Making of Memory in South Africa.* Cape Town: Oxford University Press.

Olick, Jeffrey, and Joyce Robbins. 1998. Social Memory Studies: From "Collective Memory" to the Historical Sociology of Mnemonic Practices. *Annual Review of Sociology* 24:105–140.

Orwell, George. 1949. *1984.* New York: Harcourt Brace.

Ottenberg, Simon. 1990. Thirty Years of Fieldnotes: Changing Relationships to the Text. In *Fieldnotes: The Makings of Anthropology.* Roger Sanjek, ed. 139–160. Ithaca: Cornell University Press.

Parezo, Nancy J., ed. 1993. *Hidden Scholars: Women Anthropologists and the Native American Southwest.* Albuquerque: University of New Mexico Press.

Paris, Erna. 2001. *Long Shadows: Truth, Lies and History*. New York: Bloomsbury.

Pelto, Pertti J., and Gretel H. Pelto. 1978. *Anthropological Research: The Structure of Inquiry*, 2d edition. Cambridge: Cambridge University Press.

Pendergrast, Mark. 1996. *Victims of Memory: Sex Abuse Accusations and Shattered Lives*, 2d edition. Hinesburg, VT: Upper Access.

Personal Narratives Group. 1989. *Interpreting Women's Lives: Feminist Theory and Personal Narratives.* Bloomington: Indiana University Press.

Pillemer, David B. 1998. *Momentous Events, Vivid Memories.* Cambridge: Harvard University Press.

Pincheon, Bill S. 2000. An Ethnography of Silences: Race, (Homo)sexualities, and a Discourse of Africa. *African Studies Review* 43(3):39–58.

Prusher, Ilene R. 2001. History Debate: Asian Anger Still Simmers over Japanese History Views. *Christian Science Monitor* August 16:7.

Radin, Paul, ed. 1926. *Crashing Thunder, The Autobiography of an American Indian.* New York: Appleton.

Radstone, Susannah. 2000. Working with Memory: An Introduction. In *Memory and Methodology*. 1–22. Oxford/New York: Berg.

Rappaport, Joanne. 1990. *The Politics of Memory: Native Historical Interpretations in the Colombian Andes.* Cambridge: Cambridge University Press.

Ray, Ruth E. 1998. Feminist Readings of Older Women's Life Stories. *Journal of Aging Studies* 12(2):117–127.

———. 2000. *Beyond Nostalgia: Aging and Life-Story Writing*. Charlottesville: University of Virginia Press.

Rosaldo, Renato. 1984. Grief and a Headhunter's Rage: On the Cultural Force of Emotions. In *Play, Text, and Story: The Construction and Reconstruction of Self and Society*. Edward M. Bruner, ed. 178–195. Washington, DC: American Ethnological Society.

Rose, Peter I. 2001. Remembrance of Horrors Past. *Christian Science Monitor* June 7:16.

Rosenberg, Harriet G. 1997. Complaint Discourse, Aging and Caregiving among the Ju/'hoansi of Botswana. In *The Cultural Context of Aging: Worldwide Perspectives*, 2d edition. Jay Sokolovsky, ed. 33–55. Westport, CT: Bergin & Garvey.

Ross, Bruce A. 1991. *Remembering the Personal Past: Descriptions of Autobiographical Memory*. Oxford: Oxford University Press.

Rotenberg, Robert, and Gary McDonogh, eds. 1993. *The Cultural Meaning of Urban Space.* Westport, CT: Bergin & Garvey.

Rowles, Graham. 1978. *Prisoners of Space? Exploring the Geographical Experience of Older People.* Boulder: Westview Press.

Sacks, Oliver. 1985. *The Man Who Mistook His Wife for a Hat*. New York: Summit.

———. 1995. *An Anthropologist on Mars.* New York: Knopf.

Sanjek, Roger. 1993. Anthropology's Hidden Colonialism: Assistants and Their Ethnographers. *Anthropology Today* 9(2):13–18.

Savishinsky, Joel S. 2000. *Breaking the Watch: The Meanings of Retirement in America.* Ithaca: Cornell University Press.

Schacter, Daniel L. 1995a. Memory Distortion: History and Current Status. In *Memory Distortion: How Minds, Brains, and Societies Reconstruct the Past.* 1–43. Cambridge: Harvard University Press.

———, ed. 1995b. *Memory Distortion: How Minds, Brains, and Societies Reconstruct the Past.* Cambridge: Harvard University Press.

———. 1996. *Searching for Memory: The Brain, the Mind, and the Past.* New York: Basic Books.

———. 1999. *Seven Sins of Memory: How the Mind Forgets and Remembers.* Boston: Houghton Mifflin.

Schneider, Bronka. 1998. *Exile: A Memoir of 1939.* Erika Bourguignon and Barbara Hill Rigney, eds. Columbus: Ohio State University Press.

Schudson, Michael. 1992. *Watergate in American Memory: How We Remember, Forget, and Reconstruct the Past.* New York: Basic Books.

———. 1995. Dynamics of Distortion in Collective Memory. In *Memory Distortion: How Minds, Brains, and Societies Reconstruct the Past.* 346–364. Cambridge: Harvard University Press.

Schuman, Howard, and J. Scott. 1989. Generations and Collective Memory. *American Sociological Review* 54:359–381.

Schweitzer, Marjorie M., and Maria G. Cattell, eds. N.d. *Multifaceted Lives: Personal and Professional Narratives of Older Women Anthropologists.* Unpublished manuscript.

Shostak, Marjorie. 1981. *Nisa: The Life and Words of a !Kung Woman.* Cambridge: Harvard University Press.

———. 1989. "What the Wind Won't Take Away": The Genesis of Nisa—The Life and Words of a !Kung Woman. In *Interpreting Women's Lives: Feminist Theory and Personal Narratives.* Personal Narratives Group, ed. 228–240. Bloomington: Indiana University Press.

Shweder, Richard A. 1997. The Surpise of Ethnography. *Ethos* 25(2):152–163.

Singer, Rena. 2001. After Apartheid, a Fresh Look at History. *Christian Science Monitor* June 6:9.

Smith, Andrea L. 1995. Social Memory and Germany's Anti-Foreigner Crisis: A Case of Collective Forgetting. In *The Labyrinth of Memory: Ethnographic Journeys.* Marea C. Teski and Jacob J. Climo, eds. 61–92. Westport, CT: Bergin & Garvey.

Spyer, Patricia. 2000. *The Memory of Trade: Modernity's Entanglements on an Eastern Indonesian Island.* Durham, NC: Duke University Press.

Steedly, Mary. 1993. *Hanging Without a Rope: Narrative Experience in Colonial and Postcolonial Karoland.* Princeton: Princeton University Press.

Stern, Kenneth S. 2001. Lying about the Holocaust. *Intelligence Report* No. 103:50–55.

Stoller, Paul. 1995. *Embodying Colonial Memories: Spirit Possession, Power and the Hauka in West Africa.* New York: Routledge.

Sullivan, Lawrence E. 1995. Memory Distortion and Anamnesis: A View from the Human Sciences. In *Memory Distortion: How Minds, Brains, and Societies Reconstruct the Past.* Daniel L. Schacter, ed. 386–400. Cambridge: Harvard University Press.

Sutton, David. 1998. *Memories Cast in Stone: The Relevance of the Past in Everyday Life.* Oxford: Berg.

———. 2001. *Remembrance of Repasts: An Anthropology of Food and Memory.* New York: Berg.

Swiderski, Richard. 1995. Mau Mau and Memory Rooms: Placing a Social Emotion. In *The Labyrinth of Memory: Ethnographic Journeys.* Marea C. Teski and Jacob J. Climo, eds. 95–111. Westport, CT: Bergin & Garvey.

Swora, Maria Gabrielle. 2001. Commemoration and the Healing of Memories in Alcoholics Anonymous. *Ethos* 29(1):58–77.

Taylor, A.C. 1993. Remembering to Forget: Identity, Mourning and Memory among the Jivaro. *Man* 28:653–678.

Teicher, Stacy A. 2001. Drumming Up Understanding Between the Generations. *Christian Science Monitor* June 5:14.

Teski, Marea C., and Jacob J. Climo. 1995. Introduction. In *The Labyrinth of Memory: Ethnographic Journeys*. Marea C. Teski and Jacob J. Climo, eds. 1–10. Westport, CT: Bergin & Garvey.

Thomas, William I., and Florian Znaniecki. 1918–20. *The Polish Peasant in Europe and America*. Vols. I–II, Chicago: University of Chicago Press. Vols. III–IV, Boston: Badger Press.

Tonkin, Elizabeth. 1992. *Narrating Our Past: The Social Construction of Oral History*. Cambridge: Cambridge University Press.

Trimble, Stephen, ed. 1995. *Words from the Land: Encounters with Natural History Writing*. Expanded edition. Reno/Las Vegas: University of Nevada Press.

Turner, Victor W. 1967. *The Forest of Symbols: Aspects of Ndembu Ritual*. Ithaca: Cornell University Press.

Tutu, Desmond. 1999. *No Future Without Forgiveness*. New York: Image/Doubleday.

Uhlenberg, Peter, and Sonia Miner. 1995. Life Course and Aging: A Cohort Perspective. In *Handbook of Aging and the Social Sciences*, 4th edition. Robert H. Binstock and Linda K. George, eds. 208–228. New York: Academic.

van Dijk, Rijk. 1998. Pentecostalism, Cultural Memory and the State: Contested Representations of Time in Postcolonial Malawi. In *Memory and the Postcolony: African Anthropology and the Critique of Power*. Richard Werbner, ed. 155–181. London: Zed Books.

van Onselen, Charles. 1996. *The Seed Is Mine: The Life of Kas Maine, a South African Sharecropper, 1894–1985*. Cape Town: David Philip.

Vansina, Jan. 1965 [1961]. *Oral Tradition: A Study in Historical Method*. H. M. Wright, trans. Chicago: Aldine.

———. 1970. Cultures Through Time. In *A Handbook of Method in Cultural Anthropology*. Raoull Naroll and Ronald Cohen, eds. 165–179. New York: Columbia University Press.

Vidal-Naquet, Pierre. 1992. *Assassins of Memory: Essays on the Denial of the Holocaust*. New York: Columbia University Press.

Vinitzky-Seroussi, Vered. 2001. Review of *Memory and Methodology*, S. Radstone, ed. *American Ethnologist* 28(2):494–496.

Watson, Rubie S., ed. 1994. *Memory, History, and Opposition under State Socialism*. Advanced Seminar Series. Santa Fe: School of American Research.

Weisner, Thomas S. 1997. The Ecocultural Project of Human Development: Why Ethnography and Its Findings Matter. *Ethos* 25(2):177–190.

Werbner, Richard. 1998a. Beyond Oblivion: Confronting Memory Crisis. In *Memory and the Postcolony: African Anthropology and the Critique of Power*. Richard Werbner, ed. 1–17. London: Zed Books.

———. 1998b. Smoke from the Barrel of a Gun: Postwars of the Dead, Memory and Reinscription in Zimbabwe. In *Memory and the Postcolony: African Anthropology and the Critique of Power*. Richard Werbner, ed. 71–102. London: Zed Books.

———, ed. 1998c. *Memory and the Postcolony: African Anthropology and the Critique of Power*. London: Zed Books.

Wolf, Eric. 1984. *Europe and the People Without History*. Berkeley: University of California Press.

Yerushalmi, Y. H. 1982. *Zakhor: Jewish History and Jewish Memory*. Seattle: University of Washington Press.

Zeleza, Paul Tiyambe, and Ezekiel Kalipeni, eds. 1999. *Sacred Spaces and Public Quarrels: African Cultural and Economic Landscapes*. Trenton: Africa World Press.

Chapter I

Balée, William, ed. 1998. *Advances in Historical Ecology*. New York: Columbia University Press.

Bourdieu, Pierre. 1977. *Outline of a Theory of Practice*. New York: Cambridge University Press.

Bové, José, and Francois Dufour. 2000. *Le Monde n'est pas une marchandise: Des paysans contre la malbouffe*. Paris: Editions La Découverte.

Burke, Peter. 1990. *The French Historical Revolution: The Annales School, 1929–1989*. Stanford: Stanford University Press.

Camuffo, D., and S. Enzi. 1992. Reconstructing the Climate of Northern Italy from Archive Sources. In *Climate Since A.D. 1500*. R. S. Bradley and P. D. Jones, eds. 143–154. London: Routledge.

Chisholm, Michael D. 1962. *Rural Settlement and Land Use*. London: Hutchinson University Library.

Connerton, Paul. 1989. *How Societies Remember*. Cambridge: Cambridge University Press.

Crumley, Carole L. 1987. Historical Ecology. In *Regional Dynamics: Burgundian Landscapes in Historical Perspective*. C. L. Crumley and W. H. Marquardt, eds. 237–264. San Diego: Academic Press.

———. 1992. *Historical Approaches to the Assessment of Global Climate Change Impacts*. Washington, DC: Committee for the National Institutes for the Environment.

———. 1993. Analyzing Historic Ecotonal Shifts. *Ecological Applications* 3(3):377–384.

———. 1994a. The Ecology of Conquest: Contrasting Agropastoral and Agricultural Societies' Adaptation to Climatic Change. In *Historical Ecology: Cultural Knowledge and Changing Landscapes*. C. L. Crumley, ed. 183–201. Santa Fe: School of American Research.

———, ed. 1994b. *Historical Ecology: Cultural Knowledge and Changing Landscapes*. Santa Fe: School of American Research.

———. 1995. Building an Historical Ecology of Gaulish Polities. In *Celtic Chiefdom, Celtic State*. B. Gibson and B. Arnold, eds. 26–33. Cambridge: Cambridge University Press.

———. 2000. From Garden to Globe: Linking Time and Space with Meaning and Memory. In *The Way the Wind Blows: Climate, History, and Human Action*. Roderick McIntosh, Joseph A. Tainter, and Susan Keech McIntosh, eds. Series in Historical Ecology. 193–208. New York: Columbia University Press.

Crumley, Carole L., and William H. Marquardt, eds. 1987. *Regional Dynamics: Burgundian Landscapes in Historical Perspective*. San Diego: Academic Press.

———. 1990. Landscape: A Unifying Concept in Regional Analysis. In *Interpreting Space: GIS and Archaeology*. K. M. Allen, S. W. Green, and E. B. W. Zubrow, eds. 73–79. London: Taylor & Francis.

Egan, Dave, and Evelyn A. Howell, eds. 2001. *The Historical Ecology Handbook: A Restorationist's Guide to Reference Ecosystems.* Society for Ecological Restoration. Washington, DC: Island Press.

Erp-Houtepan, A. van. 1986. The Etymological Origin of the Garden. *Journal of Garden History* 6(3):227–231.

Francis, M., and R. T. Hester, Jr., eds. 1990. *The Meaning of Gardens: Idea, Place, and Action.* Cambridge: MIT Press.

Goody, Jack. 1987. *The Interface between the Written and the Oral.* Cambridge: Cambridge University Press.

Gunn, Joel D. 1994. Global Climate and Regional Biodiversity. In *Historical Ecology: Cultural Knowledge and Changing Landscapes.* Carole L. Crumley, ed. 67–97. Santa Fe: School of American Research.

Gunn, Joel D., Carole L. Crumley, Bailey K. Young, and Elizabeth Jones. N.d. A Landscape Analysis of Western Europe during the Early Middle Ages. In *Human Impact on the Environment: An Archaeological Perspective.* Charles L. Redman, Steven R. James, Paul R. Fish, and J. Daniel Rogers, eds. Washington, DC: Smithsonian Institution Press.

Hammett, Julia E. 1992. The Shapes of Adaptation: Historical Ecology of Anthropogenic Landscapes in the Southeastern United States. *Landscape Ecology* 7(2):121–135.

Harvey, J. 1981. *Medieval Gardens.* Beaverton: Timber Press.

Herrmann, D. H., and R. Chaffin. 1988. *Memory in Historical Perspective: The Literature before Ebbinghaus.* New York: Springer-Verlag.

Holling, C. S. 1986. The Resilience of Terrestrial Ecosystems: Local Surprise and Global Change. In *Sustainable Development of the Biosphere.* W. C. Clark and R. E. Munn, eds. 292–317. New Rochelle: Cambridge University Press.

Hunt, J. D., and J. Wolschke-Bulmahn, eds. 1993. *The Vernacular Garden.* Washington, DC: Dumbarton Oaks.

Labrunie, G. 1984. *Proverbes et dictons de Bourgogne.* Paris: Rivages.

Le Dantec, D., and J.-P. Le Dantec. 1990. *Reading the French Garden: Story and History.* J. Levine, tr. Cambridge: MIT Press.

Leone, M. P. 1984. Interpreting Ideology in Historical Archaeology: Using the Rules of Perspective in the William Paca Garden, Annapolis, Maryland. In *Ideology, Power, and Prehistory.* D. Miller and C. Tilley, eds. 25–35. Cambridge: Cambridge University Press.

———. 1988. *The Recovery of Meaning.* Washington, DC: Smithsonian Institution Press.

Lévi-Strauss, Claude. 1963 [1962]. *Totemism.* Boston: Beacon Press.

Magny, Michel. 1995. *Une histoire du climat: Des derniers mammouths au siècle de l'automobile.* Paris: Editions Errance.

Marquardt, William H., and Carole L. Crumley. 1987. Theoretical Issues in the Analysis of Spatial Patterning. In *Regional Dynamics: Burgundian Landscapes in Historical Perspective.* C. L. Crumley and W. H. Marquardt, eds. 1–18. San Diego: Academic Press.

McGaugh, James L. 1995. Emotional Activation, Neuromodulatory Systems, and Memory. In *Memory Distortion: How Minds, Brains, and Societies Reconstruct the Past.* Daniel L. Schacter, ed. 255–273. Cambridge: Harvard University Press.

Miller, N., and K. L. Gleason, eds. 1994. *The Archaeology of Garden and Field.* Philadelphia: University of Pennsylvania Press.

Netting, Robert McCormick. 1993. *Smallholders, Householders: Farm Families and the Ecology of Intensive, Sustainable Agriculture.* Stanford: Stanford University Press.

O'Neill, R. V., S. J. Turner, V. I. Cullinan, D. P. Coffin, T. Cook, W. Conley, J. Brunt, J. M. Thomas, M. R. Conley, and J. Gosz. 1991. Multiple Landscape Scales: An Intersite Comparison. *Landscape Ecology* 5(3):137–144.

Pielou, Edith. 1975. *Ecological Diversity.* New York: Wiley.

———. 1984 *The Interpretation of Ecological Data: A Primer on Classification and Ordination.* New York: Wiley.

Pugh, Simon. 1988. *Garden—Nature—Language.* Manchester: Manchester University Press.

Schacter, Daniel L. 1995. *Memory Distortion: How Minds, Brains, and Societies Reconstruct the Past.* Cambridge: Harvard University Press.

Schama, S. 1995. *Landscape and Memory.* New York: Knopf.

Searleman, Alan, and Douglas Herrman. 1994. *Memory from a Broader Perspective.* New York: McGraw-Hill.

Taverdet, G., and F. Dumas. 1984. *Anthologie des expressions en Bourgogne.* Paris: Rivages.

Terrio, Susan. 2000. *Crafting the Culture and History of French Chocolate.* Berkeley: University of California Press.

Thacker, C. 1979. *The History of Gardens.* Berkeley: University of California Press.

Tonkin, Elizabeth. 1992. *Narrating Our Pasts: The Social Construction of Oral History.* Cambridge: Cambridge University Press.

Turner, Monica G., Virginia H. Dale, and Robert H. Gardner. 1989. Predicting across Scales: Theory Development and Testing. *Landscape Ecology* 3(3–4):245–252.

Van Deventer, A. Elizabeth. 2001. *Redefining the Farm, Redefining the Self: Enduring Struggles in the Historical Transformation of Agriculture in Burgundy, France.* Ph.D. dissertation, University of North Carolina, Chapel Hill.

Vansina, Jan. 1965. [1961] *Oral Tradition.* H. M. Wright, tr. Harmondsworth: Penguin Books.

———. 1985. *Oral Tradition as History.* London and Nairobi: James Currey and Heinemann.

von Thunen, Baron. 1966 [1838]. *The Isolated State.* Carla M. Wartenberg, tr. Oxford and New York: Pergamon Press.

Westmacott, Richard N. 1992. *African-American Gardens and Yards in the Rural South.* Knoxville: University of Tennessee Press.

Chapter 2

Arensberg, Conrad. 1959. *The Irish Countryman.* Gloucester: Peter Smith.

Arensberg, Conrad, and Solon T. Kimball. 1968. *Family and Community in Ireland.* Cambridge: Harvard University Press.

Ayers, Pat. 1990. The Hidden Economy of Dockland Families: Liverpool in the 1930s. In *Women's Work and the Family Economy in Historical Perspective.* Pat Hudson and W. R. Lee, eds. 271–290. Manchester: Manchester University Press.

Black, Clementina. 1983. *Married Women's Work.* London: Virago Press.

Blewett, Mary. 1990. *The Last Generation.* Amherst: University of Massachusetts Press.

Buckley, Anthony D. 1983. Neighbourliness—Myth and History. *Oral History Journal* 11(1):44–51.

Cohen, Marilyn. 1994. Religion and Social Inequality in Ireland. *Journal of Interdisciplinary History* 25(1):1–21.

———. 1997. *Linen, Family and Community in Tullylish, County Down, 1690–1914.* Dublin: Four Courts Press.

Cohen, Miriam. 1977. Italian-American Women in New York City, 1900–1950: Work and School. In *Class, Sex and the Woman Worker.* Milton Cantor and Bruce Laurie, eds. 120–143. Westport, CT: Greenwood.

Franzoi, Barbara. 1984. Domestic Industry: Work Options and Women's Choices. In *German Women in the Nineteenth Century.* John Fout, ed. New York: Holmes & Meier.

Glassie, Henry. 1982. *Passing the Time in Ballymenone.* Philadelphia: University of Pennsylvania Press.

Joyce, Patrick. 1991. *Visions of the People.* Cambridge: Cambridge University Press.

Kane, Eileen. 1972. The Changing Role of the Family in a Rural Irish Community. *Journal of Comparative Family Studies* 10(2):141–162.

Leavitt, Judith Walzer. 1986. Under the Shadow of Maternity: American Women's Responses to Death and Debility Fears in Nineteenth-Century Childbirth. *Feminist Studies* 12(1):129–154.

Lewis, Jane. 1984. *Women in England.* Bloomington: Indiana University Press.

McDougall, Mary Lynn. 1977. Working-Class Women During the Industrial Revolution, 1780–1914. In *Becoming Visible.* Renate Bridenthal and Claudia Koonz, eds. 255–279. Boston: Houghton Mifflin.

Meacham, Standish. 1977. *A Life Apart.* Cambridge: Harvard University Press.

Neill, Margaret. 1994. Homeworkers in Ulster, 1850–1911. In *Coming into the Light.* Janice Holmes and Diane Urquhart, eds. 2–32. Belfast: The Institute for Irish Studies Press.

Oren, Laura. 1973. The Welfare of Women in Laboring Families: England, 1860–1959. *Feminist Studies* 1(3–4):107–125.

Popular Memory Group. 1982. Popular Memory: Theory, Politics, Method. In *Making Histories.* Richard Johnson, Gregor McLennan, Bill Schwarz, and David Sutton, eds. 205–252. Minneapolis: University of Minnesota Press.

Reeves, Maud Pember. 1979. *Round About a Pound a Week.* London: Virago Press.

Rice, Margery Spring. 1981. *Working Class Wives.* London: Virago Press.

Roberts, Elizabeth. 1977. Working-Class Standards of Living in Barrow and Lancaster, 1890–1914. *Economic History Review,* 2d series, 30:306–314.

Rose, Sonya. 1992. *Limited Livelihoods.* Berkeley: University of California Press.

Ross, Ellen. 1982. Fierce Questions and Taunts: Married Life in Working-Class London, 1870–1914. *Feminist Studies* 8(3):575–602.

———. 1983. Survival Networks: Women's Neighbourhood Sharing in London Before World War I. *History Workshop Journal* 15:4–27.

———. 1993 *Love and Toil: Motherhood in Outcast London, 1870–1918.* Oxford: Oxford University Press.

Rowntree, Seebohm. 1913. *How the Labourer Lives.* London: Longmans.

Silverman, Marilyn, and P. H. Gulliver. 1995. *Merchants and Shopkeepers: A Historical Anthropology of an Irish Market Town.* Toronto: University of Toronto Press.

Stearns, Peter N. 1972. Working-Class Women in Britain, 1890–1914. In *Suffer and Be Still.* Martha Vicinus, ed. 100–120. Bloomington: Indiana University Press.

Thompson, Paul. 1978. *The Voice of the Past: Oral History*. Oxford: Oxford University Press.

Chapter 3

Ableman, Paul. 1999. *The Secret of Consciousness: How the Brain Tells the 'Story of Me.'* New York: Marion Boyars Publishers.

Archibald, Robert R. 1999. *A Place to Remember: Using History to Build Community*. Walnut Creek, CA: AltaMira Press.

Collingwood, R. G. 1994 [1946]. *The Idea of History*, Revised edition, with lectures 1926–1928. Jan Van Der Dussen, ed. Oxford: Oxford University Press.

Davis, Miles, with Quincy Troupe. 1989. *Miles: The Autobiography*. New York: Simon & Schuster.

Friedländer, Saul. 1979. *Quand vient le souvenir* (When Memory Comes). Helen R. Lane, tr. New York: Farrar, Straus, & Giroux.

Kammen, Michael G. 1991. *Mystic Chords of Memory: The Transformation of Tradition in American Culture.* New York: Alfred A. Knopf.

Nora, Pierre. 1989. Between Memory and History. *Representations* 26(3):9–25.

Rickman, H. P., ed. 1961. *Meaning in History; W. Dilthey's Thoughts on History and Society*. London: George Allen & Unwin Ltd.

Thelen, David. 2001. Memory. In *Encyclopedia of American Cultural and Intellectual History*. Mary Kupiec Cayton and Peter W. Williams, eds. 567–575. New York: Charles Scribner's Sons.

Chapter 4

Borowski, Neil. 1991. U.S. Census Bureau, *Inquirer* Analysis. Unpublished report.

Bowman, Daria Price, and Maureen LaMarca. 1997. *Pleasures of the Porch: Ideas for Gracious Outdoor Living*. New York: Rizzoli.

Carvajal, Doreen, and Neil A. Borowski. 1991. Asians, Latinos Flock to Philadelphia. *Philadelphia Inquirer*, March 1:B1,4.

Cattell, Maria G. 1989. *Old Age in Rural Kenya: Gender, the Life Course and Social Change*. Ph.D. dissertation: Bryn Mawr College.

———. 1991a. Aging-in-Place: Older Persons' Assessment of Urban Neighborhood Resources. Final report to the Retirement Research Foundation. Unpublished report.

———. 1991b. Aging-in-Place: Memories from Old Olney. *Olney Times*, October 17.

———. 1991c. Eating in Olney: A Multicultural Adventure. *Olney Times*, November 17.

———. 1992a. Community as Family: Neighbors, Friends, Community and Social Care among Older Persons in a Changing Philadelphia Neighborhood. Paper presented at the annual meeting of the Gerontological Society of America, Washington, D.C.

———. 1992b. Aging-in-Place: Older Persons' Assessment of Community Resources. *Association for Anthropology and Gerontology Newsletter* 13(1):5–6.

———. 1994. Environments for Living: Insider Views of an Urban Neighborhood as a Resource Environment for Elderly Residents. Poster presented at the annual meeting of the Gerontological Society of America, Atlanta.

———. 1996. Remembered Community: Elders' Memories in Constructions of Place and Self in a Philadelphia Neighborhood. Paper presented at the annual meeting of the Oral History Association, Philadelphia.

———. 1997a. "I'm Staying Right Here": Philadelphia Elders' Creativity in Fighting Frailty. Paper presented at the annual meeting of the Society for Applied Anthropology, Seattle.

———. 1997b. Mini-Versailles in Philadelphia: Gardens as Personal Resources for the Elderly. Paper presented at the annual meeting of the Central States Anthropological Association, Milwaukee.

———. 1999. Elders' Complaints: Discourses on Old Age and Social Change in Kenya and Philadelphia. In *Language and Communication in Old Age*. Heidi Hamilton, ed. 295–317. New York: Garland Press.

Clark, Dennis J. 1973. The Philadelphia Irish: Persistent Presence. In *The Peoples of Philadelphia: A History of Ethnic Groups and Lower-Class Life, 1790–1940*. Allen Davis and Mark Haller, eds. 135–154. Philadelphia: Temple University Press.

Csikszentmihalyi, Mihaly, and Eugene Rochberg-Halton. 1981. *The Meaning of Things: Domestic Symbols and the Self*. Cambridge: Cambridge University Press.

Golab, Caroline. 1973. The Immigrant and the City: Poles, Italians, and Jews in Philadelphia, 1870–1920. In *The Peoples of Philadelphia: A History of Ethnic Groups and Lower-Class Life, 1790–1940*. Allen Davis and Mark Haller, eds. 203–230. Philadelphia: Temple University Press.

Goode, Judith, and Jo Anne Schneider. 1994. *Reshaping Ethnic and Racial Relations in Philadelphia: Immigrants in a Divided City*. Philadelphia: Temple University Press.

Goode, Judith, Jo Anne Schneider, and Suzanne Blanc. 1992. Transcending Boundaries and Closing Ranks: How Schools Shape Interrelations. In *Structuring Diversity: Ethnographic Perspectives on the New Immigration*. Louise Lamphere, ed. 173–213. Chicago: University of Chicago Press.

Kaminsky, Marc. 1992. Introduction. In *Remembered Lives: The Work of Ritual, Storytelling, and Growing Older*. Marc Kaminsky, ed. 1–97. Ann Arbor: University of Michigan Press.

Keith, Jennie. 1986. Participant Observation. In *New Methods for Old Age Research: Strategies for Studying Diversity*. Christine L. Fry and Jennie Keith, eds. 1–20. Westport, CT: Bergin & Garvey.

Lawton, M. Powell. 1986. *Environment and Aging*, 2d edition. Albany, NY: Center for the Study of Aging.

Marsella, Anthony J., George DeVos, and Francis L.K. Hsu. 1985. *Culture and Self: Asian and Western Perspectives*. New York: Tavistock.

Miller, Frederic M., M. J. Vogel, and A. F. Davis. 1988. *Philadelphia Stories: A Photographic History, 1920–1960*. Philadelphia: Temple University Press.

Myerhoff, Barbara. 1978. *Number Our Days*. New York: Touchstone.

———. 1992. Life History among the Elderly: Performance, Visibility, and Re-membering. In *Remembered Lives: The Work of Ritual, Storytelling, and Growing Older*. Marc Kaminsky, ed. 231–247. Ann Arbor: University of Michigan Press.

Philadelphia City Planning Commission. 1981. *1980 Census, Special Population Summary for Philadelphia Census Tracts*. Technical Information Paper 81–11, revised edition. Philadelphia.

PHMC (Philadelphia Health Management Corporation). 1985. *Neighborhood Health Profile No. 10: Olney-Oak Lane and Olney-Feltonville*. Philadelphia: PHMC/PCA (Philadelphia Corporation for Aging).

Rowles, Graham D. 1978. *Prisoners of Space? The Geographical Experiences of Older People*. Boulder: Westview Press.

———. 1983. Geographical Dimensions of Social Support in Rural Appalachia. In *Aging and Milieu: Environmental Perspectives on Growing Old*. Graham D. Rowles and R. Ohta, eds. 111–130. New York: Academic Press.

———. 1984. Aging in Rural Environments. In *Elderly People and the Environment*. M. Powell Lawton and J. F. Wohlwill, eds. 129–155. New York: Plenum.

Rubinstein, Robert L. 1987. The Significance of Personal Objects to Older People. *Journal of Aging Studies* 1:225–238.

———. 1989. The Home Environments of Older People: A Description of the Psychosocial Processes Linking Person to Place. *Journal of Gerontology* 44(2):S45–53.

———. 1992. Anthropological Methods in Gerontological Research: Entering the Realm of Meaning. *Journal of Aging Studies* 6(1):57–66.

Shweder, Richard A., and Robert A. LeVine. 1984. *Culture Theory: Essays on Mind, Self, and Emotion*. Cambridge: Cambridge University Press.

Singer, Milton. 1984. *Man's Glassy Essence: Explorations in Semiotic Anthropology*. Bloomington: Indiana University Press.

Stafford, Philip B. 1996. *The Evergreen Project: A Report to the Community on Environments of Older Adults*. Bloomington: The Evergreen Project.

Sutherland, John F. 1973. Housing the Poor in the City of Homes: Philadelphia at the Turn of the Century. In *The Peoples of Philadelphia: A History of Ethnic Groups and Lower-Class Life, 1790–1940*. Allen F. Davis and Mark H. Haller, eds. 175–201. Philadelphia: Temple University Press.

Turner, Victor W., and Edward M. Bruner. 1986. *The Anthropology of Experience*. Urbana: University of Illinois Press.

Chapter 5

Barth, F. 1969. *Ethnic Groups and Boundaries*. London: Allen & Unwin.

Baumann, G. 1996. *Contesting Culture: Discourses of Identity in Multi-ethnic London*. Cambridge: Cambridge University Press.

Boyarin, Jonathan, ed. 1994. Introduction. In *Remapping Memory: The Politics of TimeSpace*. vii–xiv. Minneapolis: University of Minnesota Press.

Fortier, A. M. 2000. *Migrant Belongings: Memory, Space, Identity*. Oxford and New York: Berg.

Francis, D., L. Kellaher, and G. Neophytou. 2001. The Cemetery: The Evidence of Continuing Bonds. In *Grief, Mourning and Death Ritual.* J. Hockey, J. Katz, and N. Small, eds. 226–236. Buckingham and Philadelphia: Open University Press.

Halpern, D. 1998. *Social Capital, Exclusion and Quality of Life: Towards a Causal Model and Policy Implications.* Unpublished Nexus Briefing Paper.

Hart, L. K. 1992. *Time, Religion and Social Experience in Rural Greece.* Boston: Rowman and Littlefield.

Herman, J. 1996. *Stones of Kolin: A Bohemian Jewish Rhapsody.* Unpublished manuscript.

Hirschon, R. 1989. *Heirs of the Greek Catastrophe: The Social Life of Asia Minor Refugees in Piraeus.* Oxford: Clarendon Press.

Hunt, J. D. 1997. Come Into the Garden Maude: Garden Art as a Privileged Mode of Commemoration and Identity. In *Places of Commemoration: The Search for Identity and Landscape Design.* J. Wolschke-Bulmahn, ed. Colloquium on the History of Landscape Architecture 19. 9–24. Washington, DC: Dumbarton Oaks.

Kenna, M. 1976. Houses, Fields and Graves: Property and Ritual Obligation on a Greek Island. *Ethnology* 15.

Klass, D., P. R. Silverman, and S. L. Nickman, eds. 1996. *Continuing Bonds: New Understandings of Grief.* Washington, DC: Taylor & Francis.

Rapport, N., and A. Dawson. 1998. Opening a Debate. In *Migrants of Identity: Perceptions of Home in a World of Movement.* N. Rapport and A. Dawson, eds. 3–38. Oxford: Berg.

Townsend, P. 1957. *The Family Life of Old People: An Inquiry in East London.* London: Routledge & Kegan Paul.

Vassiliadis, N. P. 1993. *The Mystery of Death.* Fr. Peter A. Chamberas, tr. Athenes: The Orthodox Brotherhood of Theologians 'The Saviour.'

Walter, T. 1996. A New Model of Grief: Bereavement and Biography. *Mortality* 1(1):7–25.

Ware, K. 1995. Go Joyfully: The Mystery of Death and Resurrection. In *Beyond Death: Theological and Philosophical Reflections on Life After Death.* D. Cohn-Sherbok and C. Lewis, eds. London: Macmillan.

Warner, W. L. 1959. *The Living and the Dead.* Chicago: Free Press.

Young, M., and P. Willmott. 1957. *Family and Kinship in East London.* London: Routledge & Kegan Paul.

Chapter 6

Anderson, Benedict. 1983. *Imagined Communities.* London: Verso.

Avruch, Kevin. 1981. *American Immigrants in Israel: Social Identities and Change.* Chicago: University of Chicago Press.

Balibar, Etienne, and Immanuel Wallerstein. 1991. *The Nation Form: History and Ideology in Race, Nation, Class: Ambiguous Identities.* London: Verso.

Behar, Ruth. 1996. *The Vulnerable Observer: Anthropology That Breaks Your Heart.* Boston: Beacon Press.

Bertaux, D. 1981. *Biography and Society: The Life History Approach in the Social Sciences.* Beverly Hills: Sage.

Briggs, Jean L. 1987. In Search of Emotional Meaning. *Ethos* 15(1):8–15.

Climo, Jacob J. 1990. Transmitting Ethnic Identity through Oral Narrative. *Ethnic Groups* 8:163–179.

———. 1995. Prisoners of Silence: A Vicarious Holocaust Memory. In *The Labyrinth of Memory: Ethnographic Journeys.* Marea C. Teski and Jacob J. Climo, eds. 175–184. Westport, CT: Bergin & Garvey.

———. 1999. *A Memory of Intimacy in Liminal Space.* In *Sex, Sexuality and the Anthropologist.* F. Markowitz and Michael Ashkenazi, eds. 43–56. Urbana: University of Illinois Press.

Crapanzano, Vincent. 1985. *Tuhami: Portrait of a Moroccan.* Chicago: University of Chicago Press.

Fabian, Johannes. 1983. *Time and the Other: How Anthropology Makes Its Object.* New York: Columbia University Press.

Fox, Richard G., ed. 1990. *Nationalist Ideologies and the Production of National Cultures.* Monograph Series No. 2. Washington, DC: American Ethnological Society.

Giddens, Anthony. 1991. *Modernity and Self-Identity: Self and Society in the Late Modern Age.* Stanford: Stanford University Press.

Goldsmith, Martin. 2000. *The Inextinguishable Symphony: A True Story of Music and Love in Nazi Germany.* New York: John Wiley and Sons.

Guarinzo, L. E. 1994. Los Dominicanyorks: The Makings of a Binational Society. *Annals of the American Academy of Political and Social Science* 533:70–86.

Gubrium, Jaber F., and James A. Holstein. 1995. Biographical Work and the New Ethnography. In *The Narrative Study of Lives.* Ruthellen Josselson and Amia Lieblich, eds. 45–58. London: Sage.

Hertzberg, Arthur, ed. 1960. *The Zionist Idea: A Historical Analysis and Reader.* New York: Meridian Books; and Philadelphia: The Jewish Publication Society of America.

Ishino, Iwao. 1995. Memories and Their Unintended Consequences. In *The Labyrinth of Memory:Ethnographic Journeys.* Marea C. Teski and Jacob J. Climo, eds. 185–201. Westport, CT: Bergin & Garvey.

Jameson, Frederic. 1981. *The Political Unconscious: Narrative as a Socially Symbolic Act.* Ithaca: Cornell University Press.

Kaminsky, Marc. 1992. Introduction. In *Remembered Lives: The Work of Ritual, Storytelling, and Growing Older.* Marc Kaminsky, ed. 1–97. Ann Arbor: University of Michigan Press.

Lutz, Catherine, and G. M. White. 1986. The Anthropology of Emotions. *Annual Review of Anthropology* 15:405–436.

Middleton, Dwight R. 1989. Emotional Style: The Cultural Ordering of Emotions. *Ethos* 17(2):187–201.

Mintz, Sidney. 1996. The Anthropological Interview and the Life History. In *Oral History: An Interdisciplinary Anthology.* David K. Dunaway and Willa K. Baum, eds. Walnut Creek, CA: AltaMira Press.

Myerhoff, Barbara. 1978. *Number Our Days: A Triumph of Continuity and Culture among Jewish Old People in an Urban Ghetto.* New York: Simon & Schuster.

———. 1985. *In Her Own Time.* Lynne Littman, Director. Center for Visual Anthropology, University of Southern California in association with Embassy Television. New York: Jewish Media Fund.

———. 1992. Life History among the Elderly: Performance, Visibility, and Re-membering. In *Remembered Lives: The Work of Ritual, Storytelling, and Growing Older.* Marc Kaminsky, ed. 231–247. Ann Arbor: University of Michigan Press.

Owings, Alison. 1993. *Frauen: German Women Recall the Third Reich.* New Brunswick: Rutgers University Press.

Peltz, Rakhmiel. 1998. *From Immigrant to Ethnic Culture: American Yiddish in South Philadelphia.* Stanford: Stanford University Press.

Rapport, Nigel. 1998. Coming Home to A Dream: A Study of The Immigrant Discourse of "Anglo-Saxons" in Israel. In *Migrants of Identity.* Nigel Rapport and A. Dawson, eds. Oxford: Berg.

Rosaldo, Renato. 1993. *Culture and Truth: The Remaking of Social Analysis.* Boston: Beacon Press.

Shweder, Richard, and Robert LeVine. 1990. *Culture Theory: Mind, Self, and Emotion.* New York: Cambridge University Press.

Shostak, Marjorie. 1993 [1981]. *Nisa: The Life and Words of a !Kung Woman.* New York: Random House.

Spiro, Melford. 1964. *Kibbutz: Venture in Utopia.* New York: Schocken Books.

Teski, Marea C., and Jacob J. Climo, eds. 1995. *The Labyrinth of Memory: Ethnographic Journeys.* Westport, CT: Bergin & Garvey.

Waxman, Chaim I. 1989. *American Aliya: Portrait of an Innovative Migration Movement.* Detroit: Wayne State University Press.

White, Hayden V. 1987. *The Content of the Form.* Baltimore: Johns Hopkins University Press.

Williams, Brackette F. 1989. A Class Act: Anthropology and the Race to Nation across Ethnic Terrain. *Annual Review of Anthropology* 18:401–444.

Wolf, Eric. 1984. *Europe and the People Without History.* Berkeley: University of California Press.

Yerushalmi, Y. H. 1982. *Zakhor: Jewish History and Jewish Memory.* Seattle: University of Washington Press.

Zerubavel, Yael. 1995. *Recovered Roots: Collective Memory and the Making of Israeli National Tradition.* Chicago: University of Chicago Press.

Chapter 7

Boyd, Maurice. 1981. *Kiowa Voices: Ceremonial Dance, Ritual, and Song,* Vol. 1. Fort Worth: Texas Christian University Press.

———. 1983. *Kiowa Voices: Myths, Legends, and Folktales,* Vol. 2. Fort Worth: Texas Christian University Press.

Connerton, Paul. 1989. *How Societies Remember.* Cambridge: Cambridge University Press.

Foster, Morris W. 1991. *Being Comanche: A Social History of an American Indian Community.* Tucson: University of Arizona Press.

Hagan, William T. 1990. *United States-Comanche Relations: The Reservation Years.* Norman: University of Oklahoma Press.

Horse, Billy Evans. 1990a. Oral presentation recorded by author, Apache, Oklahoma, July 14.

———. 1990b. Recorded conversation with author, Carnegie, Oklahoma, July 10.

———. 1991a. Recorded conversation with author, Anadarko, Oklahoma, June 20.

———. 1991b. Recorded conversation with author, Carnegie, Oklahoma, July 11.

Hymes, Dell. 1981. *"In Vain I Tried to Tell You": Essays in Native American Ethnopoetics*. Philadelphia: University of Pennsylvania Press.

Kavanagh, Thomas W. 1996. *Comanche Political History: An Ethnohistorical Perspective, 1706–1875*. Lincoln: University of Nebraska Press.

Kiowa Gourd Clan. 1976. *Kiowa Gourd Clan Ceremonials: July 1–4, 1976*. Photocopy of program in author's possession.

Lassiter, Luke Eric. 1997. "Charlie Brown": Not Just Another Essay on the Gourd Dance. *American Indian Culture and Research Journal* 21(4):75–103.

———. 1998. *The Power of Kiowa Song: A Collaborative Ethnography*. Tucson: University of Arizona Press.

———. 1999. Southwestern Oklahoma, the Gourd Dance, and Charlie Brown. In *Contemporary Native American Cultural Issues*. Duane Champagne, ed. 145–166. Walnut Creek, CA: AltaMira Press.

———. 2000. Authoritative Texts, Collaborative Ethnography, and Native American Studies. *American Indian Quarterly* 24(4):601–614.

———. 2001. From "Reading Over the Shoulders of Natives" to "Reading Alongside Natives," Literally: Toward a Collaborative and Reciprocal Ethnography. *Journal of Anthropological Research* 57(2):137–149.

Lowie, Robert H. 1916. Societies of the Kiowa. In *Societies of the Plains Indians, Anthropological Papers of the American Museum of Natural History* 11(11):836–851.

Mooney, James. 1898. *Calendar History of the Kiowa Indians*. Seventeenth Annual Report of the Bureau of American Ethnology, Part 1. Washington, DC: Government Printing Office.

Nye, Colonel W. S. 1969 [1937]. *Carbine and Lance: The Story of Old Fort Sill*. Norman: University of Oklahoma Press.

Prucha, Francis Paul. 1985. *The Indians in American Society*. Berkeley: University of California Press.

Satethieday Khatgomebaugh. 1994. Promotional flyer in author's possession.

Tedlock, Dennis. 1983. *The Spoken Word and the Work of Interpretation*. Philadelphia: University of Pennsylvania Press.

Teski, Marea C. 1995. The Remembered Consciousness of a Polish Exile Government. In *The Labyrinth of Memory: Ethnographic Journeys*. Marea C. Teski and Jacob J. Climo, eds. 49–58. Westport, CT: Bergin & Garvey.

Teski, Marea C., and Jacob J. Climo, eds. 1995. *The Labyrinth of Memory: Ethnographic Journeys*. Westport, CT: Bergin & Garvey.

Wallace, Ernest, and E. Adamson Hoebel. 1952. *The Comanches: Lords of the South Plains*. Norman: University of Oklahoma Press.

Weeks, Philip, ed. 1988. *The American Indian Experience, A Profile: 1524 to the Present*. Arlington Heights: Forum Press.

Chapter 8

Aguirre Beltrán, Gonzalo. 1992. *Teoría y Práctica de la Educación Indígena.* Mexico: Universidad Veracruzana, Instituto Nacional Indigenista, Gobierno del Estado de Veracruz: Fonda de Cultura Económico.

ANPIBAC. 1980. *I Congreso Nacional: Los Indígenas y su política educativa.* Mexico: ANPIBAC.

Bauman, Zygmunt. 1998. *Globalization: The Human Consequences.* Oxford: Polity Press.

Bhabha, Homi. 1997. Of Mimicry and Man: The Ambivalence of Colonial Discourse. In *Tensions of Empire, Colonial Cultures in a Bourgeois World.* Frederick Cooper and Laura Stoler, eds. 152–160. Berkeley: University of California Press.

Bonfil Batalla, Guillermo. 1981. *Utopía y Revolución: El pensamiento politico contemporáneo de los indios en América Latina.* Mexico, D.F.: Nueva Imágen.

———. 1989. *México Profundo: Una civilización negada.* Mexico: Grijalbo.

Bourdieu, Pierre. 1984. *Distinction: A Social Critique of the Judgement of Taste.* Cambridge: Harvard University Press.

Burke, Peter. 1991. Heu domine, adsunt Turcae: A Sketch for a Social History of Post-Medieval Latin. In *Language, Self and Society, A History of Language.* Peter Burke and Roy Porter, eds. 23–50. Oxford: Polity Press.

Cahill, Spencer E. 1998. Towards a Sociology of Person. *Sociological Theory* 16(2):131–148.

Cimet, Adina. 1997. Incomplete Allowance: Jews as a Minority in Mexico. *Estudios Interdisciplinarios de America Latina y Caribe* 8(2):105–124.

Coombe, Rosemary J. 1995. The Properties of Culture and the Politics of Possessing Identity: Native Claims in the Cultural Appropriation Controversy. In *After Identity, A Reader in Law and Culture.* Dan Danielsen and Karen Engle, eds. 251–270. New York: Routledge.

Dietz, Gunter. 2000. Entre Estado y Nación y Comunidad Indígena: la identidad del magisterio bilingue purhepecha en México. *Estudios Interdisciplinarios de America Latina y Caribe* 11(2):93–112.

Foucault, Michel. 1977. *Language, Counter-memory, Practice: Selected Essays and Interviews.* Donald F. Bouchard, ed. D. F. Bouchard and Sherry Simon, tr. New York: Cornell University Press.

García Canclini, Néstor. 1995. *Consumidores y Ciudadanos: conflictos multiculturales de la globalización.* Mexico, D.F.: Grijalbo.

Gruzinski, Serge. 1993. *The Conquest of Mexico.* Oxford: Polity Press.

Guerrero, Francisco Javier. 1998. Fundamentalismo Indígenista. *Excélsior* March 22:8.

Harvey, Neil. 1998. *The Chiapas Rebellion: The Struggle for Land and Democracy.* Durham, NC: Duke University Press.

Jímenez Ricardez, Ruben. 1997. Las rezones de la sublevación. *Chiapas* 3:55–72.

Joyce, Patrick. 1991. The People's English: Language and Class in England, 1840–1920. In *Language, Self, and Society: A Social History of Language.* Peter Burke and Roy Porter, eds. 154–190. Oxford: Polity Press.

Kiernan, Victor. 1991. Languages and Conquerors. In *Language, Self, and Society: A Social History of Language.* Peter Burke and Roy Porter, eds. 191–210. Oxford: Polity Press.

Krauze, Enrique. 1999. Chiapas, redención o democracia. *Letras Libres* 1(1).

La Grange, Bertrand. 1997. *Marcos, La genial impostura*. Mexico: Nuevo Siglo Aguilar.

La Grange, Bertrand, and Maite Rico. 1999. El otro subcomandante. *Letras Libres* 1(2).

León Portilla, Miguel. 1992 [1969]. *Visión de los Vencidos, Relaciones Indígenas de la Conquista*. Mexico: UNAM.

———. 1997 [1964]. *El Reverso de la Conquista*. Mexico: Joaquín Mortiz.

León y Gama, Antonio. 1990 [1792]. *Descripción Histórica y Cronológica de las Dos Piedras*. Mexico: INAH.

Lomniz, Claudio. 1998. Krauze y su fábrica de la historia. *Milenio* May.

Los Mexicanos Pintados por si Mismos; reproduccion exacta del original de 1853 hecha en lithcraft. Mexico, D.F.: Studio Mexico.

Merleau-Ponty, Maurice. 1973. *Consciousness and the Acquisition of Language*. Evanston IL: Northwestern University Press.

Mehta, Uday S. 1997. Liberal Strategies of Exclusion. In *Tensions of Empire: Colonial Cultures in a Bourgeois World*. Frederick Cooper and Ann Laura Stoler, eds. 59–86. Berkeley: University of California Press.

Paz, Octavio. 1998. Epitafio sobre Ninguna Piedra. *Vuelta* 22:258.

Perez Enriquez, Maria Isabel. 1989. *Expulsiones Indígenas: Religión y Migración en tres municipios de los Altos de Chiapas: Chemalhó, Larrainzar y Chamula*. Mexico, D.F.: Claves Latinoamericanas.

Saramago, José. 2000. *Chiapas, Rostros de la Guerra* (War Faces). Cd. Obrera, Mexico, D.F.: Publicaciones Espejo.

Todorov, Tzvetan. 1982. *The Conquest of America*. New York: Harper & Row.

Williams, Raymond. 1977. *Marxism and Literature*. Bristol: Oxford University Press.

Wood, Gordon S. 1998. The Bloodiest War. *The New York Review of Books* April 9:41–44.

Chapter 9

Abercrombie, Thomas A. 1998. *Pathways of Memory and Power: Ethnography and History among an Andean People*. Madison: University of Wisconsin Press.

Agosin, Marjorie. 1996. *Tapestries of Hope, Threads of Love: The Arpillera Movement in Chile, 1974–1994*. Albuquerque: University of New Mexico Press.

Allende, Isabel. 1999. Pinochet Without Hatred. *New York Times Magazine* January 17:24–27.

Ancan Jara, Jose. 1997. Indian City: Urban Mapuches: Reflections on a Modern Reality in Chile. *Abya Yala News* 10(3):12.

Anderson, Jon Lee. 1998. The Dictator Profile. *The New Yorker* October 19:44–57.

Aylwin, Jose. 1998. Indigenous Peoples' Rights in Chile: Progresses and Contradictions in a Context of Economic Globalization. Paper presented at the Canadian Association for Latin American and Caribbean Studies XXVIIIth Congress, Vancouver.

Bateson, Mary Catherine. 1990. *Composing a Life*. New York: Plume/Penguin Books.

Berger, Peter L., and Thomas Luckmann. 1966. *The Social Construction of Reality: A Treatise in the Sociology of Knowledge*. New York: Anchor Books.

Bourdieu, Pierre. 1977. *Outline of a Theory of Practice*. New York: Cambridge University Press.
Bourdieu, Pierre, and Lois J. D. Wacquant. 1992. *Invitation to a Reflexive Sociology*. Chicago: University of Chicago Press.
Camnitzer, Luis. 1994. Art and Politics: The Aesthetics of Resistance. *NACLA Report on the Americas* XXVIII(2):38–46.
Castañeda, Quetzil. 1997. On the Correct Training of Indios in the Handicraft Market at Chichen Itza: Tactics and Tactility of Gender, Class, Race, and State. *Journal of Latin American Anthropology* 2(2):106–143.
Cleary, Edward L. 1997. *The Struggle for Human Rights in Latin America*. Westport, CT: Praeger.
Clifford, James. 1988. *The Predicament of Culture: Twentieth-Century Ethnography, Literature, and Art*. Cambridge: Harvard University Press.
———. 1997. *Routes: Travel and Translation in the Late Twentieth Century*. Cambridge: Harvard University Press.
Derechos Chile. 1999. *Human Rights in Chile—Then and Now*. At www.derechoschile.com/english/about.html.
Dorfman, Ariel. 1998. *Heading South, Looking North: A Bilingual Journey*. New York: Farrar, Straus & Giroux.
Fairclough, Norman. 1989. *Language and Power*. New York: Longman.
Garcia Canclini, Nestor. 1993. Memory and Innovation in the Theory of Art. *South Atlantic Quarterly* 92(3–4):423–443.
Hayner, Priscilla B. 2001. *Unspeakable Truths: Confronting State Terror and Atrocity*. New York: Routledge.
Kleymeyer, Charles David, ed. 1994. *Cultural Expression and Grassroots Development: Cases from Latin America and the Caribbean*. Boulder: Lynne Rienner.
Lawson, Dominic. 1999. Getting to Know the General. *The Sunday Telegraph*, Review Section, July 18:1–2.
Lutz, Catherine A., and Jane L. Collins. 1993. *Reading the National Geographic*. Chicago: University of Chicago Press.
Marcus, George E., and Fred R. Myers. 1995. The Traffic in Art and Culture: An Introduction. In *The Traffic in Culture: Refiguring Art and Anthropology*. George E. Marcus and Fred R. Myers, eds. 1–51. Berkeley: University of California Press.
Montecino, Marcelo. 1994. *Nunca Super Sus Nombres*. Coleccion Mal de Ojo. Santiago: LOM Ediciones.
Myerhoff, Barbara. 1992. *Remembered Lives: The Work of Ritual, Storytelling, and Growing Older*. Marc Kaminsky, ed. Ann Arbor: University of Michigan Press.
Neruda, Pablo. 1978. *Memoirs*. London: Penguin.
Teski, Marea C., and Jacob J. Climo. 1995. Introduction. In *The Labyrinth of Memory: Ethnographic Journeys*. Marea C. Teski and Jacob J. Climo, eds. 1–10. Westport, CT: Bergin & Garvey.
———. N.d. Memory Practices: Culture and the Creation of Memory Repertoires. Unpublished manuscript.
Turner, Victor. 1982. *From Ritual to Theatre: The Human Seriousness of Play*. New York: PAJ Publications.

Warren, Kay B. 1992. Transforming Memories and Histories: The Meanings of Ethnic Resurgence for Mayan Indians. In *Americas: New Interpretive Essays*. A. Stephan, ed. 189–219. New York: Oxford University Press.

———. 1998. *Indigenous Movements and Their Critics: Pan-Maya Activism in Guatemala*. Princeton: Princeton University Press.

Chapter 10

Anson, Bert. 1970. *The Miami Indians*. Norman: University of Oklahoma Press.

Callendar, Charles. 1978. Miami. In *Handbook of North American Indians*, Vol. 15, *The Northeast*. Bruce Trigger, ed. Washington, DC: Smithsonian Institution Press.

Crow, Warder. 1936. Manuscript. Wabash County Historical Society.

Friedman, Jonathan. 1994. *Cultural Identity and Global Process*. London: Sage.

Glenn, Elizabeth J., B. K. Swartz, Jr., and Russel L. Lewis. 1977. *Archaeological Reports*. Number 14. Muncie: Ball State University.

———. N.d. Ethnohistory Report on Francois Godfroy's Salamonie Reserve. Typescript.

Greenbaum, Susan. 1990. Anthropological Report on the Miami Nation of Indians of Indiana: Social and Political Organization, Territorial Distributions, Social Relations and Cultural Identity. First Computer Concepts, Inc.: Typescript.

Halbwachs, Maurice. 1980 [1950]. *The Collective Memory*. Maurice Halbwachs, J. Ditter, Jr., and V. Y. Ditter, tr. New York: Harper & Row.

Hall, Robert. 1997. *An Archaeology of the Soul: North American Indian Belief and Ritual*. Urbana: University of Illinois Press.

Jeske, Robert. 1996. World Systems Theory: Core, Periphery Interactions and Elite Economic Exchange in Mississippian Societies. *Journal of World Systems Research*, vol. 2, art. 10 at csf.colorado.edu/jwsr/archive/vol2/v2_na.htm (accessed March 26, 2001).

Kinietz, Vernon. 1991. *The Indians of the Western Great Lakes, 1615–1760*. Ann Arbor: University of Michigan Press.

Mann, Robert. 1999. The Silenced Miami: Archaeological and Ethnohistorical Evidence for Miami-British Relations, 1795–1812. *Ethnohistory* 46(3):399–428.

Poinsatte, Charles R. 1969. *Fort Wayne During the Canal Era 1828–1855: A Study of a Western Community in the Middle Period of American History*. Indiana Historical Collections, vol. 24. Indianapolis: Indiana Historical Society.

Rafert, Stuart. 1982. *The Hidden Community: The Miami Indians of Indiana, 1846–1940*. Ph.D. dissertation, University of Delaware.

———. 1996. *The Miami Indians of Indiana: A Persistent People, 1654–1994*. Indianapolis: Indiana Historical Society.

Rafert, Stewart, and Lemoine Marks, eds. 1991. Testimony Pursuant to Congressional Legislation of June 1, 1872 Taken Before the Commission Appointed by the Secretary of the Interior to Make Partition of the Reserve Granted to Me-shin-go-me-sia in Trust for His Band by the Seventh Article of the Treaty of November 28, 1840 between the United States and the Miami Tribe of Indians. Testimony taken at the School House on the reservation adjoining the Union Baptist Missionary Church from May 14, 1873 until July 7, 1873. Typescript.

Rolland, Lewis Whitson. 1914. *Centennial History of Grant County*. Chicago: Lewis.
Sahlins, Marshall. 1985. *Islands of History*. Chicago: University of Chicago Press.
———. 1988. Cosmologies of Capitalism: The Trans-Pacific Sector of the World System. *Proceedings of the British Academy*, LXXIV:1–51.
Teski, Marea C., and Jacob J. Climo, eds. 1995. Introduction. *The Labyrinth of Memory: Ethnographic Journeys*. Westport, CT: Bergin & Garvey.
Trowbridge, C.C. 1938. *Meearmeear Traditions*. Vernon Kinietz, ed. Occasional Contributions from the Museum of Anthropology of the University of Michigan, No. 7. Ann Arbor: University of Michigan Press.
Urry, John. 1990. *The Tourist Gaze: Leisure and Travel in Contemporary Societies*. London: Sage.
Wepler, William. 1984. *Miami Occupation of the Upper Wabash Drainage*. Archaeological Resources Management Service, Report of Investigation 16. Muncie: Ball State University.
White, Richard. 1991. *The Middle Ground: Indians, Empires and Republics in the Great Lakes Region 1600–1815*. Cambridge: Cambridge University Press.
Winger, Otho. 1943. *The Frances Slocum Trail*. North Manchester, IN: L.W. Schultz.

Index

About the Contributors

Robert R. Archibald, Ph.D., has been President of the Missouri Historical Society since 1988, where he has overseen the recent renovation and expansion of the Missouri History Museum and the development and implementation of the Society's mission to facilitate inclusive community discussion. In addition to his activities in the fields of history and museum work, Archibald is active in the concerns of his present community of St. Louis and is a nationally known speaker and consultant on issues of museum practice and administration, the humanities, environmental responsibilities, and community collaboration. His most recent book, *A Place to Remember: Using History to Build Community,* was published by AltaMira Press in 1999.

Maria G. Cattell, anthropologist and Research Associate at The Field Museum of Natural History, has taught at Franklin and Marshall College, Lebanon Valley College, and Millersville University. Her research focuses on older people and social change, families, intergenerational relationships, gender, and power. She has been doing long-term research among Abaluyia in Kenya since 1982 and has also carried out research projects among Zulus in South Africa and with older white ethnics in Philadelphia. With Steven Albert she wrote *Old Age in Global Perspective: Cross-Cultural and Cross-National Views* (1994).

Adina Cimet was born in Mexico City and studied sociology at National Autonomous University (UNAM), Mexico City. She studied at the London School of Economics, where she received M.A. and M.Phil. degrees, then Columbia University where she received her Ph.D. in sociology. Cimet taught contemporary civilization courses in Columbia University and is affiliated with YIVO Institute for Jewish Research at Columbia University. She is a consultant to the Barnard-Columbia

Center for Urban Policy Research, and contributed to conferences and teaching courses in the National Autonomous University (UNAM) and Iberoamericana University (UIA), Mexico. Her most recent book is *Ashkenazi Jews in Mexico: Ideologies in the Structuring of a Community* (1997).

Jacob J. Climo, Professor of Anthropology, teaches social and medical anthropology at Michigan State University. He has conducted research and taught anthropology in Mexico, Ethiopia, Israel, and the USA. His current research focuses on intergenerational relationships, including: intimate relationships that are distant in time and space, the ethnography of memory in cross-cultural perspective, aging and elder care in rich and poor countries, grandparents who parent their grandchildren, and narratives of the quality of family relationships between aging parents in America and their adult children who live in Israel. His books include, *The Labyrinth of Memory: Ethnographic Journeys* (co-edited with Marea C. Teski, 1995) and *Distant Parents* (1992).

Marilyn Cohen is Assistant Professor of Anthropology at Montclair State University in New Jersey. She has published widely on the Irish linen industry, editing an interdisciplinary volume entitled *The Warp of Ulster's Past: Interdisciplinary Perspectives on the Irish Linen Industry, 1700–1920* and *Linen, Family and Community in Tullylish, County Down, 1690–1914.*

Carole L. Crumley (Ph.D., Wisconsin-Madison, 1972) is Professor at the University of North Carolina, Chapel Hill (1977–present). Her major interests include European archeology and ethnography, historical ecology, epistemology of complex systems, state societies, geographic information systems (GIS), and remote sensing. Her recent publications include: *Heterarchy and the Analysis of Complex Societies* (with R. Ehrenreich and J. Levy, 1995); *Historical Ecology: Cultural Knowledge and Changing Landscapes* (1994); *Regional Dynamics: Burgundian Landscapes in Historical Perspective* (with W. H. Marquardt, 1987).

Doris Francis is an anthropologist living in Santa Fe, New Mexico, where she teaches university courses in aging and is conducting research on the Girard Collection of amulets and ex-votos for the Museum of International Folk Art. *The Secret Cemetery*, her ethnography of cross-cultural London cemeteries and mourning practices, written in collaboration with Leonie Kellaher and Georgina Neophytou, is scheduled for publication by Berg Press in 2002.

Leonie Kellaher is Director of The Centre for Environmental and Social Studies in Ageing at the University of North London. As an anthropologist, she has published extensively on residential care.

Luke Eric Lassiter is an Associate Professor of anthropology at Ball State University in Muncie, Indiana. His books include *The Power of Kiowa Song: A Collaborative Ethnography* (1998), *The Jesus Road: Kiowas, Christianity, and Indian Hymns* (co-authored with Clyde Ellis and Ralph Kotay, 2002), *Powwow: Native American Performance, Identity and Meaning* (co-edited with Clyde Ellis, 2003) and *Representation, Identity, and Practice in Selected Souths* (co-edited with Celeste Ray, 2003).

Cheryl Natzmer is a historian with the Michigan Historical Museum where she facilitates object-based learning programs. She is a doctoral candidate in the anthropology department at Michigan State University. Prior to returning to graduate school at midlife, she worked with a variety of nonprofit, performing, and visual arts organizations and was Director of the Rutherford Barnes Collection, a gallery devoted to contemporary Latin American Art. Her research centers on the social and political functions of creative expression in society.

Georgina Neophytou conducted the study of Greek Orthodox cemeteries for the University of North London 'Landscape as Garden' project. She is a doctoral candidate in sociology at the London School of Economics.

Larry Nesper is an assistant proffessor of anthropology at the University of Wisconsin, Madison. His book *The Walleye War: The Struggle for Ojibwe Spearfishing and Treaty Rights* (2002) exemplifies his interest in the cultural and historical dimensions of contemporary American Indian political and economic projects in the Great Lakes region.